SUPER
YOU

EMILY V. GORDON

Illustrations by **HANNAH NANCE PARTLOW**

RELEASE YOUR INNER SUPERHERO

SUPER
YOU

SEAL

Seal Press
A Member of the Perseus Books Group
1700 Fourth Street
Berkeley, California

sealpress.com

Library of Congress Cataloging-in-Publication Data
Gordon, Emily V.
Super you : release your inner superhero / Emily V. Gordon.
pages cm
Includes bibliographical references and index.

ISBN 978-1-58005-575-8
1. Self-actualization (Psychology) I. Title.
BF637.S4G6697 2015
158—dc23
2015017391

10 9 8 7 6 5 4 3 2 1

Cover design by Faceout Studio, Jeff Miller
Interior design by Kate Basart/Union Pageworks
Printed in the United States of America
Distributed by Publishers Group West

This book is dedicated to you—to all the people you have been, all the people you are now, and all the people you will be

Contents

Introduction: Finding Your Bat Signal

M y own personal Bat Signal clicked on when I was in college. I was between identity crises, overweight, unsure of how to deal with any of my emotions, and generally unhappy with myself in myriad ways, plus I used words like "myriad." I spent my time scaring the normals with my pink-and-black-striped hair whilst projecting an up-for-anything, cool-girl persona that I held on to tightly, to the exclusion of anything else. One night I was dragged to a Top 40 dance club by a couple of friends. I hated every minute of it—no one was going to get me to dance like one of these brainwashed idiots. Don't get me wrong—it wasn't that I don't like dancing; I love dancing. I had taken dance classes as a kid and adored how free it made me feel, and even now, in the midst of my self-loathing, I passionately flailed around my bedroom as if chased by bees, ignoring everything wrong with me, focusing on the beat from my tiny CD player. I just refused to show such passion in public, afraid that it would betray the badass exterior hiding my incredibly fragile interior, concerned that it would be "off-brand." When we'd first arrived at the club, one of my friends said, "I've had such a long week, I just really need to dance and de-stress." That simple statement cut deep. I too had had a long week, and I too would have really benefited from letting loose—to whatever music was playing that night. But the life I'd set up for myself didn't allow for dancing.

So I started thinking: Am I living the life I want to live if I can't even dance? Is this how I pictured my life when I was a little kid yearning for the awesomeness of being an adult? And if not, why not? Am I even allowed to live the life I want to live? Whose permission would I need to live it? What does *off-brand* mean anyway, and what is my brand?

To answer your question, no, I didn't dance that night. This is my life, not an inspirational sitcom moment; a sea change like that takes time. I didn't dance for years, but that tiny question in that admittedly lame nightclub clicked on a little light, far away and hard to see, that gave me something to squint at, off in the distance, and move toward. In short, it gave me a mission. My mission was to become a girl who had the confidence to dance in public. If I were Bruce Wayne, she'd be my Batman. She'd be the version of me not so weighed down by my own "stuff." She'd be a superhero, but only to me. I started slowly creeping toward that tiny mission as if it were my own personal Bat Signal.

The Bat Signal, by the way, is how residents of Gotham call Batman in times of extreme distress. The Bat Signal tells Batman he's needed, and serves to remind him to be … Batman. It also tells ne'er-do-wells they'd better run. My guess is that you came into this already knowing what a Bat Signal is. If you did, good for you, and if you didn't, now you know. I often use comic books, video games, or other nerdy pop-culture references in my writing; it helps me understand the more complicated parts of the world a little more easily since, culturally, it's the ocean I swim in. For example, yesterday I compared committing to a romantic relationship to Harry Potter's prophecy to kill Voldemort. Nerdy and pop-culturey analogies just make sense to me, but even if sci-fi, magical teenagers,

and comic books aren't your thing, I promise there's a lot in here that can resonate with you, hopefully helping you move in the direction of your choosing. The concepts and important stuff are easily accessible and plainly written—the superhero stuff is just the sugar on top. You won't even have to know Black Widow's origin story.

I once worked as a therapist at a facility for young men—teenage boys, really—removed from their homes for behavioral problems. We talked a lot about goals and expectations, but I always felt those terms were somewhat nebulous and "therapisty." So one day I asked them to draw themselves as superheroes with tricked-out suits. I gave no other instructions. They loved this. Teenage boys can't resist drawing weapons that melt the faces of thine enemies. Once they'd finished, I threw on the therapeutic element: I asked them to identify every piece of equipment drawn on their suits, and to come up with the personal strength it represented. Shoulder laser guns became the ability to understand that others' behavior isn't about them! Protective helmets became anger management skills!! As we talked about the kinds of equipment, I got to hear about coping skills they'd have never admitted to wanting otherwise. They really got into seeing themselves like that—not as a list of qualities they *should* be, and are constantly failing at, but as slightly improved heroes armed with tangible equipment that helped them in emotional battles.

This happened way back when superhero movies were few and far between and starred actors like Christopher Reeve (Superman) and Michael Keaton (Batman), when superheroes were a novelty to most people. Since then, superhero films have filled the multiplexes, giving us a host of ripped gorgeous bodies and amazing CG (Computer

Generated) villains to marvel over—universally, we seem to be obsessed with caped crusaders with complicated backstories and noble callings. Over that same period I moved on from being a therapist to writing full-time, including writing a regular advice column. There I received questions from men and women who easily could have been me, with the same kinds of hopes and fears that I've had, who struggled to figure out how the past fit into the present, who grappled with weaknesses just as I have, who just wanted to understand themselves. I've spent many years, in therapy offices and on Tumblr, talking to all kinds of people about how they construct their identities and how they wish they could make improvements. The more conversations I have, the more I realize that the struggle to know, understand, and like oneself is truly universal. I also realize that some people believe self-esteem and emotional well-being are things we either have or don't have, rather than being things that are attainable, that we can work toward. Even worse, some of us believe that emotional well-being is a luxury, whereas I see it as a basic part of living. And though these struggles are universal, they can make us feel completely lonely, because we don't talk enough about this stuff. But there's no need to be lonely- we're all here together.

Let's take Wonder Woman, for example. Female superheroes are often not given the same glorious backstories and dramatic calls to action as male superheroes, and they're certainly not as well-known—there's a Marvel superhero named Squirrel Girl who looks like a squirrel and has the ability to control squirrels, but never is this power explained—but *everyone* knows Wonder Woman. Born Princess Diana of Themyscira, a tiny isolated island, Diana lived with an all-female tribe called the

Amazons. One day a man named Steve crashes his plane onto their island, and she finds him and nurses him back to health. She falls in love with him, and ends up escorting him back to "civilization" to protect him and work to fight evil and injustice there. (Funny how civilization needs more help than the uncivilized Amazons.) As an Amazon she has superior combat skills; she also has a Lasso of Truth, a tiara-cum-missile-like weapon, two indestructible bracelets, and later, an invisible jet. (By the way, more recent versions of Wonder Woman have recast her as [1] created from clay, or [2] an orphan in New York City, but this is my favorite origin story for her.) Steve was soon backburnered, and Wonder Woman took on the task of saving the world. Do I love that she became a superhero because of a man? It's not my favorite thing. But do I love how she took her own love for a man and then expanded into a career and a new identity that made her happy? Absolutely. Ultimately it's that level of intentionality and choice, and those incredibly specific bracelets, that attract me to superheroes.

Because that's what superheroes have: a specific set of skills, a specific identity, clearly identified weaknesses they've learned to work around, dramatic origin stories they have to deal with, and the choice, every single day, to go out and fight crime. Even a cursory look at a few popular superheroes shows how neatly they break down into these basic categories.

Quick and Dirty Superhero Breakdown

SUPERHERO	WHAT'S THEIR "THING"?	POWERS	ORIGIN STORY	WEAKNESSES	MUST DO THE RIGHT THING?
BATMAN	Bats	Good at fighting, lots of tech	Parents killed in front of him; bonded with bats	Kind of a hermit weirdo	Yes
SUPERMAN	Being super	Literally everything	Alien from another planet	Kryptonite	Yes
BUFFY SUMMERS, THE VAMPIRE SLAYER	Being "the Slayer"	Combat training, lots of attitude	Destiny chose her; will she choose to fulfill it?	Being in high school	Yes
WONDER WOMAN	She's an Amazon	Lasso of Truth, indestructible bracelets	Traveled from her homeland to civilization to protect a dude and fight for justice	Powerless if you bind her bracelets together	You betcha

Now, notwithstanding the fact that each of us is unique, and yes, we're all complex and special snowflakes, but: Could you add yourself to this chart? Could you explain what your "thing" is, and what made you who you are today? Are you honoring your past with what you're doing today, or is it the thing that's holding you back? Do you know what your strengths are? And since we're already asking questions, why don't we give ourselves the opportunity to be our own symbol of hope and justice and truth—why don't we become the heroes we deserve?

Since this book is called *Super You*, and it calls on you to *release your inner superhero*, what does that mean? What is a Super You, and what would be gained by creating one?

We're going to find all this out together. A Super You, in the plainest of terms, is the best version of yourself that you can achieve at any one moment. Super You is who you want to be—and that can mean anything. For me, my current Super You is a magic cocktail of confidence, the ability to know what to bring to a dinner party, and the courage to look past her own privilege to truly understand others.

She works hard but doesn't overwork herself. She can represent herself fully as a professional without downplaying her skills, and she goes to the gym for exercise without trying to lose weight. Your Super You may be unafraid to tackle big projects or face rejection. Your Super You may sometimes have terrible days and act like a brat. Your Super You may vow to eat vegetables every day but also may count sweet potato fries as a vegetable. With this book, I want to help you figure out where you are now, and where you'd like to be—and then help you map out concrete steps to actualizing your Super You. (Note that, ideally, our Super Yous are actualized enough to know that being actualized doesn't work all the time.)

Do you have a sense of what that Super You version of yourself might look like? If not, don't worry, we're going to figure it out.

We're here (both on this Earth and within this book) to progress. It's not that you need to change to be good enough—we are all already good enough—it's about making the choice to be different, if you want to. For those of you who think reading a book like this is a tacit acknowledgment that you aren't living up to your potential—that you're accepting yourself as less than optimal—let's get this out of the way now: no matter where you are in your life, and no matter why you're looking at this book, there is always room to grow and understand and change, and there is always an opportunity for self-examination and self-improvement. And I would love to be involved in yours.

Here's where I could start talking about various approaches to wellness, positive psychology and the five factors of happiness, the intricacies of rewriting one's narrative, emotional intelligence, the sources of self-worth, and all that—but instead I'm going to try to keep you awake. You see, before I spent six years as a practicing couples and family therapist, I spent many years earning a bachelor's and then a master's degree in mental health, so I know a fair amount about the workings of the brain and heart and spirit. But I've also spent even more years earning my stripes as a person, so I really know how annoying "wellness literature" can be. I went through long periods of being incredibly unhappy with myself, and when I tried reading books on self-esteem and wellness and all that, I couldn't get past the first few pages. In my preparation for becoming a therapist, I slogged through such books out of educational obligation. And while they're all quite useful, they are also either (1) exceedingly dry and clinical, or (2) so cloyingly saccharine and "You go, girl!" that I found them difficult to read, mostly because my eyes wouldn't stop rolling long enough to focus on the words.

For years I'd held on to the hope that there had to be some way to talk about self-esteem and emotional development without sacrificing humor, warmth, and the feeling that you're not alone in your struggles. That hope and the draw-a-superhero activity, as well as seeing my two-hundredth *Batman* movie, my mental health training, my own life experiences, and how I think about emotional well-being eventually coalesced into what you're reading now.

And while this book is intended for everyone, it definitely focuses on women from their teens to their forties; this is because

I can personally relate to the millions of things that go into a woman's self-esteem (and lack thereof), and because women have generally been my readership so far. Though I have experienced life only as a Caucasian straight cis-female and really can only speak to that experience, this book focuses more on your experiences of *your* life, and the emotions behind them; for that reason, it's my hope this book will apply to a wide range of people. I also intend my relationship advice to be applicable to all romantic unions, though at times my language defaults to hetero relationships. There was a slogan for a deodorant brand a few years ago—okay, *quite* a few years ago—that went: "Strong enough for a man, but made for a woman." I think of this book as being strong enough for a woman, but made for everyone.

Coming Soon to Your Local Psyche

So let's talk about you, and why you're here. You're ostensibly reading this in hopes of figuring out some things within yourself, and for that effort I applaud you. Perhaps you're stuck in a rut and want to make some changes in how you see and think about yourself. Maybe you like yourself just fine but also like the idea of becoming the superhero version of yourself. Possibly you're wondering what the hell superheroes have to do with self-esteem. In fact, I think it may do some good to go over this together. I suggest you grab yourself a notebook and keep it handy, because along the way I'm going to ask you to jot down a lot of stuff. So, once you have that notebook, write your answer to the following question: what are you hoping right now to get out of this book?

Whatever that goal is, try to keep it in mind as you read further. Think of what you want to get out of this book as your own Bat Signal for the rest of our journey together. We'll dig into your overall goals for your life further down the road, but for now, we're just thinking about what you want to get out of reading *this*. And if it changes later on, that's fine too; just write that one down as well.

That kind of flexibility—acknowledging when the tide has changed, and flowing with it—is a vital part of the Super You outlook.

You didn't ask, but one of the most important things I want you to get out of this book is to awaken you to the idea of living life with as much intentionality as possible. I'm using the word "intentionality" in its therapeutic context, so get ready, therapisty term coming up:

Intentionality, when it comes to our own behaviors and lives, means acting in a deliberate, purposeful manner. It means striving to stay aware of the myriad (that word again!) factors that go into our decision-making, and into our thoughts and feelings and behaviors. We are all changing at all points in time, in tiny, imperceptible ways as well as in monstrous, life-altering ways. This constant flux can offer great opportunities for steering toward our chosen direction. The thing is, many of us rarely take advantage of these opportunities; some of us don't even know they're there. Intentionality, for me, is about learning to understand myself enough to make my choices with purpose, even if those choices aren't always the best ones. Because if I just float through my life, functioning on autopilot and accepting that the way

I think and feel and act is just "how it is," without attempting to control "how it is," I'll never get anywhere more evolved, better, or even just different from what I've got right now. I'll just stay in autopilot. But if I can pay more attention to what is happening within me during the good and bad times, I have the opportunity to consider my choices more carefully, based on my wants and needs—and make choices that I can use to grow into the person I want to become. In short, I know myself. We'll talk a lot about intentionality throughout this book.

Using myself as a guinea pig, I've spent the last few years developing the different aspects of becoming a Super You. Slowly that drawing exercise, as well as my own personal Bat Signal, morphed into a paradigm of thinking about my identity—both the identity I currently had, and the one I wanted to occupy. To me, both are incredibly important.

Identity is something I struggled with mightily as a teenager: I went from being an oversized girl who towered over the kids in her elementary school class and desperately wanted to fit in (or just fit) to an oversized teenager who was constantly advertising—with her nineties-era alternative wardrobe and attitude—that she didn't want to fit in. With my ripped fishnets and my anger at the "normals," I understood the importance of having a goal identity—it's just that it wasn't the healthiest choice for me. While striving to be badass on the outside, I was desperately plumbing my depths on the inside, trying to figure out who I was and what was important to me. I thought that when I became an adult I was supposed to just "settle in" to who I was and be fine from then on. That certainly wasn't the case with me. Every major life change—marriage, divorce, moving across the country, career turnaround—sent me spinning off into the familiar panic of "Who am I? Who am I now? How do I show others who I am?" And I imagine I'm not alone in that. For years after I stopped seeing clients, I would introduce myself at parties by saying, "I'm Emily. I used to be a therapist, but I don't see clients anymore ... but I guess I'm always going to be a therapist at heart. Can we define ourselves by a job we're no longer doing? Anyway, did you try the artichoke dip?"

I am fun at parties, you guys.

But it's in these kinds of transitional times, which are inevitable in life, that thinking of myself in aspirational, superhero terms helped me come to more of an understanding of who I am, and who I want to be. I've had a lot of transitional times, and a lot of identities, and a lot of superhero prototypes, because no Super You is set in stone. The best version of yourself today isn't the same as the best version of yourself ten years ago, or even two years ago. Much like every new actor cast as Batman has a new take and a new suit (nippled or non-nippled), your Super You will continue to grow and change and adapt to new situations. And I'll reiterate, it's not that you *need* to change—it's that we're all continually changing, whether we like it or not. I just think it would work out better all around if we have a little more control over what we become.

After we get a sense of who we are, our Super You IDENTITY, we're going to need Super You MISSIONS to help us step into that more evolved identity. Every superhero has a mission, and that mission is usually to "uphold justice"—so we're going to turn that into what "justice" means to you. What does the best version of yourself do on a day-to-day basis? What's the first thing she does in the morning, and the last thing at night? Now, how can we convert those

actions into concrete goals, so we know how we can uphold our own justice?

Once we settle on an identity to fulfill and goals to reach for, we'll be ready to discuss the RIGHTS AND RESPONSIBILITIES of being our super selves—because as every Spiderman movie has taught us, with great power comes great responsibility. What are your responsibilities to others, and your responsibilities to yourself? When we're treated poorly by others, what choices do we have in the matter? Do we have to love ourselves every day? Does a Super You have to put up with friends who are passive-aggressively rude? What about those friends who're always in crisis, needing you to help make things okay? Every superhero has to have a personal code of conduct, so to speak, and so does every Super You. We can develop that code together.

After that, we'll talk about our relationship to our EMOTIONS, and how that can change over time. It's best when our emotions sit in our car's passenger seat, only advising on directions. But too many of us either (1) let our emotions drive, or (2) hog-tie them and shove them in the trunk—both of which can be problematic. A big part of becoming a Super You is learning to understand your emotions and make them work for you, rather than the other way around.

So once we have our emotions on track, from there we'll start developing a basic set of TOOLS for getting out of emotional jams. And by "tools" I really mean self-care skills, but since "self-care skills" sounds clinical and corny, we're going to call them tools. We're going to discuss what, ahem, self-care skills are, why they're so important, how to find the ones that work for you, and how to make sure you always have some in your toolbag (or wallet or messenger bag or designer purse), ready to use. You'd be amazed at how many of us walk around without a single self-care tool, let alone a cool-looking bag to hold them in.

From there, we'll start teasing out your own SUPERPOWERS and learn how to deal with some common Super You WEAKNESSES. This is important, because it's all too easy to underuse the one and over-stress about the other. I used to jokingly dismiss my superpowers, and I treated my weaknesses as dark secrets to hide at all costs. But our superpowers are the unique things that make us best qual-ified to live our lives, and not utilizing them seems as pointless as Superman taking a cab. Besides, Superman doesn't see his aversion to Kryptonite as a personal flaw to be fixed—it's just an obstacle for him to navigate. Then why should I hide my Kryptonite?

After understanding what I had to work with personality-wise, I started evaluating the methods I used to protect myself from the harsh reality of … reality—to see if they were actually doing me any good, or if they were just dragging me down. What purpose did those CHEAP, FAULTY WEAPONS of suspicious origin, like sarcasm and a holier-than-thou attitude, serve for me, and how did they keep me from actually growing? We'll cover all this.

The final piece of my Super You puzzle was thinking about my ORIGIN STORY, since apparently origin stories in superheroes are all the rage these days. It's not enough to see superheroes as they are now, shining and proud and kicking ass—moviegoers want to see how they became that way, because origin stories are a large part of what defines a superhero. And that makes sense: since we're not genetic mutants grown in a pod, we all have pasts, and more importantly we all have filters we view our pasts through. The thing is, I didn't real-ize for a long time how the origin story I told myself about my hum-ble beginnings affected how I felt about myself, and affected how I

developed. Origin stories are a large part of what defines us too—just sometimes in directions that aren't helpful to us. So rethinking and rewriting my own origin story also became a part of my Super You plan. When we reach that part of the book, I'll challenge you to really dig deep into your own story to understand it from multiple angles. Because it's when we're able to see our stories from a distance that we can start changing the way those stories affect us.

Once all your pieces are in place, we'll talk about how your Super You will function in the real, day-to-day world. Becoming the best version of yourself is useless if it only comes out when you're alone, if you're not able to hang on to your new identity at work, with friends, or on dates, especially since these times are often when we need a hero the most. While some superheroes do work alone, the superhero versions of ourselves cannot—we must be able to deal with the weirdness that is everyday life without losing a sense of ourselves, or a sense of self-esteem.

Then, once we're done with all that, it'll be time for you to spin off into the world as a bold, badass superhero who continues to work on herself *while* being badass.

The Obligatory Superhero Reality Check

Of course, all of this work could be done without superheroes, to be sure, but using them as a framework has become important to me, so I'm hoping it will be useful to you as well. Superheroes don't hate themselves in their "alter ego" forms, they accept who they are, they just also make an effort to be a more ass-kicking version of themselves. But I also want to clarify a few things. I am not using superheroes, or superhero mythology, to make light of anyone's identity, self-esteem, or past. These are, to me, the things that make people who they are, and they are precious. I am not turning emotional wellness work into a game here. Instead, I want to loosely use superhero mythology to offer a filter through which to objectively and actively work on ourselves while having a little bit of fun. Superheroes, with their well-documented powers and weaknesses and stories, merely provide a whimsical and relatable blueprint of how we can think of ourselves.

I'm also aware that superheroes aren't always seen as the most mentally healthy of creatures, and I tend to agree with that. Leading a double life—one being a lithe burglar and one being a cat-themed reluctant crime fighter—isn't the goal here whatsoever. Dressing up in weird costumes and beating people up, even if those people are bad guys, isn't necessarily the best way to deal with your anger. And it's not like I think neglecting your own personal life because you've roped yourself into this life of fighting crime (and there's always crime to fight) is a healthy pursuit of purpose. No part of this book recommends that you create a double life to devote yourself to, to the exclusion of all else. And besides, superheroes often drown in the expectations put upon them by their fans, the police, and their sense of justice—it's why so many of them seem so tortured. Cultivating your Super You isn't about trying to live up to expectations put on you by external forces—your Super You's expectations come from you and you alone. You will be functioning as your own superhero, and all that will be expected of you is to identify, embrace, and encourage the best parts of yourself, and learn to frame yourself a bit more positively. When you fail, as we all will, you aren't letting anyone down—you're merely taking the next step in your journey to become the superhero you set out to be.

Let's Do This

I have created, with a lot of trial and error, a version of myself that I can be happy and comfortable with—a version of myself that dances if she wants to dance. Now I'd like to help you do the same, and there is no time like the present. If you were looking for motivation to make some changes in your life, let reading this book be your motivation. Motivation is thought of as this magical, glorious, divine energy that takes you over when you need it most, but I have found that that's mostly bullshit. The process of change isn't always about having some deep insights into yourself and then deciding to alter your behavior as a result; sometimes it's about making the changes whether or not you're "feeling them"—and then letting your insights catch up.

This is extremely important, so keep it in mind: *coming to a deep understanding about yourself does not automatically lead to change in your behavior*. Sometimes it does, but sometimes behavior change kick-starts understanding. What we'll be doing in this book is approaching life improvement in two distinct ways: planning out small, concrete, manageable changes to make and gaining some insight about our current thoughts, feelings, and behaviors. It is the combination of the two that, for me at least, seems to lead to long-lasting change. In our time together, you'll have the opportunity to gain some new habits while gaining new understanding about old habits.

Now let's say you're trying to read this book but keep putting it down because it seems too overwhelming to take on right now, that you're thinking, "I'll read it once I get through [insert excuse here]." For those of you feeling that, I challenge you to stay with me and to start today. Self-esteem work isn't intended to be done once you "get your shit together" or are at least less stressed-out. Self-esteem work is just as important as eating and sleeping—but that doesn't mean you have to completely overhaul your life. There is no one sweeping change that I recommend; real alterations are done in tiny, little increments that you repeat and then add to daily. Sometimes life-upending, enormous changes are cathartic and worthwhile, but they can also be overwhelming, and can doom you to failure if they are too drastic. I get overwhelmed easily when faced with large changes—then I panic, and shut the whole thing down (sorry, CrossFit!). So for me, tiny changes is the only way to go. Plus, the tinier the change, the less excuse we have for rationalizing why we cannot possibly make the tiny change until "things calm down a bit."

When I make changes that will be uncomfortable but that I know need to happen, I always try to keep in mind the following simple truth: *my life is happening either way*. Whether I'm seeking fulfillment and improvement or just trying to keep my head above water and get through it, the days are passing by just the same. Life isn't something to be lived only in perfect circumstances—it's something that should nourish us daily. Some days are more business-like and stressful than others, sure, but we can't save up the "good stuff" for when our lives seem ready for it—because they may never seem ready for it.

One last thing. You don't have to be a comic book fan or even a nerd to get something out of this book. All of us have a sense of self, and all of us could stand to become a bit more emotionally healthy; and that's all you need to start creating your Super You. Becoming the superhero version of yourself is all about learning to respond

to the trials and tribulations of life in a way that makes you a stronger, wiser, and more positive human being. It's about learning to grow from bad experiences rather than just adding them to the pile of things that have gone wrong in life. As many great helpers have said before, life is happening either way. Change is mandatory, growth is optional, and greatness is inside all of us.

Let's get started.

CHAPTER 1

Identity: Who Would You Like to Be Today?

In my thirty-six years I have had many different personas. In fact, having personas has kinda been my thing—at least, I thought it was until I started talking about it and writing about it. As it turns out, we all live our lives under some persona or another.

Meet the Incarnations of My Super You

I was a kid with a constantly spinning, anxious mind and a sensitive disposition. Though I would cry at the drop of a hat, I was generally happy—I just couldn't seem to quiet my mind, ever. When I was three my mother took me to a neurologist because I kept complaining I had "swirlies in my head." He hooked up a bunch of things to my head and talked to me, and the meds they gave me to go to sleep made me seem drunk, which had to be hilarious to the workers at the fast food restaurant where we stopped on the way home. The diagnosis? Precocious. I clung to this label fiercely. I wanted to present myself as clever, hoping that identity would help anchor me in the constant swirling in my brain, would help explain my weirdness. I loved being my family's precocious baby girl who had elaborate backstories for all of her stuffed animals. I was Clever Girl.

Then I had an early growth spurt, and from the age of eight on, my size became my private obsession. I towered over the boys and girls in my class, hating myself for sticking out when it seemed most important to be just like the other kids. I shrunk down in school pictures. My posture was terrible. On the school bus one day, while I was sitting with a good friend, our knees propped against the seat in front of us, she casually, innocently commented: "Look, your legs are like, twice as big as mine." I was mortified and heartbroken—she had called out my secret. I quit taking dance classes, furious that my body had betrayed me and made me such a target. Every day my panic and self-loathing grew. My size seemed to be my identity now, as I was teased by friends and playground jerks alike. I wondered if it'd be like that forever. I had good friends and a lovely family, but none of that seemed to matter anymore. I felt cast out by my own looks. I was Monster Girl.

By the time I hit my teenage years, grunge was in full swing and my anger found a new home. I saw that I could express myself with the music I listened to and the way I dressed and adorned myself. I felt somewhat relieved that there seemed to be an escape valve for my self-loathing. Not everyone dyes her hair and gets piercings

because she's angry with herself, and it certainly wasn't the only reason I was doing it (it also looks damned awesome). But for me, dressing like a dead baby doll gave me control over my looks and my body, which had felt so out of my control for so long. I was still going to be ugly, sure, but I was going to be ugly on my own terms, thank you very much. I became Freak Girl, and I relished making others uncomfortable. I relished being unique. Of course, in my quietest, most private moments, I had some awareness that I wasn't actually that unusual—I was dressing exactly like all of my "freak" friends. It's just that what I really needed at that point was a community. After feeling so alone for so long, I needed to see myself reflected in the eyes of my friends.

A few years down the road, with a few terribly unhealthy relationships and a few misunderstood women's studies classes under my belt, I felt the need to project that I was independent and incredibly cool with anything. If I looked punk rock on the outside, I reasoned, my look would protect me from people knowing how squishy and sensitive I was on the inside. I had been hurt by boys who were careless with my heart, and frankly, *I* had been pretty careless with my heart, so I decided to put up an enormous wall around my heart and my feelings and pretend it didn't matter. And I told myself that to acknowledge other people's ability to hurt me was to acknowledge that they mattered, so I refused to do either. Outwardly, I was the party girl who would carry your drum equipment while you flirted with other girls. I was just going through the motions. Inside, I was numb. I wasn't like the other girls. I was the Punk Rock Stepford Wife!

I packed my emotions down tight for a few years, refusing to let myself feel anything. So after Punk Rock Stepford Wife came a slew of emotions, and once I started feeling again, I felt hard. It felt good. I put myself in therapy and tried taking care of myself a bit more. I married a very nice man. I devoted myself to my education, and then to my career as a therapist, and I became Therapist Girl. I loved my work, and I loved being seen as an even-handed, emotionally in-touch person who could still rock combat boots. "I'm a therapist," I'd say, "but I'm not one of those hippie therapists." The distinction seemed important to me. During this period I moved to a big city for the first time, after which my husband and I divorced, amicably. After so many years of being part of a unit, being newly single in a new city was exhilarating and terrifying. I obsessed over how to introduce myself to people. I briefly became Divorced Girl.

I fell in love again, this time as a truer version of myself, and threw myself into my career and my social life with every ounce of my being. Everything seemed rosy for a while until I became incredibly sick in my late twenties. I was hospitalized for a few weeks, during part of which my survival was in question. The entire thing hit me like a ton of bricks. I had been taking better care of myself, but clearly not enough to see how sick I'd been getting. On top of all that, suddenly everyone was clucking over me and my fragile body, giving me sad "poor you" eyes. I hated it. My illness briefly brought back the Punk Rock Stepford Wife, as I was unable to fully process how scary the entire ordeal was, as well as unwilling to accept other people seeing me as weak. I pushed myself hard, desperate to pass as "well"; it took some time before I actually started listening to my body, giving it the space I needed to recover. Once well again for real, my heart was no longer in seeing therapy clients. I wanted to write full-time, but felt terrified and unmoored by the idea of starting over. I no longer needed Punk Rock Stepford Girl, but I wasn't sure what my next persona was. I became Confused Girl. I took

every gig offered me, sometimes for free, and introduced myself weirdly to strangers. Slowly, and especially as more and more work came in, I started getting more comfortable with calling myself a writer. And here's where we are today. I suppose I'd call myself Entrepreneur Girl these days.

How Do You Make an Identity?

Does any of this sound familiar to you? Whether or not you can distinctly identify your personas to the point of naming them, if you look back at your life, can you see the different values and beliefs you held reflected in how you projected yourself and how you thought about yourself? For a long time I believed that I adopted personas because I wasn't ready to be myself, that I felt too vulnerable to just "be me." This led to a mini existential crisis. Oh my god, what does "being me" even mean? Am I the same person alone as I am with friends, or relatives, or strangers?

I no longer believe those personas weren't me. They all were the real me, just with varying personality traits dialed up or down based on what life called for at the time. It is my belief that who we are is constantly in flux—that every single person actually encompasses multitudes. To see more of what I mean, try answering these questions in your Super You companion notebook:

> How would you describe yourself if you were a contestant on a competition show where you wanted the home audience to feel sorry for you, and therefore vote for you?
>
> How would you describe yourself if you were a contestant on a dating show where you wanted someone to choose you over two other potential dates?

> **How would you describe yourself at a family reunion where you've been asked to introduce yourself to relatives you don't know?**

Your answers to these questions all describe accurate versions of you. Presenting, inhabiting, or inhibiting one version over another is something we all do throughout our lives—think job interview versus going on a date—but somehow that technique has been lost on us internally. If we contain multitudes, why don't we give ourselves the benefit of the doubt when we're alone instead of claiming somewhat unflattering versions of ourselves as the real versions? The truth is that who you are when you're alone is *and* isn't your real self. Every person has flattering, positive qualities as well as less flattering, more private, funky qualities—and all of them are useful.

I say this because I went down a rabbit hole of soul-searching, from which I eventually came to a few vital realizations.

Realization I: Who I Am Depends on a Lot of Factors. One of Those Factors Is a Group of Core Values and Beliefs About Myself.

I approach how I define myself as building a recipe. Your *core values and beliefs* are the ground beef/chicken/tofu/protein that you start off with; your *identity* is everything else you add to make that protein a meal. You might go in one direction and end up with tacos, or in another direction and end up with lasagna. There's a pretty excellent quiz online at www.viacharacter.org that can identify your character strengths after you answer 120 questions. It's like a BuzzFeed quiz, but slightly more useful.

If 120 feels like too many questions, I've come up with a few of my own to help guide you in understanding your core values and beliefs. As you answer them, reflect on your entire life, not just how you're feeling right at this moment. If you struggle with any question, answer it the way you think someone you're close to would, and then consider whether that answer resonates for you. No one else will see these answers, so try to dig deep, continually asking yourself whether you're answering how you're "supposed" to or if it's how you actually feel. (If you already feel pretty solid on your core values, please feel free to skip these questions.)

★ Who in your life is important to you, and why?

★ What news stories do you gravitate toward?

★ The last few times you felt happiness, what were you doing? Whom were you with?

★ Think back to when you last felt fulfilled, useful, and competent. What were you doing?

★ What is ideal downtime for you?

★ When do you like yourself the most?

★ When do you like yourself the least?

★ What are you proud of?

★ What are you afraid of?

★ What do you try to protect within yourself?

As for my own answers to these questions, and when I reflect on the entirety of my life, I see a few clear recurring themes. I am loyal to my family and my close friends. I am incredibly, perhaps overly,

fond of animals. I believe there is power in a group of people coming together as one, which is why I think of church, comedy shows, and movie theaters as spiritual places. I am passionate about social justice, and I get satisfaction out of seeing tasks completed, almost to the exclusion of quality. I sometimes believe that I don't deserve good things. I have confidence in my abilities in a few key areas and tend to avoid things I'm not confident in. I have a fear that at any time people will discover I'm incompetent—I also believe I'm incompetent in a lot of things. I'm both extremely sensitive and embarrassed about how sensitive I am.

Now, given that these are my core values and beliefs, it's easy to imagine that they all derived from me. But it's interesting to note that it's possible just to inherit values and beliefs from other people, taking them on without questioning whether or not they apply to us. So let's poke around a bit and see if we can figure out where each of your beliefs originated, how much you believe them yourself, and how emotionally healthy each self-belief is for you. Here are a few of my own examples.

Belief: I believe that I am pretty competent in my work as a writer.

Where did this belief originate? **From editors and people who read my work online and tell me that they like it.**

Do I agree with this belief intellectually? **Most days.**

Is my agreement/disagreement emotionally healthy for me? **I would prefer to agree with this belief every day.**

Belief: I believe that I should be a good southern girl and not let anyone make too much of a fuss over me, because I don't deserve it.

Where did this belief originate? **From the women in my family, who put everyone's needs in front of their own, often to the point of personal harm.**

Do I agree with this belief intellectually? **I disagree with it, but old habits die hard.**

Is my agreement/disagreement emotionally healthy for me? **It is healthier for me to disagree.**

The examples above are my own, but I'd like for you to try this exercise for yourself. Just because you believe something deep down in your bones doesn't always means it's *your* belief. A Super You does her best to challenge the beliefs that don't work for her. See if you can do the same.

Once you've gained a sense of your core beliefs, where do you go from there?

Realization 2: Identity Is a Construction That Evolves over Time.

Okay, so we have the protein base of our meal, but what recipe are we currently making? What factors influence what we make? Millions of things—like how competent we feel, our close relationships, socio-economic status, body image, and life changes—can influence both how we think of ourselves and how we define ourselves.

Here's the important thing: your identity isn't some mystical ball of energy handed to you like a gift from the mountain. You construct it, and you're constructing it all the time whether you're aware of it or not. So since we're working on living with more intention, let's put a bit more intent in how we construct ourselves. I can't tell you how helpful it was for me to look back at all the versions of myself and realize that, like it or not, they were all my design. The same is true for you: this boat you're driving is under your control. Some of us try to abandon it when things get rough, throwing up our hands and saying we're just doing our best to stay afloat, but even if our choice is to abandon control, *that is still a choice*. Some of us may be allowing our parents, boyfriends, girlfriends, or others to construct our identities for us—but even if that's the case, that's a responsibility we gave them, and it's our job to take it back. We've always been in charge, even if we haven't always realized it.

Creating a Super You is how we get ourselves comfortable with the idea that we've always been creating ourselves. Making internal changes is how we come to grips with our own power over ourselves. Since changes are always happening to us anyway, wouldn't you rather be proactive about them?

As I mentioned before, all my major external life changes have sent me into minor identity crises. This doesn't mean I question the very core of who I am; it's just that I rearrange all the parts of me that are *built* on that core so I can adjust to my new reality. In short, I have to change the recipe, and that is stressful. Life changes that can alter how you think of, and therefore construct, your identity can include:

- ⚡ Beginning therapy

- ⚡ Being diagnosed with an illness

- ⚡ Changing jobs

- ⚡ Changing your appearance

- ⚡ Coming out

-  Getting married

- Having a baby

- Learning new information

- Leaving any type of relationship

- Losing a job

- Losing a loved one

- Moving far away

- Starting a new hobby

- Starting any type of relationship

The environment we're in affects how we construct ourselves. Changes, even when they are positive, can throw how we think about ourselves into chaos and uncertainty. If you find yourself feeling uncomfortable and unmoored, often it's because your current identity isn't serving your needs, and needs to be restructured. Identity crises aren't signs that something is wrong with you; they're merely signs that things are changing—and that it's time for you to change with them.

Here's an example of how a few even minor-seeming life changes can affect your identity. Growing up, I preferred hanging with guy friends. We liked the same stuff—horror movies and sketch comedy— and if I'm totally honest, hanging out with girls often reminded me of how unattractive and "weird" I felt. So I stuck with the boys, and ended up rejecting many feminine things about myself, deciding that anything "girly" was synonymous with "stupid." I refused to wear skirts. I hated most other girls on sight. This construction of myself was based on my insecurity about the feminine parts of me. Then, in college I reconnected with an old friend who had, in the years since we'd been kids, both come out and started performing as a drag queen [new relationship]. That friendship, combined with a class in gender studies [learning new information], opened my eyes to the importance of feminism—and of my own femininity. I went from never wearing skirts to only wearing skirts. (Seriously, I only wore skirts for about two years, if we're including a pair of pants with a built-in skirt that I rocked for a time. It was the nineties.) My identity as a self-loathing female who wanted to hang with the guys was changing, and my old identity, which had served me well when I didn't believe in myself, was no longer useful to me.

So essentially: your identity = your core values and beliefs + the environment you're in + how you respond to that environment.

Realization 3: Every Identity We Construct (Whether We Mean to or Not) Serves Us in Some Capacity.

In my life I've been a Monster Girl, a Punk Rock Stepford Wife, and a Confused Girl, and though it would have been nice not to have gone through those ebbs and flows of self-loathing, I appreciate each of those Girls. Those were my proto-superheroes, trial versions of my Super You. Parts of them have stuck with me, and parts have been discarded, but again, I appreciate all of them as part of the process. I've talked with many women who think of themselves as "broken" or "stupid" because they've made choices that seemed self-destructive, but I think they're neither broken nor stupid. To my mind, every choice they made likely reflected how they were doing their best with what was available.

Let me repeat that, because it's important: every choice you make is a reflection of you doing your best with what you have in front of you.

For example, my Punk Rock Stepford Wife was a hard, walls-up kind of girl, but at that point in my life I couldn't handle being vulnerable to other people. That persona protected me until I felt ready to exist without those walls.

So let's say you get involved with men who treat you terribly; that may be your clue that you don't believe yourself worthy of a quality mate. Or you may have everything you thought you wanted and still be unhappy; that may be a sign that you feel you don't deserve happiness, or that your ideas of your "dream life" weren't entirely your own. Take a minute now to acknowledge that, regardless of whoever you have been in the past, and whoever you are right now, those identities did and do their best to help usher you through the world. Plus, we can learn lessons from how they protected and enabled us, and take those lessons forward. We'll talk about that a bit more later; for now, just acknowledge them as a valuable part of yourself.

Realization 4: Self-Esteem Only Partially Comes from the Self.

Self-esteem is supposed to be the esteem in which you hold yourself, right? And absolutely, your beliefs about what you deserve in life, and the values you hold, are a vital part of determining how you feel about yourself. But it's a disservice to pretend that other

factors don't also play a part, because they absolutely do. Research has shown that, as children develop, how they *initially* think of themselves is a reflection of how their parents regard them. As they age, the regard of additional people—teachers and other adults and eventually their own friends—gets added to the mix of how they feel about themselves. So does that process just stop when we become adults and are expected to rely on ourselves alone? I don't think so. I have my core values and beliefs, I have my thoughts on how to respond to things, but I don't exist in a bubble. I am affected by someone praising me on Twitter, by making huge mistakes at work, by my parents telling me they're proud of me, by my husband whistling when I get dressed up.

There was a time when I wanted never to allow the opinions of others to solely shape my self-esteem, so I embarked on a long quest of trying to rid myself of the influence of others in how I felt about myself. In the end I realized that was impossible—not to mention that I felt like a failure for not being able to be independent. So I started looking at my self-esteem for what it is for me: a balance of how I regard myself and how I am regarded by those around me. But pay attention here, because this next part is vital: just as your self-esteem cannot come only from you, it cannot come only from other people either. Frequently in life I have taken others' opinions about me as my own, allowing them a majority role in how I regard myself. I have done this for many reasons: out of laziness, out of fear of self-examination, out of comfort with keeping things as they were. While all these reasons are completely valid, adopting someone else's opinion of me as my own is not self-esteem—it's just allowing someone else to determine my identity for me. On the flip side, living as if my opinion of myself weren't influenced by the world around me is both impossible and incongruous with the fact that I value my relationships above all else. So instead of lamenting that I'm impervious to the world around me, I'd rather embrace that fact and figure out how to incorporate such influence into my identity in a way that's a boon to my self-esteem.

If Our Identities Are in Flux and Created as a Recipe, Then Who Do I Want to Be?

Okay, so at this point I hope you have a sense of your current self-constructed identity. You have a sense of what she believes, how she serves you, where her beliefs about herself come from, and the basic values on which she was built. Are you tacos? Are you beef Bolognese? You might even want to name her. (Probably not a food name though, unless tacos define you.) You know who you are, and you understand that, warts and all, your selves are constructed. The next step is figuring out what kinds of changes you'd like to make in your life.

But first, it's worth restating that, for almost all of you, who you are right now is absolutely functional and making it work (thanks, Tim Gunn) in your day-to-day life. You do not have to go through this process; you are surviving just fine without creating a version of yourself to strive for. You can easily, healthily, and happily get through life without being a Super You. And that's great. All the same, it couldn't hurt to know the way of the Super You. As I will continually stress throughout this book, we are all constantly changing to adapt to the world around us; it's my hope that we can become a bit more intentional in where we end up.

So, for those of us who want to continue now, figuring out what changes need to be made is significantly more difficult than just saying, "Yeah, I need to change." Anyone can say that. I like to start with a few general questions. So if who you are now is You, and who you would like to become is Super You, let's talk about how things will be different in this superhero version of yourself that we are intentionally constructing.

Go through each of these questions twice. For the first round, ask yourself how You would answer this question. For the second round, ask how Super You would answer this question. The answers might not always be different, but even subtle differences can help us set our missions.

MOST RIDICULOUS SUPERHERO ALTER EGOS

He-Man is Prince Adam by day, but the only difference between the two is that He-Man is more tan and wears fewer clothes.

Robin, of Batman and Robin fame, is an acrobat named Dick Grayson who travels with his acrobat family, The Flying Graysons.

★ What's your general mood?

★ How do you respond to stress?

★ How do you react when hurt?

★ How do you unwind?

★ What do you get out of romantic relationships?

★ What's the first thing you do in the morning?

★ What does a perfect day look like?

★ What do you get out of family interactions?

★ What are you doing for work?

So let's look at the Super You answers that are different from your You answers. Maybe Super You will hang out with your friends more, or you'll give yourself more you-time. Perhaps, rather than dating whoever asks you out, Super You will date guys because you're interested in them and think they have a lot to offer. Maybe your Super You goes back to school, or looks for a better job. Overall, looking at your different answers, you might find there are some areas you don't want to change at all, and some you want to completely overhaul.

But let's check in: how difficult was it to come up with ways you'd like your life to be different? It can be tough sometimes to envision what the future could be, especially if we've been going with the flow in our lives so far, simply swept with the current. Sometimes all you know is that you want things to be different, but you struggle with what "different" would be. Luckily, there are two incredibly basic "working shit out" techniques I learned as a therapist that I use personally, professionally, and over long brunches with pals. Both of these techniques, though simple, can make you feel like a superhero once you've mastered them.

Super You Assessment Tool I: What *Won't* You Be Doing?

If you were to ask people how to be a law-abiding citizen, the answers would likely be pretty diverse. Since a million different things that citizens do are considered law-abiding, building a

recipe based on what a law-abiding citizen *does* is too hard to pin down. So sometimes we must start with what we *won't* be doing. A law-abiding citizen won't be committing crimes—won't be drug dealing, won't be stealing, won't be murdering. Simple, right?

Though this approach is a bit tougher when applied to ourselves, it can be a fantastic place to start. So let's say you'd like to make some changes in your life, for example with diet. It feels too vague to say: "I'll be eating healthier!" But how about: "I *won't* eat after 1:00 AM anymore"? Instead of: "I'll make men respect me," perhaps make it: "I *won't* accept booty calls. (Though I may still make booty calls.)" Instead of: "I'll get better about my anxiety," maybe try: "I won't bite my nails." So take some time to consider: when you've achieved Super You status, what won't you be doing anymore, for better or for worse? Making a list of what you won't be doing also helps you get a sense of what might fill the void: concrete, observable behaviors, which are essential for intentional change and yet very hard to come up with on your own. This leads us perfectly into the next skill . . .

Super You Assessment Tool 2: The Reality Show

Repeat after me: *concrete, observable behaviors*. Say it again. Here's an interesting fact I learned as a therapist: even though mental illness is mostly internally experienced, it is diagnosed from the concrete behaviors professionals observe in the patient. Why is that? It might be because humans are miserable at self-reporting. When we're struggling, we're so "in it" that it can be difficult to describe what it feels like, and so we may over- or underrepresent ourselves. It might also be because, in order for progress to be tracked, the patient needs to be seen making behavioral changes. Or it might be because professionals like to feel their assessments are important. Who knows, but it's how things work.

When doing work on oneself, it's extremely important to get a certain amount of objective, emotional distance from one's self. I don't mean that you should take no responsibility for your behavior, and I don't mean that you shouldn't be "in the moment" in your life. What I mean is that, all day, every day, we walk around with every bit of the cultural and emotional baggage that we've picked up from being a human being for however many years we've been alive. We each swim in our own ocean of understanding: about how our culture works, how people work, and especially how we work. But here's the thing: we're sometimes too awash in this ocean of context to properly evaluate the things that happen to us. Our own context can cloud over our life experience, sometimes to our detriment.

So how do we go about objectively assessing ourselves? We can adopt a trick I used to evaluate clients based on their (say it with me) concrete, observable behaviors. I'll show you what I mean with a quick scene.

Interior: A busy office—day

Amanda, a professional-looking young woman, is in the middle of a business meeting. Also present are **Daniel**, her young hip boss, and **Rayanne**, a potential client. We join them mid-meeting.

Amanda: . . . and these are just a few of the reasons why I think working with our company will bring you a 30 percent increase in profits in the next six months.

Rayanne: This all sounds very impressive. Daniel, you've got a good manager on your hands.

Daniel: Thanks, Rayanne! Yeah, Amanda is one of our best. Not so great at making coffee, though—she spilled all of the beans on the floor of the kitchen yesterday. I had no coffee! I thought we weren't going to make it!

Daniel and **Rayanne** laugh good-naturedly and continue discussing business. **Amanda** blushes, looks down, and does not speak for the rest of the meeting.

End scene.

So what happened here? If this were a reality show (albeit a boring one), you'd see Daniel making a joke during a business meeting and Amanda essentially shutting down. You'd wonder what on Earth was going on. Depending on your own context, you'd maybe think that Amanda was being overly sensitive, or that Daniel was being a jerk. What you'd find out in the talking-head segments of the reality show is that Daniel was raised in a family where compliments are immediately deflected and minimized in an effort not to seem highfalutin'. So when Rayanne complimented Amanda, Daniel felt the need to assure Rayanne that he appreciated her compliment but also had humility about his employees. In Amanda's talking-head interview, you'd find out she was raised by a family who did not tolerate mistakes whatsoever. Even tiny mistakes she made as a child were held over her head and used to insult her. So when Daniel joked with Rayanne about the coffee beans, Amanda felt immediately shamed and did what she did as a child, which was to shut down.

But watching this scene from afar, as we just did, we are divorced from all that baggage and forced to analyze the situation based only on what we can see. We are forced to look at the situation the way a therapist would. Would it be a better world if everyone could understand other people's baggage and approach them with sensitivity? Sure, maybe. But I'd also like Amanda to progress to a point where she understands that not everyone is her father, and I'd like Daniel to take some lessons in being a manager and not bring his own stuff to work. Were I Amanda's therapist, I'd have a few recommendations for her that work in tandem: (1) understanding that her past clouded how she responded to a gentle (albeit stupid) joke in a business meeting, (2) learning to evaluate her interactions with others based solely on those interactions, and (3) learning to acknowledge her past's influence and then decide how she wants it to affect her—rather than letting it affect her automatically.

This ability to acquire distance from one's inner turmoil in order to see day-to-day life as objectively as possible is an incredibly helpful skill. It's one that I started in an unhealthy way in my early twenties (we'll discuss that soon), and it may be the most important thing I got out of my therapist training. For practice, I'd love for you to select a few interactions you've had in the recent past—perhaps an emotionally heavy one, an interaction with a stranger, and a conversation with your significant other—and try to replay those interactions as if you were watching them on a reality show. As you replay each, try to

ignore your emotions around the interaction—and realize that that's how the other person experienced your interaction. Your emotions and context are incredibly useful to your wellness, but we should never forget that our emotions and contexts are ours and ours alone; they are not plain to everyone else. Rather than letting those emotions and that rich emotional history ruin our interactions, we need to make them work *for* us, and getting some emotional distance is a great first step for this. So practice the reality show technique for a couple of past interactions. Then, if you can remember, try it when you're in the middle of a new interaction.

Now that we're getting to know ourselves a bit better—who we've constructed ourselves to be in the past and the present—and now that we have a few techniques for evaluating our behavior and environment a bit more scientifically, let's start talking about our Super You goals for the future.

CHAPTER 3

Missions: Should You Choose to Accept Them

So let's talk about goals. The word "goals" for me conjures up a million different images, and none of them good: of coaches yelling at players, of clients doing the minimum necessary to technically meet a standard I'd set, of dieters wanting more mashed potatoes when they've eaten their daily calorie allotment. Goals, while wonderful, have developed a reputation for being too lofty, too "not me," too unattainable, too lame. So let's begin this chapter about goals by not calling them goals.

All superheroes have something big they're working toward. They may want to stop terrorists, or protect America, or fight crime in Gotham. But things like that are never truly complete, so superheroes call what they're trying to accomplish "missions."

When you're your own superhero—your Super You—though your missions will likely be slightly smaller-scale than stopping terrorism, they will be yours, and they'll be no less important. You've already set one mission for yourself—what you want to get out of this book—but it's time to get a little more specific about what your Super You will be doing in the future. So let's throw a few ideas out there. What will wellness look like for you? How will you know you're feeling it? Do you want to be less tired? Stand up for yourself at work? Feel more focused every day? Express yourself more? Do you want to no longer be afraid to say no to people? Spend time with people who care about you? It may not sound as exciting as crime-fighting, but Super You's job is to fight internal crime, and be on the side of justice and well-being.

So, since the things we need to work on aren't as obvious as crime or terrorism, how do we figure out what needs to change in order to make change?

Therapists have these things they create with clients called *treatment plans*. They sound fancy, but they're not. A treatment plan solidifies the work the therapist and client will do together; it also justifies to insurance companies that therapists and clients are working together. For the purposes of explaining a treatment plan, I'm gonna use that "goals" word again, if you'll forgive me. A treatment plan spells out what's causing the client distress (problem); lists the physical manifestations of that problem (symptoms); and sets goals based on those symptoms, broken down so it's clear when each milestone has been met (goals). One fun and weird term frequently used in treatment-plan

THERAPY TERM *alert*

language is "AEB." AEB stands for "as evidenced by," and is used to justify either a problem or a goal. Here, I'll show you.

Problem: Client is lethargic as a result of depression.

Symptom: Client does not attend school and is not eating regularly.

Goal: Client will become more energetic AEB attending school four days a week and eating at least two meals a day. Client will be able to express why attending school is healthy.

See? This is where concrete, observable behaviors come in. The client is depressed, but if we set a goal of "be happier," or if we set the problem as being just "depression," we'd be failing the client. That's because the goal is too vague, the problem is too vague, and nothing is observable. Plus, it seems unattainable to go from "be depressed" to "be happy." So instead what we do is break the depression down into tiny pieces, and tackle each piece with both emotional work and behavior changes. For example, Wonder Woman's mission is "to bring peace to the outside world" as evidenced by "stopping Maxwell Lord from mind-controlling Superman and wreaking havoc" or "dueling her sister, Nubia, who claimed to be Wonder Woman."

To apply the magic of AEB to your own life—let's say you'd like to express yourself more—what concrete, observable goal could we set so we'll know when it's met? Maybe "expressing yourself more" means that you'll vocalize a restaurant preference even if you don't care where you go. Or, if your mother starts ragging on your sister, you'll stop her and ask that she please not insult one child in front of the other. Do you see the difference between these specific examples and the wiggle room allowed in "expressing yourself more"?

If you think it's somewhat problematic to base treating mental health issues on (what we hope is) the outward expression of mental disturbances, you're not wrong. It's not a flawless system. I had a client who set a treatment goal of peeing on his clothing less than twice a week. Did that goal directly address the feeling that urged my client to pee on his clothes? No. But the hope is that good, insightful change can come from addressing particular behaviors *on top of* the work of discussing the internal stuff that leads one to want to pee on one's clothes. In this case, the client felt that peeing on his clothes was the only way to clean them, and he was trying to work on hygiene. As I've mentioned in this book, it takes addressing both the behaviors *and* the thought patterns behind them to make real changes.

Before I was a therapist I believed that change came from having some sort of divine insight about myself, followed by a bold pronouncement, followed by a one-woman show in some dingy theater. "And that's when I learned," I'd opine in the spotlight, "that the only person I needed to be dating was myself." Sometimes changes do come that way, but more often they come simply from doing things that a healthier person does while trying to assimilate her own baggage. The good warm fuzzy feelings, that divine motivation? It'll come, but you've got to earn it. Alcoholics Anonymous frequently uses the expression "Fake it 'til you make it" to describe being functionally sober, and I'm a big fan of that expression, even though I don't think it exactly fits our work here. It's hard to fake being happy, but if to your mind happy people have lunches with friends and take walks in the park, then perhaps we can start with lunch with friends and see if the feelings follow. And if we're talking brain chemistry, it so happens that if you smile to *try* to be happy, the same synapses fire as when you smile *because* you're happy. Even the science supports faking it. So, while you're lunching with friends, you may not feel as if you're happy enough to warrant such frivolity, but hey, you're still doing it, right? I suppose a better expression would be putting the actions cart in front of the feelings horse. Or would it be an actions horse in front of the feelings cart? Regardless, you can see why AA went with the simpler expression.

But let's go back to talking about the Super You missions you'd like to establish. First, some basics of how this works. Crafting a Super You mission has four distinct parts: (1) the area where you'd like to make changes, (2) how you are now, (3) how you'd like to be different, and (4) how being different will look. Plus, the process of mission creation can start at many different entry points. For example, it can start with picturing what your better life will look like overall and working backward; or it can start with what you *won't* be doing (which we covered in the last chapter); or it can start with the area of your life you are most dissatisfied with. There is no wrong way to figure out the right missions for you. And while we're not going to make a treatment plan, since we're not at a mental health facility, we are going to create a modified version of one, starting with whatever part you feel comfortable filling in first. I'll show you how.

Let's imagine a person, who is not at all similar to me, and start with the one thing she does know: she dislikes her body.

Sample Super You Mission-Setting Table: Step I

AREA WHERE YOU'D LIKE TO MAKE CHANGES	HOW YOU ARE NOW	HOW YOU'D LIKE TO BE DIFFERENT	CONCRETE, OBSERVABLE INDICATIONS THAT THINGS ARE DIFFERENT
?	I hate my body. I'm ashamed of it.	?	?

I'd say to this person, who is *definitely* not me: Okay, you hate your body and feel shame around it. How would you like to feel?

Sample Super You Mission-Setting Table: Step 2

AREA WHERE YOU'D LIKE TO MAKE CHANGES	HOW YOU ARE NOW	HOW YOU'D LIKE TO BE DIFFERENT	CONCRETE, OBSERVABLE INDICATIONS THAT THINGS ARE DIFFERENT
?	I hate my body. I'm ashamed of it.	I'd like to feel healthy and also proud of my body the way it is.	?

So I—I mean, she—wants to change her body image a bit; this is an issue for the best of us. And the worst of us. Everyone, really. So we'd add "body image" to the chart. Notice I said "change her body image." I didn't say "change her body." And health is always an amazing goal to go for. So now let's figure out the AEB: if we're watching her reality show, divorced from all the churning feelings inside her, how would we know when she feels healthy and proud of her body?

Sample Super You Mission-Setting Table: Steps 3 and 4

AREA WHERE YOU'D LIKE TO MAKE CHANGES	HOW YOU ARE NOW	HOW YOU'D LIKE TO BE DIFFERENT	CONCRETE, OBSERVABLE INDICATIONS THAT THINGS ARE DIFFERENT
BODY IMAGE	I hate my body. I'm ashamed of it.	I'd like to feel healthy. I'd also like to feel proud of my body the way it is.	I would exercise three times a week minimum, for at least 20 minutes. I would go to pool parties I'm invited to. I would wear skirts in public. I would take that dance class I've been too embarrassed to take.

See how things can build on each other? Try filling in a few of your own Super You Mission-Setting Tables in your notebook. Think back on everything you've read so far, and start where you're comfortable. To magically turn those oservable behaviors into missions, change the "I would" part to "I will" (so "I would wear skirts in public" becomes "I will wear skirts in public"), and make a list of them. These, my friend, are your Super You Missions. Find one that you could do either today or tomorrow, and then, today or tomorrow, take that step: accept that mission. And keep this list handy, because we'll be talking about it throughout this book.

And since you asked (you're like, "but I didn't!"), I thought maybe I'd set some missions too—missions I have for those of you reading this book. I don't want to shape any of the changes you will be making whatsoever. But there are some basic thoughts that, if I've done my job correctly, I am hoping you'll take with you for the rest of your days, like little presents from me. Be aware that I'm breaking my own rules here and keeping these missions a little vague and not attached to specific behaviors—that's because this isn't for just one person, but for all of you.

I want you to finish this book with an increased awareness of yourself—your day-to-day moods, feelings, and annoyances. I want you to live less of your life on autopilot. Autopilot isn't always a bad thing; autopilot is your body and mind working together, putting up defenses to get you through stressful times, letting you focus on one thing to the exclusion of other things. But too many of us are *living* on autopilot. Autopilot doesn't fix stress or confusion or misery; it just pushes it away, protecting us from it. I want you to have more coping skills than just autopilot at your disposal.

Similarly, *I want you to finish this book with a commitment to living your life with intention.* Living with intention is the natural extension of being more self-aware, because it means self-awareness plus decision-making. It means that you are aware of what's best for you, and that you will be making decisions for yourself. But note that those two things needn't be related. Sometimes you're going to make mistakes. Sometimes you're going to know exactly what to do and do the "wrong" thing anyway. Sometimes you'll only stumble upon doing the "right" thing. I just want you to be more in charge of the direction your life is heading in, and take pride in that ownership.

I want you to leave this book knowing that you are valuable, if you didn't know that already. You are valuable, your thoughts and feelings are important, and you deserve to be treated with respect and love and cheeky silliness. I want you to leave here treating yourself as you would a new romantic partner or a longtime best friend.

Your missions for yourself—plus my missions for you—are all we need to get started. Now, I know some of you may be thinking; "Wait, is this it?" Yes, this is it. It's this simple. It bears repeating: rarely do huge sweeping changes stick as well as tiny ones. Your list of Super You Missions, which I expect you'll be adjusting and changing as you proceed, is a big step, even if it doesn't necessarily feel like a big step. And since we're all changing all the time anyway, the best way to start taking control of those changes is slowly. Some of these changes will come to you easily, and will then just need to become habit. Some will take time to feel comfortable doing. What's more, some changes will take place on the inside, where no one but you can observe them.

Fundamentals: Rights, Responsibilities, Choice, and Control in a Superhero World

o we've gotten to know ourselves a bit, and we've figured out what we want to change in our lives—this is great news. Now let's take a step backward and talk about some of the fundamentals of good emotional health—the fundamentals of being a Super You. Let me tell you a story.

I once knew this girl who was yelled at by a stranger in a restaurant for something she did not do. She listened to the stranger quietly, almost politely, and then apologized for upsetting her. She spent the rest of the day feeling guilty about upsetting someone. Guilty! When asked later why she didn't tell the stranger that grown-ups shouldn't yell at other grown-ups because it's disrespectful and creepy, she said, "I didn't realize I had that option."

Of course this girl was me, and of course I didn't realize, back then, that I had the option of not accepting being yelled at by a stranger for something I didn't do. The stranger in question was a woman at a buffet restaurant who thought I had broken in line in front of her kid and wanted to let me know how she felt about it. (Note: I am not a line breaker. It feels important to let you know that.) But because I was young, because she was older than I was, and because I didn't have a sense of what was okay and not okay concerning my own personal boundaries and sense of well-being, I not only allowed it to happen, but also felt guilty about an infraction I did not commit. This wasn't the first time I didn't understand my rights in a situation, and it certainly wasn't the last. When I think about how much of the ickiness in my life can be chalked up to not understanding the differences among four interrelated and yet completely disparate concepts—rights, responsibilities, choice, and control—well, all I can say is, "Yikes." I have let angry people have their way, I have gone further sexually than I intended to out of "not wanting to be weird," I have stayed in miserable situations because it felt easier than changing, I have taken on the responsibility of someone else's happiness and felt guilty and terrible when I failed, I have been saddled with responsibilities I didn't want because I didn't want to say no—I have been in all of these boats, and I imagine some of them are familiar to you too. So let's go through these terms now and define them as they relate to Super You.

Control

Control is one of those weird concepts that can be positive or negative depending on the connotation, the person saying it, or whether or not you are referencing panty hose. Control-top panty hose are a blight on humanity. Plus, it can be tricky to fully comprehend what we can control in this life and what we cannot. A lot of inner turmoil comes from people either giving up all control and wondering why they feel terrible, or attempting to control everything around them and wondering why they feel terrible. What a Super You understands, even if she forgets now and then, is that you cannot control anyone other than yourself. Period. You can influence how other people behave, sure, or you can force people to do what you want for a little bit, perhaps—but really, the only control you have in this life is over yourself.

You cannot control:

- How other people perceive you

- Whether a car plows into you on the way home from work

- Whether aliens come and kidnap you

- Whether anyone celebrates a holiday the way you celebrate

- Whether your boyfriend acts like an asshole in front of your work friends

- Whether your children turn out artistic

- Whether your friends want to hang out with you

- Whether your romantic partner cheats on you

- Other people's feelings toward you

- What fashion trends will be happening next year

- Literally anything other than your own behavior

I think the idea of control is scary to all of us. Not being in control can leave us feeling weak and vulnerable to the millions of things that can go wrong in the universe. Plus, understanding that we can control only ourselves means that, when it comes to how we operate, the buck stops with us. We can make changes, we can influence people, we can be a cog in the machine, but we can only do any of that so far as controlling our own actions allows us. Bill Gates, the manager of your closest fast food chain, Malala Yousafzai, and that guy from your high school who is still living at home and clearly depressed but covering it up with binge drinking—all of these people can control only themselves. But how they choose to conduct themselves and influence others varies widely. To me, the difference between the people who are successful and fulfilled and those who are frustrated and freaked-out has always had to do with accepting what we can and cannot control, and then doing our best to enact changes within that.

SUPERHEROES WITH MIND-CONTROL ABILITIES THAT CONTRADICT WHAT I'M SAYING HERE

→ Professor X of the X-Men (for good)

→ Emma Frost of the X-Men (for evil)

→ Jean Grey of the X-Men (mostly for good)

→ Psylocke of the X-Men (for good)

→ Mandarin of the Avengers Universe (for way evil)

I'm a bit of a control freak, but (I like to think) in the loveliest way—I am just the person most likely to organize an outing to the movies, to set up flights for travel, or to drive if there's a car full of people to be driven around. It's not that I think my way is the best way, it's just that I don't love hanging out in the "in between" spaces between decisions. I want things to be done so I don't have to think about doing them—my control freakness is more about eliminating my anxiety than anything else. I frequently say, "Okay, so what information are we waiting on to make this decision?" when my husband and I are discussing things like vacations, or house repairs, or switching cat foods. (I'm a real handful.)

That anxiety about school projects or dinners with friends or house parties used to be all-encompassing for me—I would never enjoy myself, because I was constantly running around, making sure everyone else was taken care of, wanting to make sure things were happening. Then I would end up kinda martyring myself, sacrificing my fun for other people's, when they would have been fine either way. It took years of watching plans fall apart without destroying people's psyches for me to realize that, not only is it not my job to make sure every plan is executed well, but it's okay if plans aren't executed well. The only thing I can control is how much fun I'm having—independent of how many snacks are at the party.

I had to come to this realization in my romantic life too. I used to think that every relationship required a certain amount of love. If I wasn't getting the amount of love equal to what I was giving out, my control freakness meant the solution was to love the guy hard enough that it was enough for both of us. Instead of: "You complete me" it was: "I will complete the gap in adoration you are showing me by adoring you twice as hard." This will never be seen in a romcom. This attitude not only kept the wool pulled over my eyes about the kinds of guys I was dating, but I guess I thought if everything was under my control in a relationship, I could protect myself from feeling hurt or sad or rejected.

The most hilarious part about trying to control everything is that it always seems to work for brief periods of time, which just reinforces the idea that you're right and the way that you're doing things is effective. But people are still people, and will never act exactly the way you want them to act. Ultimately, wanting to control anything other than yourself leaves you feeling even more hurt and sad and rejected, because when stuff goes differently from how you thought it would, as stuff tends to do, you have the added benefit of feeling at fault. So many of us ambitious and anxious people fall into the trap of wanting to micromanage all situations and lives around us. Why? Because it's comfortable and miserable and brain-occupying.

If you're a parent, this notion of control is slightly different, because you actually do have a human being relying on you for safety and sustenance and life lessons. To be a parent is to be a control freak of sorts, but that should only be to keep your kids from hurling themselves off a picnic table onto concrete. You still cannot control them. Those human beings you created will not take on all the qualities and lessons you want to impart—they may take on some of them, if you're lucky. And they certainly won't do flawless things with the stuff they do take. Those little human beings are human beings, just like you. They'll make mistakes you've never dreamed of, and they'll surprise you, and get hurt, and hurt others, and sometimes you'll spend weeks or months wondering what you did wrong. Remember the process of building a recipe, which starts with a protein base and then goes anywhere it wants to from there: your job as a parent is to give kids their protein base and then sit back as they do something completely nuts with it, like make Jell-O Beef Soufflé. You cannot stop them from making Jell-O Beef Soufflé. Your children will not be perfect, but they will be perfectly yours.

If you're a control freak in any regard, let's let today be the day we take a deep breath and accept this home truth: *you can only control yourself.* I personally need this either tattooed on my forehead or cross-stitched and framed on my wall. Let that information swim around in your head and let it be the relief that it is. You no longer have to concern yourself with what your roommates or friends or significant others are doing. You can leave all of that mess alone. It's exhausting to try to control the actions and emotions of others—and besides, aren't you tired of it? I can hear you saying, "Well, if other people would do their jobs I wouldn't have to control everything!" And I totally get that, because I've screamed it at the skies myself. But it doesn't matter. Trying to *will* people to love you, to clean up after themselves, to understand and adopt your views on feminism, or to enjoy themselves more just isn't going to happen, because you are not magical. You may be on your way to your Super You, but you will never be Supernatural You.

If we peel back the control freak in us, we may see a few of the mysteries behind those inner workings. We may see an emotional life that feels out of control, and where controlling external factors is a way of coping with that inability to control internal emotions. Or we may see a fear of being vulnerable to others, which can lead to thinking that, if we can control all the factors of our lives, no one will ever see us as weak or sad or weird. Or maybe we'll see a person whose attempts to control others are just a way to avoid dealing with herself. But

YOU CAN ONLY CONTROL YOURSELF

regardless of the reasons behind our control freakish actions, understanding the limits of our control in the world is our first lesson of the Super You Basic Credo. We are all captains of our own ships, and we have enough to worry about just keeping ourselves afloat. The minute you take on, as your duty, others' joy/career/well-being, you have entered into an unhealthy alliance with them. I've worked with many parents who tried to force their children to be more "normal," and I've worked with many jilted lovers desperate to win back their ex. In both cases, by trying to convince yourself you can somehow control the other person's choices, you are only setting yourself up for frustration and disappointment. One of the scariest things in life is realizing how little control you have in this world. All you can really control, ever, are your own actions. That's it. It is your job to focus on you, because that's all you can focus on.

Locus of control. Though it sounds like some sort of evil insect, it's actually incredibly relevant to becoming a Super You. The idea behind locus of control is simple: how much do you believe that you can control your own life? People with an external locus of control believe that their lives are controlled by external factors that don't involve them, like other people, the environment, or destiny. They believe that they cannot influence or change these factors. People with an internal locus of control believe that their lives are in their own hands—and in their abilities and reactions to things. We should all strive for a more internal locus of control. One, that goes with the idea that you can only control yourself. Two, it's mentally and emotionally more beneficial for you to believe your life is under your own control and not determined by teachers/coworkers/the haters. It's a bit of responsibility too, because if your life is under your control, then you can't sit back and relax as things go wrong, blaming everything on others. If things go wrong, even if it's because of outside factors, it's still your job to make them right again. Quite frankly, it can be exhausting to have an internal locus of control—but it's also empowering, and necessary for a Super You.

Rights

If you're reading this and you're American, you've definitely read the Bill of Rights in school, right? The first "right," or the First Amendment, is the oft-invoked one about freedom of speech.

> **Congress shall make no law respecting an establishment of religion, or prohibiting the free exercise thereof; or abridging the freedom of speech, or of the press; or of the right of the people peaceably to assemble, and to petition the Government for a redress of grievances.**

The forefathers loved run-on sentences, huh? Is there any version of this very cranky-sounding set of dry, flowery words that our government put forth centuries ago that applies to us? When I was in graduate school I found a Personal Bill of Rights in a book called *The Anxiety and Phobia Workbook* by Edmund J. Bourne, PhD; it resonated so much with me that I photocopied it and kept it in my bag for years. I connected with some of the rights because I absolutely agreed with them; with some others, I suppose they resonated with my Super Me, someone who liked herself more than I did. I made

truly believing in these rights one of my missions, and from time to time I'd check in to see where I was with each of them.

Now I'd like you to do the same. And note, by no means is this list exhaustive, but it's a good starting point. For each of the twenty-five rights, I ask you to rate how much you believe it is true for yourself, on a scale of 1 (I don't believe this at all) to 5 (I believe it 100 percent).

WEIRD COMIC BOOK FACT

In 1954, the Comics Code Authority was formed to allow the comic book world to regulate its own content. It included such gems as:

➡ Crimes shall never be presented in such a way as to create sympathy for the criminal.

➡ Females shall be drawn realistically without exaggeration of any physical qualities.

➡ In every instance good shall triumph over evil.

Great code, but it made for some boring comic books.

Personal Bill of Rights*

SCALE	1 I DON'T BELIEVE THIS AT ALL	2 I KINDA BELIEVE THIS	3 SOMETIMES I BELIEVE THIS	4 MOST DAYS I BELIEVE THIS	5 I BELIEVE THIS 100%
1. I have the right to ask for what I want.					
2. I have the right to say no to requests or demands I can't meet.					
3. I have the right to express all of my feelings, positive or negative.					
4. I have the right to change my mind.					
5. I have the right to make mistakes and not have to be perfect.					
6. I have the right to follow my own values and standards.					
7. I have the right to say no to anything when I feel I am not ready, it is unsafe, or it violates my values.					
8. I have the right to determine my own priorities.					
9. I have the right *not* to be responsible for others' behavior, actions, feelings, or problems.					
10. I have the right to expect honesty from others.					
11. I have the right to be angry at someone I love.					

*Reprinted with permission from *The Anxiety and Phobia Workbook*

12.	I have the right to be uniquely myself.		
13.	I have the right to feel scared and say "I'm afraid."		
14.	I have the right to say "I don't know."		
15.	I have the right not to give excuses or reasons for my behavior.		
16.	I have the right to make decisions based on my feelings.		
17.	I have the right to my own needs for personal space and time.		
18.	I have the right to be playful and frivolous.		
19.	I have the right to be healthier than those around me.		
20.	I have the right to be in a non-abusive environment.		
21.	I have the right to make friends and be comfortable around people.		
22.	I have the right to change and grow.		
23.	I have the right to have my needs and wants respected by others.		
24.	I have the right to be treated with dignity and respect.		
25.	I have the right to be happy.		

How was this for you? How many fives did you get? How many hovered in the ones and twos? Did any rights in particular resonate with you? When I first read these, Right 19, "I have the right to be healthier than those around me," punched me in the gut. I think I audibly gasped—it seemed so foreign to me that I would have the luxury, let alone the right, to be healthier than anyone else. I'm hoping you'll make these rights your own, periodically checking in with them as I did. (You can find these rights online.)

Now for a bigger question: do you have any personal rights of your own to add? There's always room to personalize a Personal Bill of Rights—it's in the title, really. I've added a couple of rights over the years myself. One is "No is a complete sentence," because I still struggle with feeling guilty about saying no, believing I must have a litany of understandable excuses. Another important addition is "I have a right to *not* want to be in a relationship," which for me applied to romantic relationships as well as friendships. Being in an intense, consuming relationship (or desperately seeking one) was the factory-setting default of how I operated. I was amazed to learn that I could live without this drama. Another one I've recently added is "I have the right to hold my own beliefs without having to explain or justify them to strangers," which I feel is pretty important if you exist on social media to any degree.

This Personal Bill of Rights is an essential part of your Super You Credo; it helps you create personal boundaries, which are your best tool for keeping yourself safe and healthy as you function in the world. Beautifully, the Personal Bill of Rights also functions as a pretty badass set of daily affirmations. Daily affirmations, for the uninitiated, are specifically constructed self-statements designed

to encourage positive thinking and healthy self-esteem. I've often found them quite cheesy, but that was before I became a Super Me and saw the value beneath the cheese. Now I just imagine they're the montage in the opening credits of my Super Me adventures TV show. These days I tie a long-sleeved T-shirt around my neck like a cape, I put a tiara on my head and my hands on my hips in a superhero stance, and I say to myself in the mirror: "I have the right to ask for what I want." "I have the right to say no to requests or demands I can't meet." Try it. It's pretty fun, and it can help on dark days.

Responsibilities Versus Choices

Most of you have probably seen at least one Spiderman movie, right? Fifteen of them have been released in my adult lifetime. In almost every Spiderman movie, Peter Parker (that's Spiderman) will have a conversation with his uncle Ben wherein old Ben tells Peter, not knowing that Peter's a superhero, that "with great power comes great responsibility." This line is a hat tip to the 1962 comic called *Amazing Fantasy* #15, which is known as the first Spiderman story. The quote is a version of a line from a U.K. Parliamentary speech, and a similar-sounding version is in the Bible too. My point is that it's a badass line, but with dubious beginnings.

Regardless of who said it first, that line has become a Spiderman line. When you're a superhero, and you task yourself with dealing with ne'er-do-wells, you do it with the understanding that your work will *never* be done. No matter what exciting, life-threatening coup you just successfully thwarted, someone will always be getting mugged somewhere. So really the line should be: "With great power comes great responsibility, but we all understand that you can't take on every single thing that happens, and no one expects you to." Luckily we're not tasking ourselves with anything so huge, but as a Super You the concern is still there—we know that we can control only ourselves, but beyond that, how do we decide what belongs on our plate, and what doesn't? Buffy Summers found out in high school that she was The Chosen One, foresworn to be the Slayer of evil. She didn't have to become the Slayer—she could have ignored it and kept being a high school student, but she made the choice to make it her responsibility. While she had a greater impetus than most of us will ever face, the question remains the same: how should we differentiate between the things we feel responsible for and the things we choose to take on in life?

For our Super You purposes, *responsibility* is something that is the required behavior of functioning, healthy human beings. And when you really break down what those required behaviors might be, there are frighteningly few responsibilities—at least in our social interactions. A *choice*, however, is something we take on on our own steam, whether willingly or unwillingly—a decision based on the information available at the time. So saying something like, "I didn't have a choice, I had to invite Farting Jonathan to the party—he made it so awkward by asking me about it so much!," while funny, would be a misrepresentation. You had no responsibility to invite Farting Jonathan to a party; you merely wanted to avoid awkwardness, so you made a choice to alleviate awkwardness by inviting him. A choice is a choice is a choice. A choice to do nothing—like not leaving a relationship that you know is unhealthy for you—is still a choice.

We are responsible for our own happiness—that is 100 percent an inside job, and no one else's. However, we are absolutely not responsible for anyone else's happiness. You can, if you like, choose to bring joy and happiness into another person's life, but at no point is that your burden to carry. I wasted much of my time and energy for years thinking it was my job to entertain the people around me, to keep them laughing so they'd see I had worth. If they stopped laughing, I feared, they'd see I was lame and would stop hanging out with me. I mistook my *choice* to make people laugh as a *responsibility*, and therefore hated doing it. These days, when I choose to make people laugh, it feels like a fun expression rather than a grim chore.

Understanding the distinction between responsibilities and choices became particularly important to me when I started writing full-time, and it became essential when I started doing a podcast about video games a few years ago. Podcast listeners become incredibly invested in the podcasts they listen to, as they spend at least an hour each week listening to your voice, and sometimes, as a result, they start believing they should have a say in the podcast content. My co-host and I were getting bombarded with emails saying: "You did this wrong!" or "I don't like how you said this, you should fix this!" or "How dare you not talk about _____!"

We got pretty stressed-out trying to satisfy all these people, and started making all these changes to how we structured the podcasts and the types of things we talked about—until we reminded ourselves of a few important things: we choose to make a podcast because we like doing it; it is our responsibility to make the best podcast we can; and it is not our responsibility to make the podcast that (all) our listeners want, because it is the listener's choice to listen or not.

The relief we felt upon these realizations was immense. We had been taking on responsibility for *other people's* choices, which was too much responsibility. And that's always going to be stress-inducing because, as we discussed before, we don't have control over anyone but ourselves. By taking on responsibility for others, we set up internal conflicts that couldn't be resolved. We also weren't focused on creating anymore; we were focused on making other people happy. I think women specifically struggle with this—at least from what I've seen in my own life: this issue of realizing that not every single thing is our responsibility.

I realize you may not have a podcast—although you probably do, given that most everyone does—but regardless of how relatable that example is, the idea of stress coming from the confusion between choice and responsibility has far-reaching implications in many areas of life. Let's go through the various roles we might play to try to suss out the differences between choices and responsibilities in each. Note that some of the choices listed below are healthier choices and some less healthy. I've included those because you, as we all will, sometimes make less healthy choices in your life. This isn't about making only positive choices; it's about understanding that, even when you're making less healthy choices, you're doing so of your own volition, for reasons that only need to make sense to you. If you choose to invite Farting Jonathan to a party because you would prefer his gassy company to feeling awkward, that is your choice, and it's an understandable choice. This is that "living with intentionality" horn I keep honking. This is about the agency you have in your own lives—agency to make amazing decisions, and agency to fuck up royally sometimes. Let's dig in.

Friend

★ You have a *choice* to be a friend to someone. It is not your *responsibility* to be someone's friend because "he needs a friend" or because you're a nice person.

★ If you decide to be someone's friend, you have a *responsibility* to put as much into the relationship as you would like to receive. If you are consistently giving 100 percent to friends who barely have the time for you, it is then your *choice* to change that situation—rather than waiting for the other person to be a better friend.

★ You are not *responsible* for your friend's well-being. It is your *choice* to try to cheer up or otherwise help her when she seems to be struggling.

★ You have a *choice* to end a relationship if it feels unhealthy for you.

Romantic Partner

★ I personally don't agree with the sentiment: "I just fell in love, I couldn't help it." You have a *choice* to act on your romantic feelings toward someone. Everyone has romantic feelings— sometimes at inappropriate times, or toward inappropriate people. But it is always your *choice* to act on them, not a "biological responsibility." (So said a boyfriend when I caught him making out with a girl from my Spanish class.)

★ When it comes to dating, you have a *choice*, not a *responsibility*. Just because someone likes you, pursues you, and seems like a nice person, you are still under no obligation to date him. In fact, you are under no obligation to have a romantic life at all.

★ If you are in a romantic relationship, you have a *responsibility* to communicate your needs and desires. Otherwise that person will have no idea of how best to be a romantic partner to you. (We'll talk about that a bit more later.)

★ You have a *responsibility* to directly express to your romantic partner when he's hurt you. You may *choose* also to scream at him—whether or not that would be a good idea.

★ You are not *responsible* for your romantic partner's well-being. It is your *choice* to offer support to him during difficult times, but you should not be his sole means of support.

★ You have a *choice* to leave a relationship that isn't meeting your needs. I would love to call this a responsibility, but the truth is that some situations are too complicated for this to be so cut-and-dried. If you are unhappy with a relationship, you do have *choices*: you can leave, or you can stay and adapt.

★ You do not have the *responsibility* to change yourself in order to meet your partner's needs. You can make a *choice* to change if you are able and would like to. And note: this goes both ways. The person you are dating is not the perfected version you see in your head; the person you are dating is the person in front of you.

Employee

★ You have a *responsibility* to do the best work that you are compensated for. (You also have a *choice* to do the bare minimum at work, but that's a separate issue.)

★ You have a *choice* to take on more work, or to work toward a promotion. It is not your *responsibility* to become a workaholic.

★ You are not *responsible* for your coworkers' quality of work. If a coworker you really like is not pulling his weight, let that be his *choice*.

★ You have a *responsibility* to advocate for yourself at work. No one else will do it for you.

★ You have a *choice*, if you are miserable in your job, to seek out other employment. I would prefer this to be a responsibility, but the reality is that jobs can be hard to come by, and sometimes we have to suck it up and do the best we can to support ourselves.

Daughter

★ You have a *responsibility* to your parents to live as healthily as possible. Not their version of healthy, but your own.

★ You have a *choice* of how you would like to relate to your parents. If you are still living under their roof, this is a little bit tougher. If you live at home and do not like how you relate to your parents, then your *choice* is to move out when you are of age to do so, and until then, adapt.

★ You have a *responsibility* to communicate to your parents how you would like to relate to them. They can choose to either accept that or not, but at least you will have fulfilled your responsibility.

★ You have a *choice* to decide whether the level of dysfunction/annoyance in your family is something you can tolerate out of respect for your family relationships. Some dysfunction—critical comments about your hair, for example—are par for the course in dealing with parents. Other dysfunction, like refusing to accept aspects of your life, or berating you emotionally, may be more than you're willing to put up with to remain healthy.

★ You may *choose* to live a life that pleases your parents, but that is your choice. You are not *responsible* for living up to your parents' expectations of you.

★ You have a *responsibility* to end any financial reliance on your parents. This is essential to giving you the ability to make choices. While you aren't their slave just because they pay your phone bill, as long as you financially depend on them, you are limited in some of the choices you can make about your emotional independence.

Mother

★ You have a *responsibility* to make sure that your child's needs are taken care of.

★ You have a *responsibility* to educate yourself on parenting skills.

★ You have a *choice* to decide what role your child will play in your life. Will your child become the thing that defines you, your entire world then revolving around that role? Will your child become part of your family in a way that allows you to take dance classes and read a book sometimes? Both choices are valid—just know that they are choices.

★ It is not your *responsibility* to be everything to your child.

★ You are not *responsible* for being a "perfect mother." It is your *choice* to attempt such a feat—though please be aware that no one yet has achieved this.

★ It is your *choice*, not your *responsibility*, to eschew your own needs in favor of your child's. Sometimes this choice is the best one to make, but it is not your responsibility as a mother to do this.

Woman

★ You have a *responsibility* to be the version of woman that is most comfortable for you, and you have a *choice* in whether doing so is important to you.

★ You have a *choice* to dress however you want.

★ You have a *choice* to procreate. This is not a *responsibility*.

★ You have a *responsibility* to keep yourself physically safe, to the best of your abilities, in a world that is sometimes unsafe for women. Unfortunately we cannot expect the world to keep us safe. You have a *choice* to determine what that level of safety is.

★ You have a *choice* in *how* to express your sexuality (if you choose to express it at all), and *whether* you express your sexuality with a partner. You have a *responsibility* to make your sexuality choices just for yourself.

Creative Person

★ You have a *responsibility* to find outlets to release your creativity.

★ You have a *responsibility* to make the best version of whatever you choose to create.

★ You have a *choice* to release your creative efforts into the world.

★ You have a *choice* in what your creative effort actually is—it is your choice to define it. Some people think we're supposed to have a hobby, a true passion in life, that should ideally be our career as well. This may or may not be true. There can be creative expression in any job, no matter how menial; there can be satisfaction in every job.

Consumer

★ You have a *choice* to consume the things you want—food/movies/TV/books/comic books.

★ You have a *choice* to stop consuming something that displeases you.

★ You have a *responsibility* to be mindful of the things you consume. This doesn't mean you should always or only consume high-quality stuff; it means that ideally you will consume, not blindly, but with intentionality.

Yourself

★ You have a *responsibility* to keep your body as healthy as you can.

★ You have a *responsibility* to provide for yourself so that you may live as comfortably as possible.

★ You have a *choice* to try to be skinny/muscular or to get a fat booty.

★ You have a *responsibility* to keep yourself as emotionally healthy as you are able.

★ Changes will come to your personality and your life whether you like it or not. You have a *choice* of whether to continually evolve to keep up with them or not.

★ With each new day, you have a *choice* either to stagnate or to push yourself to be better. Both options are necessary, and both options are valid.

This is by no means an exhaustive collection; there are a ton more roles that could be added. This list merely serves to get us to start thinking about the distinction between *responsibility* and *choice*—and to see the difference between them. This is especially important because sometimes our behaviors can become so ingrained that we automatically approach some choices as if they were responsibilities. For the next few days, as you go about your day, keep your Super You notebook handy. I urge you to start keeping tabs on the specific actions you take throughout the day. For each action, ask yourself two things: (1) whether it's a responsibility or a choice, and (2) whether it's something your Super You would do. Becoming aware of internal processes that are currently on autopilot is incredibly important, both in getting to know yourself and in making specific changes for yourself.

The Super You Credo is complete! It's a fourfecta (that's a trifecta made of four things) of control, rights, choices, and responsibilities. They are the basics of being a healthy, functional person. If you don't believe that now, keep coming back to it; my hope is that someday you will.

CHAPTER 4

Head Versus Heart: Making Emotions Your Bitch

So by now we're well aware that all we can control is ourselves, but how do we do that? Specifically, how do we do that with our emotions? Emotions are the most nebulous and yet most influential system our bodies have—they can't be quantified in any objective sense, there's no "emotional center" of the body— and yet many of us spend our lives as slaves to our emotions, or running from them so desperately we don't have the energy to do anything else. If you were a cyborg crime fighter, then your emotions would be the software that your cyborg runs on. (This is where superhero examples come in—they sound cooler than telling you we're going to be "getting in touch with our emotions.") So, what is your relationship to that software? Does it work seamlessly, anticipating and understanding your every request, or does it leave you impatiently staring at a screen, waiting for things to catch up? Are you able to switch between your old-school, childlike annoyance with your parents and your grown-up fondness and acceptance of them—within milliseconds? This chapter is devoted to discussing how well your emotional software works for you. And while there are nearly infinite ways for you to relate to your emotions, for the sake of keeping this book under one million words, I'm going to talk about just two types of malfunctions your emotional software can experience: overload, for those of us whose feelings drown and confuse and surprise us; and defragmentation, for those of us whose feelings are so muffled and overly intellectualized we barely feel anything at all. Obviously, this is a continuum, with these being the extremes at either end—most of us will land somewhere in the middle. In fact, we're supposed to be somewhere in the middle, experiencing both highs and lows but mostly feeling even-keeled, understanding where our emotions come from and savoring their sweet weirdness. Wherever you are on that continuum, I'm hoping to help you move more toward that center.

For those of you not there yet, note that you're in good company, as I've only recently found a steady spot in that emotional center myself—having developed a consistent, easygoing, mutually beneficial relationship with my emotions. For most of my life, I've whipsawed from one side of the continuum to the other, feeling out of control at both ends. While I've come to accept that swinging from overly feeling my emotions to overly intellectualizing my emotions must have been necessary for me to grow into and develop my own personality, all the same, the journey could have been less

embarrassing and less painful. So I want to share what I've learned in the hopes that your journey can go smoother than mine.

A Somewhat Embarrassing Look Back at Emily's Emotional Journey

Part 1: The Childhood Years

For the first half of my life or so, I was firmly planted in the "drowning in emotions" camp of dealing with my feelings. When I was eight or nine, I sobbed uncontrollably for three hours when my mother accidentally struck a raccoon while driving us home from a beach trip. I can still see that raccoon's little lifeless body flopped across the highway, and if I'm honest, it still kinda saddens me. If someone said a harsh word to me in school or piano class, I thought my world was crashing down around me. At a slumber party in elementary school, the hostess's older aunt came into the living room to say hello to us girls before being driven back to her care facility, and the sight of her, frail and sick and sweet, was so upsetting that I started crying. We all started crying, the whole slumber party, all of us suddenly confronted with our own mortality. (Again, fun at parties.)

Part 2: Pre-Adolescence

If you hadn't guessed, the situation didn't improve in my pre-adolescence, when minor tiffs with friends or boyfriends would have me keening and snotting noisily in class like a figure in a Shakespearean tragedy. After the first dozen times this happened, rather than patting my back and telling me everything was going to be okay, my friends learned to ignore me when I cried. I didn't blame them. There was no comfort for me. I felt adrift in a sea of my own emotions—and during these years, my main emotions were heartbreak, sorrow, the pain of alienation, and the utter despair of not being good enough. "Not good enough" consumed me, and intense crying was the only way I knew how to try to get it out of me. Outside of class teachers would ask how I was doing, but despite their kindness I felt them fighting not to roll their eyes at my stories of heartbreak and betrayal and sick aunts. That's the thing: I knew I warranted a few eye rolls. I knew that how I was feeling was a bit much. If someone had asked me in the middle of my hysterics if I wished I could stop, I would have said yes: I desperately wished I could stop; I just couldn't figure out how.

Please understand: I think being emotional and giving yourself permission to be vulnerable and shed tears are great and brave things that are undervalued in our world—but this wasn't that. I was walking around so emotionally raw that it interfered with my life.

Part 3: The Teenage Years

That sea of misery and embarrassment and longing kept churning and churning until, in my teen years, it turned into overwhelming rage. Now, it's not unusual for teenagers to be angry—I think that may be part of the developmental process of becoming an adult—but my anger wasn't useful to me, or engaging, or motivating. It just was, and it wasn't manageable. All-encompassing and exhausting, it was my reason for rejecting others. I'd feel alienated, get angry, and then push people away with my anger—further alienating

myself. All the emotions I always carried weighed me down; I felt pregnant with them. So, as I'd done with crying as a child, having a good hysterical rage was the only way I knew how to give birth. When I discovered angry, dark, heavy music in high school, I felt an almost palpable lightening of my heart. Instead of my hurricane of tears and fury, I now had another form of release. I could rage to music, and what's more, I could do it in public, around other people, and consider it a form of entertainment! I could make friends based on my fondness for obscure German bands! I could go see those bands live, and marvel at the community I felt there. I could wear fishnets and huge band shirts and Doc Martens and have my rage validated. I remained adrift and self-absorbed, but I also felt grateful to have an outlet for my emotions that didn't involve embarrassing myself in class.

Part 4: Adulthood, First Attempt

After many exhausting years of being consumed, and with a little bit of college, a few heartbreaks, and some brain development under my belt, I came up with a foolproof plan to fix my problem. Putting myself out there, raging or crying or otherwise, was giving people too much power over me, I decided. I wanted my power back, and I didn't like feeling so vulnerable. I saw my emotionality as a weakness only. The wisest thing to do, clearly, would be to lock all those feelings away as much as possible. This was easier said than done and took a while to perfect, but it started with me visualizing a literal box inside my brain that I could lock my emotions into. When upsetting things happened to me, I would take a very deep breath, I would open the box, and I would picture the little cartoon ladies from the opening credits of *The Carol Burnett Show* (I realize that this is an archaic reference for most of you, but Google them; they are perfect for this visualization) and shove my emotions into a tiny box. I would grit my teeth and push everything down, and I found that I weirdly did feel fine.

Fine. Not a raging storm, but fine. Amazingly, this was my first taste of getting objective emotional distance from myself, a technique I still use a lot, just in a healthier way these days. We talked about the idea of emotional distance a bit with the "reality show" technique earlier, and we'll talk about it more in future chapters. Back then my emotional distance was about shutting my emotions out. Now it's about observing them, and myself, from afar so that I can take better stock of them. Being cheated on? It sucked. Everything sucks. Who cares? Realizing that I no longer fit into yet another pair of jeans because I was gaining weight so rapidly? Who cares, fuck you. It seemed unrelated to me at the time, but today I find it interesting that when I was in my prime emotion-stuffing phase I was also in my prime emotional-eating phase. Perhaps I thought that eating ham pinwheels—a real thing I created out of pizza dough, ham, and cream cheese—would somehow help keep down all the feelings that overwhelmed me. I reveled in my new-found freedom. After all those years of my emotions controlling me, now I was the one controlling them. I was in control of myself, I thought, even though I was now so afraid of my emotions that I felt my only choice was to imprison them. I wasn't feeling anything, and that seemed like a luxury after so many years of feeling everything way too deeply.

DROWNING
expectations
fatigue
ANGER
ANXIETY
pain
...What ocean?
love
VULNERABILITY
RAGE
FEAR

Part 5: Adulthood, Second Attempt

From a safe distance, I progressed from not feeling my emotions at all to being able to intellectualize the trials and tribulations of my life, analyzing them and having a witty take on them so quickly that feeling them was no longer an option. I skipped the feeling step entirely. It's a great skill for writers and creators to have, to process things so quickly and have something to say about them so soon after they've occurred, but skipping over actual feelings is not the best skill for a healthy psyche. Rather than "Who cares?" being my dominant attitude, it would be "Sure, it sucks to be cheated on, but that guy thought Africa was a country, and besides, all relationships are temporary, ultimately. So I'm fine." I'm fine I'm fine I'm more than fine, I'm intellectual. The Clever Girl persona I had loved as a child was back, and I was able to entertain groups of girlfriends with my hilarious tales of bad boyfriends, and why love is a sham. I marveled at how evolved I was, how in control I was, how lovely it felt to have the storm subsiding inside me. I was so busy marveling at myself that I didn't notice how drab and lifeless everything felt. How blank. How sterile. How cynical.

I had my cherished distance, but it had come at a cost: I wasn't able to make connections with the people in my life who mattered, and I wasn't forging any new relationships that went any deeper than witty nights out together. I confused gossiping about horrific dates with making intimate connections with others. And I would have been sad, if I'd been able to be sad. What I was actually feeling was afraid: afraid of letting my emotions take over again. What I didn't understand is that you are *supposed* to feel a variety of emotions. You are supposed to experience the highs and the

lows and the blankness too. You are sometimes supposed to feel full of chaos, and sometimes you are supposed to feel like a robot, devoid of human emotion. When you aren't experiencing a variety of emotions, you either keep yourself from appreciating the complex magic show that our brains and hearts create for us, or you become exhausted from feeling the same two feelings to death. I had gone from one extreme to another, but they both lacked variety. And what a Super You needs is variety.

I am grateful to my "robot phase," as it honed my ability to get distance from myself. And I still use emotional distance with myself regularly, but the truth is that our emotions *aren't* separate from us. They are us. They are within us. They are created by our brains and our preconceptions and our moods and thoughts. They should be a badge of pride, a gorgeous and complex piece of machinery that occasionally has the capacity to surprise us but mostly functions under our command. Wonder Woman's compassion is considered both her greatest strength and her greatest weakness by some nerds. Rather than being a cold, hard, crime-fighting machine, she is in love with a man, she cares about humanity, and she cares about justice. Caring is a tool that the bad guys can use against her, but it's also the thing that keeps her fighting so hard. And so it is with us and our emotions. They help us make decisions, alert us to things we may not be aware of, and keep us connected to people. But for too many of us, our emotions aren't doing any of that. For too many of us, our emotions are a mystery, and we are slaves to them. Wherever you are with your emotions is exactly where you're supposed to be right now. But where does a Super You want to be with her emotions?

A Super You Makes Her Emotions Her Bitch

"Making your emotions your bitch" is a crass phrase that I use mainly because it makes me giggle, but the goal here is to take your emotions from wherever they are—the driver's seat of the car, the silent passenger locked in the trunk, or the whiny kid in the backseat—and put them firmly in the front passenger seat, riding shotgun with you and your thoughts. Your emotions are there for your pleasure and for consultation, but they need to know their place, which is right beside your thoughts. Figuring out how to work with your emotions instead of being bullied by them or running from them takes time, it takes experimentation, it takes being wrong, and it takes really listening to yourself. It takes logic, gut instinct, intelligence, and heart. Now, I needed to go through my extremes of emotion in order to land where I am today. But, with help, I could have done it a bit faster and escaped with fewer battle scars. Wherever you are, dear reader, whoever you are: in writing this book for you I am just trying to help your journey be a little less painful and less drawn-out than mine was. So let's start with baby steps—namely, when we were babies.

When we are born, our only real emotions are comfort/contentment—"good"—and discomfort/discontent—"bad." Being fed, having a dry diaper, seeing that big person who feeds you—these things are good. To make this clinical and lame-sounding, these things are stimuli, and the baby goo-goos that we do when we take in positive stimuli are our reactions. Lots of other stimuli bring out bad reactions—things like being hungry, full diaper, not seeing the big person who takes care of you. Make sense?

Now, that palette of emotions expands a bit when we get older into four basic emotions: happy, sad, scared, or angry. As we age we add on complex layers to those four basics, to create emotions like "scared we're going to lose a mate to that really hot person," which is jealousy; or "happy to see a person you care about alive but mad that he decided to jump off a balcony at a party," which is relief; or "happy that we had something really good happen but also want to downplay it so as not to seem like we're showing off," which is what we call a humblebrag. I used to have a poster that showed illustrated versions of ninety-six emotions in a big grid, and part of my sessions with children was having them shoot a sticky dart at a random emotion and then we'd talk

FUN FACT ABOUT BABIES AND CREATIVE PEOPLE

Babies pay attention to everything around them in a general sense, because they haven't learned what's important yet. Adults focus on one or two things in a room and learn to tune out the "background noise" of other stimuli. Creative people, it is thought, retain some of that ability to focus on everything just a little bit.

about what it meant, what its root emotions were, and when the child had felt that emotion. It was a helpful exercise for both parties (besides the fun of getting hit with a lot of sticky darts), because I noticed that I'd never myself actually thought about the deeper, more fundamental emotions behind complex feelings like discouragement or sympathy. I also noticed how jealousy was made up of different emotions for me than for an eight-year-old boy than for my supervisor. So be aware that the things that make up your complex emotions won't always match those of other people. Especially keep this in mind the next time you're arguing with your partner.

So now: *how* to make your emotions your bitch is detailed in the steps that follow—keeping in mind that the process of making your emotions your bitch will never be complete; it will need to be re-evaluated as you grow and mature. Not everything here will apply to you, since it's impossible to address everyone's needs in one book, but, I hope this will be a good starting point. For each step of getting your emotional life more under your command, I will address the two extremes that I've both experienced and seen in others: the hotheaded superheroes, those of us who easily get consumed and weighed down by our emotions—think Hulk and his constant Hulking-out when angry; and the automaton superheroes, those of us who either don't feel any connection to our emotions or process them so quickly that we can spit out opinions on our feelings without ever feeling them. For this, think less popular superhero The Vision, a cyborg created by Ultron in *The Avengers*.

Step I: Digging in to Your Emotions

The first step to making your emotions your bitch is, simply, to start thinking about complex feelings for yourself, and to dig down within to see what those feelings are made of when you experience them. I could add a list of emotion words here, but we all have the Internet. I highly encourage you to Google "emotion list" and then, in your handy-dandy notebook, go through each emotion and ask yourself a few questions:

★ How does this emotion feel to you?

★ Do you think you feel this emotion differently than other people do, or similarly?

★ What primary emotions (happy, sad, scared, angry) can you break this down into?

★ Are you afraid to feel this emotion, or would you welcome it?

★ How did you feel this emotion as a kid? How do you experience it now?

★ When was the last time you felt this emotion? What was happening?

★ Do you like how you handle this emotion?

For all you Emotional Hulks out there, this may not be a terrible difficult task. So just keep it simple, focusing on only one situation and the cocktail of feelings that went with it; don't try to cover every last detail. This is also a chance for you to think about the situations that tend to set you off—essentially, the kinds of emotions that certain stimuli evoke in you.

For you Intellectualizing Visions, while you should certainly take a glance at the more complicated feelings, I'm more interested in your feelings of happiness, sadness, fear, and anger. How do you remember experiencing them as a small child? What triggered these emotions in you way back then? Do you remember a situation in which you were *supposed* to feel one of these more complex emotions but didn't? Why did you think you were supposed to feel that way? What was stopping you from feeling it? When you're protecting yourself from your own emotions, there actually is an emotion at work here: fear. What are you afraid of feeling if you start really sitting with your emotions?

Step 2: Getting in the Moment

I've referred to sitting with your emotions a few times now, so let's make sure we're on the same page of what that means. Thinking about your emotions in past situations may be somewhat workable, but what does it mean to actually sit with yourself and experience your emotions as they are happening? It means stopping everything and focusing on yourself. This is much harder than it seems. It's so much easier in life to focus on others instead of ourselves, and when we do focus on ourselves, to keep it on something simple, like our bangs. Being alone with yourself can be tough, and some people spend their entire lives trying to avoid it, but it's a necessary thing for a Super You to do. Our emotions aren't simple. They aren't always fun to feel. They aren't easily fixed. Emotional Hulks just let the emotions take over without keeping a sense of their intellect, whereas Intellectualizing Visions just focus on anything other than what's going on inside their hearts and bodies. Whichever direction you're coming from, here's how we start getting more in control of our emotions: by increasing our self-awareness.

How-To: Mega Awareness

To follow is my Super You spin on an established technique for "increasing mindfulness." (You can Google that term if you want to go your own route, eschewing the cape.) This is a technique that I

use specifically for snapping me back into myself and helping me to feel without being overwhelmed by feeling. If you were a super-hero, this would be a combination of a freeze ray and Spidey-Sense, Spiderman's incredibly vague psychic ability to know when some-one is about to attack him. Since we are Super Yous, we're going to call this technique Mega Awareness.

So much of the time we're on autopilot: as we drive to work, eat breakfast, or just sit at our computers refreshing Twitter over and over again. Two of the universal Super You Missions I mentioned earlier are acting with intention and increasing self-awareness—both of which are the exact opposite of being on autopilot. Mega Awareness helps to break us out of autopilot and gets us to start focusing on ourselves again.

I start by sitting down and, if possible, I close my eyes. Closing your eyes keeps you from being distracted by how you look or what the world looks like around you. I start at my feet, consid-ering: How does it feel to be wearing these shoes right now? Are they comfortable? How are my feet resting on the floor? Are they tapping? I experience what it's like to sit where I am sitting, as me. No one else experiences sitting just like me.

Next, I move up my legs: How do they feel in these pants? Am I cold or warm? Is there a breeze? Are there any weird smells? Are my hands clenched? Balled up? Resting in my lap? Are my nails ragged? Is my forehead sweaty? Is my heart beating fast, slow, or normally? So, now you: focus on your heartbeat for a bit, listening to its rhythm, detecting its speed. Then move on to your breathing: Is it fast? Labored? Slow? Phlegmy? Take inventory of all the ways that you're existing in the moment you're in without judging or edi-torializing. If you are sweaty, be sweaty—note that information and then let it go. Be observant of yourself. Put your hand on your stomach and take deep breaths, focusing on making your stomach push outward as you inhale. This is breathing from your diaphragm. Feel your body moving as you take these deep breaths. Inhale for a count of seven, hold for a count of seven, and exhale for a count of seven.

Once you do this breathing for a few rounds, and have become reasonably comfortable existing in your body at this moment, start focusing on your feelings. Let's say your heartbeat or breathing was on the fast side: those are bodily cues that you're feeling distress. What are you feeling? Are there many feelings? If you need to look at a list of emotion words, feel free. Can what you are feeling be boiled down to happy, sad, scared, or angry? What does it feel like to feel these emotions? Have you ever felt this way before? When? What was the situation? Are you comfortable feeling these emotions, or does it suck?

After sitting with how these emotions feel for a few minutes, start asking what you *think* about these emotions. Why do you think you're experiencing them right now? What brought them on? Give yourself five to ten minutes to really think about them. If doing that feels stupid or goofy, then you're on the right track. The ego does amazing things to protect itself, including making you think that what you're doing is stupid.

While Mega Awareness can be used for recalling past situations, with practice it can also be called upon in the present. When something stressful or upsetting is happening, it can help get you out of the loop of over- or underreacting and get you to focus on yourself and what to do next. We'll talk more about that in the next step.

Emotional Hulks, your challenge here will be taking those deep breaths and rooting your brain deeply in yourself so that you can experience how your body is reacting. Take care to spend time on this step—as you feel emotions deeply, you may think you have this down pat, but there is a difference between experiencing emotions and being overrun by them. Let your emotions communicate with you rather than yell at you. Sit with yourself until they quiet down a bit, enough that you can understand them. I'll refer to Tim Gunn again here: you should be wearing the dress rather than letting the dress wear you.

Intellectualizing Visions, if you're having trouble with this, ask a friend if (and how) he can tell when you are happy, sad, scared, or angry. Ask about your demeanor, your facial expressions, or how you communicate. Our friends will sometimes be better at reading us than we are at reading ourselves.

So, to wrap it up: practice practice practice sitting with yourself and feeling how your body feels in the moment. Then let that logic transfer into feeling your feelings.

Step 3: Diagramming!

And now, a quick and incredibly simplified lesson in brain development. Not simplified because you can't handle it, but simplified because I'm not an expert in brain development. This is a way I've come to think about emotions that is helpful to me, but isn't the most scientific, so if you want to pooh-pooh it, I will not stop you. I will say that it's something I would pull out when working with tantrummy teenagers, because it would have been helpful for me to see a diagram like this when I was a teenager. Think back to how we talked about how babies react to simple stimuli, when everything feels either good or bad. We experience a stimulus, like being awake too long or having a poopy diaper, we experience feeling bad, and we react by crying. Easy.

Stimulus to Physical Reaction Table 1: Babies

STIMULUS	SENSATION/EMOTION	PHYSICAL REACTION
POOP IN DIAPER	Uncomfortable (a.k.a. bad)	Cry

When we get a bit older, we develop the ability to think about the emotions we're feeling, so our reactions to stimuli change. We pause during the emotional reaction to a stimulus to give ourselves time to *choose* an action. Instead of it being stimulus–emotion–reaction, now it looks like this:

Stimulus to Physical Reaction Table 2: Kiddies

STIMULUS	SENSATION/EMOTION	THOUGHTS ABOUT THAT EMOTION	PHYSICAL REACTION
A KID HITS YOU AT RECESS.	Physically hurt, embarrassed, a little scared.	I can't let anyone see me crying.	Hit the kid back and then run away to cry in the bathroom.

As you see in the above chart, rather than responding solely based on being hurt and embarrassed, our kid selves also have thoughts about those feelings, and instead of responding to just the feelings, we respond based on the feelings *and* the thoughts. This is a huge step in cognitive development. Note too that

experiencing that crucial, halting step of forming thoughts about our emotions doesn't always lead to making the best decisions in how we react; but the "rightness" or "wrongness" of the reactions isn't the focus here—the focus is merely on the new step of reacting to the thoughts. Rather than primitively reacting to our emotions alone, we're thinking through the environment, who we are, and our relation to the people around us *before* reacting. That's cognitive development at work.

For many years, when I was drowning in my emotions, I ignored the "thoughts about that emotion" step and reverted back to baby status. A boy ignored me, I felt rejected and embarrassed, and like a baby, I would cry. A lot. And let me tell you, it was kind of a bummer to let all this brain development just go to waste.

So the next step of making emotions your bitch is exploring and understanding the cognitive process that is at work inside your brain for every stimulus you experience. Even if you're ignoring a step of it, or understanding all the steps and then still making weird decisions about how to react, this process is still at work, and we need to learn to pay attention to it, to make it less automatic. I'd like you to think back to a couple of events, whether innocuous or portentous, that you've had recently: interactions you've had with bosses, or a significant other, or your parents—anything that elicited a reaction from you. Then diagram—literally write down—the stimulus, the resulting emotions, the thoughts about those emotions, and your physical reaction, as shown in the table above. Start with any of the four that seems the most obvious and clear to you, and fill in the other parts accordingly. Try not to sanitize your answers or judge yourself for them—you're just trying to get a sense of how your process works. It's a good idea to use it regularly, to be practiced in it, so it's available to you in times of stress and emotional upheaval.

Emotional Hulks, your job here will be to get very honest—and deep—with yourself while going through this exercise. You may discover, through diagramming, that some of your reactions are not a result of the stimulus you've been presented with, or that some of your thoughts are irrational and not at all related to your emotions. When I first started doing this, I would have to start with my reaction, because often I was in the dark about why I was reacting the way I was. I would freak out at a deli counter guy and then realize, days later, that I was actually upset about a phone call with my mother that I was avoiding thinking about. While the deli counter guy didn't deserve my freak-out, he's the one who got it, because I wasn't ready to let my mother have my freak-out. It's a beautiful dance, really, when you figure it all out.

And for you Intellectualizing Visions, this should be pretty easy. When doing this exercise, you may find that the thoughts come to you way easier than the emotions. When I was in this phase of myself, I found that my "thoughts about that emotion" column was fuller than the emotion column itself. "It isn't good to be cheated on because it creates distrust in future relationships," I could write confidently, without properly letting myself feel betrayed or hurt. If you find yourself writing emotion words without feeling them, I challenge you to keep digging back to the last time you remember feeling that particular emotion, whatever it is, and remember what that felt like in your gut, not just in your head.

Here are a few examples from my past week.

Stimulus to Physical Reaction Table 3: Emily

STIMULUS	SENSATION/EMOTION	THOUGHTS ABOUT THAT EMOTION	PHYSICAL REACTION
ROWDY CROWD AT MY STAND-UP SHOW LAST WEEK. PEOPLE WERE RUDE TO STAFF.	Mad. Seething mad rage.	This staff works for free and doesn't deserve this.	Gave some free video games to the staff.

Stimulus to Physical Reaction Table 4: Emily Redux

STIMULUS	SENSATION/EMOTION	THOUGHTS ABOUT THAT EMOTION	PHYSICAL REACTION
~~MY HUSBAND DOESN'T NOTICE THAT I'VE GOTTEN MY BANGS TRIMMED.~~ I EMAILED A PITCH TO AN EDITOR AND HAVEN'T HEARD BACK.	Anxious. Nervous. Feeling like a fraud.	Well, I guess I'm just invisible and that was a dumb pitch. What was I thinking?	Snapped at my husband.

Notice how I revised the stimulus on that second one. That's because understanding ourselves isn't always easy. It's also because there are two things that can trip us up, whether we're Hulks or Visions, while working through this table: feeling anger, and misinterpreting the stimulus.

How Anger Can Trip You Up When Digging in to Your Emotions

Anger is a fascinating emotion to me. It can be motivating, it can be debilitating, it can be righteous, it can be blinding, and it can be incredibly protective. It's that last one we don't talk about enough. What do I mean by "protective"? Well, how often have you been incredibly angry with a friend or romantic partner, only to simmer down later and realize that what you were actually feeling was hurt? Anger is an emotion that we often throw on top of something more painful—like feeling hurt or scared or embarrassed—because those emotions are too difficult to feel. They're too ego-crushing. While anger is consuming, and can be destructive, it doesn't crush your ego. Anger keeps you feeling righteous. I try to think of it as a pill with a candy-flavored coating. The pill itself is made of hurt, but that's too upsetting to our ego's stomach, so a bright red anger coating is added to make it easier on the stomach. "Nothing to see here, boss!" our adorable psyches say to us. "You're doing just fine with your righteous anger! Keep going!" Our psyches do a lot of things to clumsily protect us that sometimes end up hurting us. Just remember that anytime you are feeling angry, which can sometimes be absolutely the best and most appropriate way to feel, try to question yourself. See if there's not another, harder-to-feel feeling under there that is sweetly shielded by your anger.

How Misinterpretation Can Trip You Up When Digging in to Your Emotions

Now we come to the other common trip-up of exploring our thoughts and feelings and reactions: misinterpreting a stimulus. A big part of being a grown-up and functioning in life, in my opinion, is simply figuring out when the shit belongs to you, and when the shit belongs to other people. "The shit" here refers to emotional stirrings that occur when things get heated or upsetting or conflicted or anything more than hunky dory between two or more people. Sometimes when people are in conflict, it's just about the conflict. But as we learned from the "Reality Show" technique in

Chapter 1, you aren't just interacting with another person: you're interacting with that person along with all the emotional baggage she brings to the situation, *and* with all the emotional baggage you bring to the situation. That's a lot; it's complicated enough to try to untangle just what you're actually reacting to, and unfortunately it's super easy sometimes to yell at your partner for something the boss yelled at you for. And since that's complicated for you, remember that it's complicated for other people too. If someone blows up at you and it seems like an overreaction, remember that it's the other person's shit that's truly weighing her down—and don't take it on as your shit. Let her shit belong to her. Similarly, it's not okay for you to take out your shit on people who aren't actually triggering you. And besides, snapping at someone else isn't even all that effective. Anger, and any of its underlying emotions, don't go away when you take them out on people—they just briefly subside. It's only in dealing with the stimulus at its source that we keep ourselves emotionally in balance.

I have so many examples of misinterpreting a stimulus—over- or underreacting based on my own shit rather than the situation at hand—that I could write a book on just that. I'd probably send copies to all my exes and old friends, and my parents too. Examples can be small—like having a bad day at work and then lashing out when your roommate leaves the door unlocked—and large—being unhappy in a marriage but, instead of addressing the marriage, taking on a ton of new hobbies in the hopes of being happier. The important thing is getting better at realizing when you've misidentified a stimulus (like "My husband doesn't notice that I've gotten my bangs trimmed" in my chart earlier) and then revising it with the underlying stimulus ("I emailed a pitch to an editor and haven't heard back"). It helps me to cross out the misidentified stimulus. And because no one's life is neat and simple, sometimes your feelings and thoughts will be the result of a mishmash of stimuli. So two bonus questions we can add to our diagram are: Was this reaction appropriate to the stimulus presented to me? Would an average person on an average day react to this stimulus in a similar manner, or does this seem like an overreaction or an underreaction? In the example mentioned above, snapping at my husband because I hadn't heard back from an editor is inappropriately aimed, so I can fix that by answering this additional question in my chart.

Stimulus to Physical Reaction Table 5: Super Emily

STIMULUS	SENSATION/ EMOTION	THOUGHTS ABOUT THAT EMOTION	PHYSICAL REACTION	WAS THIS AN APPROPRIATE REACTION?
MY HUSBAND DOESN'T NOTICE THAT I'VE GOTTEN MY BANGS TRIMMED. I EMAILED A PITCH TO AN EDITOR AND HAVEN'T HEARD BACK.	Anxious. Nervous. Feeling like a fraud.	"Well, I guess I'm just invisible and that was a dumb pitch. What was I thinking?"	Snapped at my husband.	Snapping at my husband is not an appropriate way to respond to him not noticing that my bangs were 2 mm shorter. Keep digging.

We'll talk about this more in chapter 10, "Being Out in the Universe", but for now, just remember always to question, within yourself, whether or not your reactions to a stimulus are appropriate to that stimulus. Diagram a few of your own emotional reactions to things from the past few days, starting with whatever step feels the most obvious—be it the emotion of "feeling overwhelmed" or the reaction of "telling a stranger to fuck off"—and then dig deep to fill in the pieces around it. And, if you can, try to keep in mind all the ways your ego could be trying to protect you during this kind of work. Ask yourself if you'd have the same reaction to this stimulus on any given day. Ask yourself if this reaction seems in line with the stimulus itself. If not, keep digging.

SUPER YOU MISSION CHECK-IN!

Before we move on, let's check in briefly with the list of missions you created earlier. Have you been able to do any of the concrete behaviors you set for yourself? Or are they still too large to take on? Are they making sense to you? Or do any of them need to be tweaked?

It is always perfectly acceptable, as you read through this book and continue thinking about yourself and your emotional health, to change your goals as you go along, making them larger or smaller depending on what you need.

Okay, now back to your regularly scheduled book programming.

Step 4: Letting Your Wants Get Involved

Once you've got a few situations diagrammed out, let's talk about how to react when things happen in real time. I'm most interested in the space between "thoughts about that emotion" and "physical reaction," because that's where we can wield the most influence. That's when we get to ask ourselves: given the situation we're in, and the emotions we're feeling, and the thoughts we're having about those feelings, *what do we want to do about it*? When my emotions were not my bitch, I often felt like they were an embarrassing distraction, an adorable antiquated folly of my youth. But emotions really can be a tremendous tool in helping us make decisions and evaluate our environment. So, once you've used your Mega Awareness and explored your thoughts about your emotions, and what brought them on, and so on, ask Super You what you want. Let's add this to our chart.

Stimulus to Physical Reaction Table 6: What Do You Want?

STIMULUS	SENSATION/ EMOTION	THOUGHTS ABOUT THAT EMOTION	WHAT DO YOU WANT?	PHYSICAL REACTION
A KID HITS YOU AT RECESS.	Physically hurt, embarrassed, a little scared.	I can't let anyone see me crying.	I want to look tough and escape.	Hit the kid back and then run away to cry in the bathroom.

This is where we get to shape ourselves. Your physical reactions should only push you toward the answer to the question "What do you want?" It's as simple as that. I know that sounds rudimentary and obvious, but you'd be surprised how often we act in ways that are in opposition to what we actually want. I think where we get tripped up is in the difference between what we actually want and what we think we're supposed to want. Let me give you permission, here and now, to want whatever you want, even if it's not the most mature and emotionally evolved stuff to want.

A list of acceptable wants:

⚡ I want this situation to improve.

⚡ I want to communicate my needs to another person.

⚡ I want to feel happier.

⚡ I want to feel heard.

⚡ I want to get out of this situation safely.

⚡ I want to keep this job.

⚡ I want to make someone feel terrible for how he treated me.

⚡ I want to punish others.

⚡ I want to stay exactly like this because I'm too scared to change.

As you can see, some of these wants are dumb—and not things a therapist would approve of, but that's okay too. The key to diagramming your emotions and thoughts is not about being a Super You, it's about really understanding yourself. It's about acting with intentionality.

Step 5: Giving Yourself a Safe Space to Experience and Release Emotions

Part of what bummed me out about growing up, and still does, is that we are no longer allowed to just throw tantrums. Don't get me wrong: I'm much happier with myself as a non-tantrummy adult than as a tantrummy one. But it's sad to me that many of the things that are considered semi-healthy outlets for children are considered no longer appropriate for adults because we've supposedly "grown out of that." While I'm okay with this being true of things like eating scabs, I still think we all deserve healthy outlets for our emotions that are as internally satisfying as throwing a nice tantrum—whether or not we choose to act on them. The next step to making your emotions your bitch, then, is giving them a safe space to play. Consider: a dog that gets regular walks and play sessions most likely won't destroy your pillows while you're gone. So, how do we do that as grown-up people? In designating a time and a place for your emotions to run wild.

How Emotional Hulks Give Their Emotions Space

The Emotional Hulk's challenge, here, is to find ways to release emotions that aren't self-destructive or relationship-destructive. Tearjerker reality shows, horror movies, and video games are all excellent ways to let off a little emotional steam so our emotions, important as they are, don't negatively impact our day-to-day lives. I personally really like slowly tearing strips of paper and dancing very hard to intense music. Various creative arts—say drawing, or sculpting with clay or with Play-Doh—and exercise—from spin class to jumping jacks—are also excellent ways to release emotions. The trick is to make sure you focus your emotions on what you're doing. I do that by literally stating the thing that I'm emotional about while doing the activity, which is why I can sometimes be found running on a treadmill chanting "Twitter trolls" under my breath.

Emotional Hulks can also try a little thing I call the Wallow. The Wallow is letting your body and mind know that you're going to give it time to experience an overwhelming tide of feelings—but on your terms. When I start feeling overwhelmed and don't know if I'm going to be able to push through, I pull out my iCal and literally schedule for myself twenty minutes to *feel emotion*. Making it an official event somehow pacifies me enough to make it to the allotted time. Then, in those twenty minutes, I sit alone, without distractions, and I devote all my energy to letting my emotional shit come out. I recall the thing that got me stirred up, I examine it from many different angles, I immerse myself in the situation. If I feel like I'm done before the timer runs out, too bad: when wallowing, you must use the full allotted appointment time, just like at the therapist's office.

HULK CRYING STORY!

In an episode of the animated series of the Incredible Hulk, Bruce Banner (Hulk's alter ego) was poisoned, and the only way to keep him alive was to keep him Hulked-out. His friends all told him that he was a monster and they didn't like him, and Hulk remained Hulk and started crying. The poison was flushed out, and afterward everyone apologized.

You wanted my attention, I tell my emotions, and now you've got it. Advise me. Help me understand what these feelings are about. I use all the tricks of Mega Awareness here as well. Once the twenty minutes are over, I'm somewhat relieved to be done feeling so hard, and I can move on to the grown-up part: processing and thinking and analyzing and comprehending my thoughts about my emotions.

How Intellectual Visions Give Their Emotions Space

Now, you Intellectualizing Visions may have a harder time finding appropriate releases for your emotions. If we're thinking about this as a continuum, with overfeeling on one end and underfeeling on the other, for Visions the goal is to start experiencing emotions in a way that is more visceral and not so much about the sociopolitical climate or how you think other people react when in the same situation. It's about inching toward a center of feeling in your gut and your heart and *then* letting your head weigh in—instead of skipping the gut and heart entirely. For Visions, moving toward the center of this continuum specifically means you will feel more pain, and that's a tough sell, I know. Why would you want to feel more pain when you're doing just fine on your own? Just like a lot of things in this book, this isn't about *needing* to make changes; it's about deciding for yourself who you want to be and then figuring out how to get there. And while Intellectualizing Visions can be perfectly healthy, some of them may feel bored with their lives. They may feel as if their day-to-day lives are shrink-wrapped, as everything they experience is somehow limited.

The best way to break out of this shrink-wrap is to start provoking emotions in yourself. Watch documentaries. Watch ASPCA commercials narrated by Sarah McLachlan where, rather than intellectualizing how spaying or neutering pets is the ultimate answer to the overpopulation problem, you force yourself to focus on the sad eyes of the sad puppies. Watch YouTube videos of children and pets welcoming soldiers home from war—dismissing any thoughts you have about war itself. Ask yourself questions like: "How would I feel if this was happening to me?" "How would I feel if this was happening to someone I care about?" Think back to times that you've felt heartbroken, or relieved, or overwhelmingly sad, even if those times were when you were a child—and sit with those feelings. Sit quietly and make yourself aware of your body. Is your heart beating faster or more slowly than usual? Are you breathing differently? Is your foot tapping? These physical signs can help cue you to your emotions. Make a pact with yourself that you will work on getting emotionally naked with yourself.

And then, when you're ready, make a pact with someone you trust that you will get emotionally naked with her, verbally expressing your emotions even if it feels difficult and wonky. Tell this person that you trust her, and explain what trusting her means to you. If it feels stupid to do this, explain that you feel stupid; even throw in why you feel stupid doing this. As I've said before, dig dig dig into yourself, and when you find a current of emotion, be it feeling "stupid" or "angry," ride that current. Write down what feeling that feeling is physically like for you. Keep away from intellectual descriptions. Write as an elementary school student would write. Rinse and repeat.

The most important thing about making emotions your bitch, and the thing that I didn't understand for a very long time, is that no matter what you are feeling and how you are reacting, it is important that you're reacting to the world mindfully. That, instead of being a mystery to you, your feelings, heart palpitations, tantrums, crying jags, stoicism, and reactions all make sense to *you*. That doesn't mean you behave like a well-adjusted little lady at all times, and it doesn't mean that you need to make sense to anyone else. But being on Team Super You requires that you do the hard work of delving into yourself and understanding where you're coming from.

For many years I was so angry—angry with my body for how it looked, angry with the rest of the world for making me care so much about how my body looked, angry with my mind for not being able to shut up and just enjoy what other people seemed to be enjoying—but I had stopped listening to myself for so long that I had no way of understanding where my anger came from, or where it should be directed. I limped along, finding outlets here and there that worked to some degree, but I wish I had taken the time to really sit with myself—"myself" being a person I didn't particularly want to be around—and really dig into my thoughts and my emotions. I didn't do this because I was afraid to know myself, afraid of what I'd find—but if I had done it, ultimately I would have been comforted by a sliver of understanding about myself. I still would not have liked myself, but maybe my crying jags in class would have gone from being something I was embarrassed of to something that I was doing because it was getting me the attention I desperately wanted. It would have helped me to realize earlier that it wasn't that I was a tiny swimmer being tossed around in a massive ocean—it was that I *was* the ocean. Now, even with this awareness, it's not as if acting with intentionality necessarily makes you a better person. I still would have raged and caused hurricanes and sank ships and made gorgeous waves for surfers, but I would have done it all intentionally, knowing it was *my* ocean. Regardless of your relationship to your ocean, it is yours, and a Super You's goal is to experience the wonder and majesty of that ocean on a daily basis.

In the next chapter, we'll talk a bit more about some tools you can use to help maintain your Mega Awareness, keep your intentionality high, and find more outlets in times of stress. In the meantime: surf's up.

Plucked from the Shadowy Superhero Research Lab: Super You's Toolbag

atman has this amazing belt filled with batarangs and other stuff. Spiderman has webs that somehow shoot out of his wrists. Iron Man has a suit that basically does everything. And Thor has a hammer. These tools make superheroes able to be superheroes. I love the idea of this applying to us, so I've done my best to employ this superhero logic to a very dorky mental health term: self-care skills. There's nothing wrong with the term, I suppose, but when I hear it I picture a person who sneezes six times in a row at a minimum and talks about new diseases all the time. A person full of phlegm. (My apologizes to the phlegmy folk out there for characterizing you so harshly.)

Self-care skills, if we consult the Internet, are "actions and attitudes which contribute to the maintenance of well-being and personal health and promote human development." Though, as in much of the mental health field, "self-care skills" is a term that merely defines the obvious, there is power in assigning meaning to what has previously been just a given.

We want to be clear-headed, clear-hearted, and clear-sinused, so let's instead take some of these important self-care skills and talk about how they can be tweaked, reframed, and added to your Super You's bag 'o tools. The idea is that the bag's always strapped to you, so the tools will always be readily available. Some of the tools you can and should use every day, some are only used for maintenance and checking system levels, and some are for emergencies. On the days when I'm feeling petulant and unhealthy (which absolutely still happens), and I just want to splash around in my own misery, it's imagining that one of my "systems" has gone haywire that persuades me to start taking the steps needed to get myself into a healthier place. If someone sidled up to me, when I'm grumbling and eating my second pizza, and said, "Hey, Emily, it looks like you need some self-care skills, wanna journal?", I'd probably punch him in the face. But if I reframe self-care skills as a standard maintenance issue of the glorious machine that is me—well, that makes all the difference. But that's just me. I will be asking you to keep track of the number of self-care skills you're using on a daily basis, so let's start defining what these tools are—you may be using some of them already without realizing their importance. These tools are essential to working toward Super You goals. In fact, using these tools on a regular basis would be a perfectly reasonable goal to set for yourself—and maybe that would be the extent of changes you want to make. Whatever works.

I've broken the tools down into seven categories, as you'll see below.

Super You Tool Category: Physical

For the beginners out there, we'll start with the basics: you've gotta keep your body healthy. We all know this. But what does that mean?

Tool: Eating Healthily

You may define this as you like, but generally a healthy diet is full of fruits, vegetables, protein, fiber, vitamins, and minerals. But it's also about more than that. It's about setting aside the time to eat meals rather than making spaghetti into a pasta cone that you can eat as you run from one thing to another. It's about eating without distractions so that you're aware of what you are eating—mindfully—rather than just shoving food in your pie-hole while you watch *Project Runway,* only to look up and realize the entire jar of peanut butter is gone. When we're eating, we should be savoring. Eating is yet another aspect of life that I want you to do with intention. And that includes indulging sometimes without beating yourself up about it. Healthy eating isn't just about the food you consume. It's also about the role food plays in your life, and keeping food's role sustaining and social rather than comforting and soothing. This is an issue that many authors have written about more eloquently than I do here. If changing your relationship to food is part of your larger Super You Missions, I suggest you start by checking out some of those books, reading up on the healthy and unhealthy roles food can play in our lives.

Tool: Getting Enough Sleep

Sleep deprivation can completely skew your worldview and seriously affect your physical and emotional health. Since sufficient sleep is the basis on which all other healthy behaviors are built, do your best to get at least seven hours of sleep a night. This may mean missing out on some social outings or TV, or not getting enough work done in a day, or not doing the dishes. While it may sound like I'm asking you to sacrifice everything for sleep, note that regular opportunity to rest and regenerate is the only way we can keep our wonderful machines functioning effectively.

GETTING A THERAPIST

You're likely reading this in hopes of moving yourself in a better direction, and that's awesome. But all the same, I highly recommend you go to a therapist, especially if you've never done it before. A lot of people don't seek therapy because they're "not crazy" or they think they have nothing to talk about. But therapy has so much to offer: it can be a lifesaver in intense, stressful times, and it's like a day at the spa at other times. It's also a very specific relationship that is unlike any other—and it's 100 percent focused on you. Therapy is a natural extension of becoming a Super You. Try it.

the **SUPerYOU** *tool Kit*

Physical

recharge

Self-Examination

Perspective

MAYA ANGELOU

The Atlantic

MAP

Bigger Picture

Social Support

Emergency

Tool: Getting Regular Medical Care

Go to a doctor when you're sick, and forge a relationship with that doctor so you're not just a patient folder to him or her. Go to a dentist twice a year. See a therapist if you feel you need someone to talk to and your friends just aren't cutting it.

Do not ignore physical symptoms in your body, hoping they'll go away—just get them checked out. Many of my friends are incredibly anxious that seeing a doctor for nagging symptoms could reveal they're suffering from an incurable, terminal disease, so they avoid doctors at all costs. Does that ring true for you? For starters, the tiny, back-of-the-mind, "what if?!?!" anxiety you're feeling can be cured only by visiting a doctor and getting things checked out—regardless of the outcome. Living with that anxiety may be more harmful than whatever else you have going on. And if you are suffering from some sort of ailment, you can't treat it if you don't know about it. I've gone to a doctor for depression and found out I was anemic. I've gotten a routine dental X-ray that revealed a tumor in my jaw that, left untreated, could have dissolved the bones in my face. So I'm not kidding when I say medical care is important.

Tool: Exercising

Okay, get ready for a soapbox here. I was fairly overweight for years, as well as unhealthy and unhappy. These things don't always go together, but for me they did. I was also weirdly defiant and secretive about being overweight—I hated myself, but I tried my best to present to the world that I didn't know I was fat, and didn't care. Part of that plan involved not exercising, as exercise meant surrendering

to how I thought the world saw me. In case it's not abundantly clear by now, this was a bad idea. My misery was compounded by my lack of activity, and my lack of activity compounded my misery; this was a rough cycle that took some force to break out of. I started slowly: took walks around my neighborhood, worked my way up to playing tennis with a friend, and eventually took dance classes. For a while I was nauseated when exercising, but at some point I realized that I'd also stopped thinking, and was just using my body as a tool to deliver a ball across a net, or get me to a spot two miles away. I'd thought of my body in a million different, terrible ways, but I'd never really thought of it as useful. I had never thought of it as a machine that does my bidding.

The point is this: every body needs exercise. We all need to sweat, and stretch, and get our hearts pumping. And most important, exercise isn't about losing weight and being appealing to others— it's about keeping the many systems of your beautiful machine in smooth working order. And to boot, it's about upping your energy level, triggering endorphin release in your brain, and (for me at least) getting the hell out of your own head for a few minutes and focusing on just staying upright and in motion. Exercise can help raise your Mega Awareness tremendously. For a girl like me who overthinks everything, exercise gives me a vacation from myself. So move along with exercise DVDs at home. Work out at a gym. Dance at a nightclub. Take walks around the block at lunch. Just move, and do it regularly. Your body isn't ugly or perfect or fat or almost there or an object to be ogled—your body is a machine. Keep it in top running order.

Super You Tool Category: Recharge

Tool: Giving Yourself Downtime

Learning to give yourself downtime and actually experiencing that downtime is incredibly important. And as we all become surgically attached to our mobile devices (I think that's a feature of the next iPhone, in fact), it's more important than ever, because your brain and your psyche, in order to perform properly, need stretches of time when they're not taking in a ton of stimuli. So what *is* downtime, or "me time"? People may intellectually know what it means, but they don't know what it means to them. Me time, as I'm defining it, is how you accumulate mental energy—not physical energy, and not social energy, but mental energy. It's a pleasant way to spend time that is not productive, as cleaning or going to the gym is. It's just straight-up indulgent stuff that you do for you and you only—and it doesn't tax your brain.

I'm a pretty scheduled girl, so I try to set aside thirty minutes for downtime every day. I know that sounds ridiculous, but it actually works. It's something I can look forward to in my schedule, and then I have a range of options to choose from. Here are a few things that I do in my downtime.

- Eat at a restaurant alone—no book, no phone.

- Get a massage.

- Get my nails done or my hair cut. (This only works if your beauty technicians aren't chatty. You may even want to ask them not to talk so you can focus on zoning out.)

- ⚡ Make cookies.

- ⚡ Masturbate.

- ⚡ Put on a cocktail dress and heels and dance around my house to loud music.

- ⚡ Read fashion mags.

- ⚡ Reread my old Sweet Valley High books.

- ⚡ Stare out the window.

- ⚡ Take a bath.

- ⚡ Walk slowly and aimlessly in pretty surroundings.

- ⚡ Watch TV. (It must have no redeeming educational value; I use this one sparingly. TV is almost too good for zoning out.)

To help me come up with my list, I thought about what I did when I was a kid in the summer and had whole days stretched out in front of me with nothing to do. I hated those boring days back then, but it turns out that a lot of what was boring to me as a kid is incredibly soothing to me as an adult.

See if you can come up with ten or twelve things for your own list—and then schedule them in.

Super You Tool Category: Self-Examination

Every good Super You has the ability to do some self-examination—both when things get frustrating and when you have some free time and nagging decisions to make. It would be amazing if we had

Google Glass for our hearts and minds, alerting us to things we may need to deal with, but we would look like assholes wearing Emotional Google Glass equipment, so instead let's talk about how we can take a look inward, and what we can do with what we find there.

Tool: Freewriting

I've found the oft-described technique of freewriting fantastic when I'm feeling overwhelmed or creatively stuck. (Note: it's different from journaling, which we'll get into later.) We humans are complex creatures, and we're capable of holding many conflicting emotional and intellectual thoughts at once. I've always found it helpful to write out those thoughts, so I make it a goal to freewrite a few times a week whether I'm feeling pent-up or not. Freewriting is exactly what it sounds like: sitting down with pen or computer and writing whatever comes into your head for ten to fifteen minutes straight. Most of my freewriting entries start: "Ugh, so here I am freewriting again, I never know how to start this …" If I'm feeling incredibly stuck, I start writing as if I'm writing to my best friend. And while there are no wrong ways to freewrite, it is important to keep writing the entire time—eventually you do get into the zone.

Tool: Running a Systems Check

Remember how we talked about emotions being the software you run on? This is where we run a systems check of that software. There are a billion emotions out there—so many that some of them haven't even been named yet. I sometimes have a somewhat icky

feeling when I'm in a heated discussion with someone and have a piece of information she doesn't have, and for a few moments I have a mean sort of giddiness before I drop the justifiable hammer. I don't have a name for that emotion, but I've definitely felt it. Maybe it's triumphsquirm? That's a long name.

I digress. We've already talked a great deal about how to make your emotions your bitch. The systems check is the down-and-dirty version of this, designed merely to give you a sense of where you are, emotionally, at any point in time. And while it works fantastically when you're having a rough day, it functions as preventive maintenance as well. You also get the added bonus of getting to know yourself a little bit better just by doing something simple. At my busiest and most preoccupied, I sometimes forget that I have needs and wants and desires; instead I treat myself like a robot designed to carry my brain from one event to the next. And while that approach can help get you through a rough patch, too many of us get stuck not checking in with ourselves for long periods, which doesn't help anyone.

So how does it work? Try to find a quiet, technology-free place where you can do this check-in for a few minutes. To follow are the systems check questions I ask myself. I call this the PELHA, to help me remember the steps of it, even though the word "pelha" means absolutely nothing.

★ P—What is your *predominant emotion* right now?

★ E—What's the *environment* you're in?

★ L—Are your emotions *lining up* with the environment that you're in, or are they a mismatch? A mismatch could indicate that how you're feeling isn't related to what you're doing now, but rather to something else.

★ H—Are there any *hidden emotions* underneath what you're feeling?

★ A—Is how you're feeling now okay with you, or do you need to take *action* to help yourself out?

This tool is important to me because, as I've mentioned, I'm not always amazing at correctly sourcing my emotions. Sometimes they're covering other, more complicated emotions. When I was in graduate school and incredibly stressed-out and anxious about my future, I went through a two-month period when I was absolutely convinced one of the tires on my car was going to blow out. I was driving a lot for school, so it made some sort of sense, but I wasn't really anxious about the tire. The tire blowout just presented a very concrete, specific, and convenient hook for me to hang my anxieties on. I wasn't doing systems checks back then, but if I had been, I most likely would have caught on to this weirdness within myself a lot sooner.

One important thing to note is that digging down to figure out where your emotions are coming from doesn't automatically mean that they will resolve themselves. I'll repeat the mantra I mentioned in the introduction to this book: "coming to a deep understanding about yourself does not automatically lead to change in your behavior." You can know what the problems are for years and still not have any idea how to change your behavior, or even any real desire to change your behavior. This is why a double-pronged approach to making changes—behavioral change (your Super You Missions that you set earlier) and emotional processing (all this fun

stuff)—is the best way to actually make an impact on yourself. Realizing that you have got a lot of anger toward your parents doesn't make that anger disappear. But understanding where your anger is coming from, combined with making concrete goals of reducing your anger, can help you overall: in having a healthier relationship toward your parents *and* your anger.

Super You Tool Category: Perspective

You know the feeling when something really terrible happens to you, and you have a moment of looking around at people going to the store or crossing the street and you think, "How the fuck are you able to go about your day. Don't you know that this just happened to me?!" I essentially lived in that space for a few years. Drowning in my emotions and racing thoughts and internal conflicts, I was too caught up even to look up to see what was going on around me—let alone how the people around me were faring. And yes, this entire book is about "focusing on yourself," but there is a difference between focusing on yourself and drowning in yourself, and I was definitely guilty of the latter. I could have used a superhero back then for sure. I probably would have scoffed at a superhero if she'd shown up at my door, ready to save me from myself.

We all struggle with our place in this world. We all want to matter to something or to someone, and when we sometimes feel insignificant it hurts. Or, on the flip side, sometimes we feel like the entire world is resting on our shoulders, like it would stop turning if we weren't there to spin it like a Harlem Globetrotter—and that hurts too. And both of these mindsets can happen in the same day—how lovely is that? This category of self-care skills is about exploring the perspective of anyone other than yourself—about understanding that your headspace isn't the only headspace, so you can properly evaluate what's happening in your life. These skills are here to help you understand and appreciate your life in the context of the rest of the world and all the stuff *it* has going on.

Tool: Journaling

This is a pretty catch-all tool, but I put it in the perspective section because I often don't have a full grasp of the emotions churning inside me until I'm able to get them out of me. Sometimes I rely on friends to help me operate the release valve on my turmoil, but sometimes the stuff is too private, which is when I rely on journaling. I write out everything that's bothering me, everything I'm afraid of, everything I'm mad about. Somehow, seeing it in front of me helps me quantify what it is exactly that I'm concerned about—and helps me realize how ridiculous my fears are, or at least helps me feel like I am facing my fears head on and seeing them for what they are by the light of my Macbook.

Tool: Exploring Empathy

People sometimes think that empathy is "feeling sorry for someone"; that's completely incorrect. I won't bore you with the official definition, but empathy is about being able to put yourself in others' shoes and imagine the world (and any given situation) as they see it, and even more importantly, as they *experience* it. When you're training to become a therapist, you learn to really flex your

empathy muscles. Often I would be assigned to clients who had done some pretty heinous things in their lives, and it would be my job to develop a rapport with them so that we could work together to build some better coping skills. I'd have a fourteen-year-old kid in front of me who'd been raised in a much tougher environment than I'd ever even thought of, and I'd need to understand how that background affected his thoughts and feelings. Or I'd have a mother convicted of child abuse in front of me who wanted to learn better ways to discipline her child—and if I'd approached her from the perspective of "this woman is bad because she hit her child," I wouldn't have been able to work with her. It's important to note that empathy is not about excusing people's behavior because they've had it rough; it's about understanding that, based on the environment they were in and the choices they saw in front of them, the actions they chose made the most sense to them at the time. It was my job to provide them with different choices—sometimes that came down to informing them there even *were* different choices.

Basically, empathy is how we come to understand the humanity in what can sometimes be inhumane actions. Plus, the empathy I learned as a therapist has only helped me in my personal life. What's great about this tool is that you can use it in lots of situations—at times of crisis, or even just to find something to journal about.

So how do we explore empathy? Come up with a scenario in your head, like coming upon a car accident, or seeing a homeless person fall down, or finding a box of kittens in the street, and write: (1) what you would think upon seeing it, and (2) how you would respond to it. Be honest—no one's grading your work here. After you've answered those two questions for yourself, try to change a few of your own variables and see how that changes the response.

How would you handle this scenario if you were rich? Poor? A different race? A celebrity? Then, move on to other people you know: your parents, your siblings, your boss, your romantic partner, your friends—even fictional characters you've spent a lot of time with. If you're feeling adventurous, try adding people you don't have a lot of interaction with—the guy who works at the convenience store, the lawyer you've consulted, the girl who walks your dog. When you're answering, dig deep into what you know about each person's background, personality, and way of doing things. Get detailed. If it's a struggle to come up with answers for other people, it might be interesting to ask them: find out how they'd actually deal with each scenario. This exercise really helps us realize just how differently we approach things despite how much we may have in common. For example, though my sister and I were raised in the same household, we have wildly different perspectives on life. (Note: we both would rescue a box of kittens.) It's important to remember that not everyone sees the world the same way you do, and that your perspective, while it may be right to you, isn't the gospel truth, and isn't always set in stone for you.

If you're having trouble imagining what someone else's environment would actually be like, the following tool can help.

Tool: Volunteering

I'm a bit of a volunteering nerd. My parents forced me to volunteer when I was too young to work, and though I hated them for it at the time, it absolutely shaped who I became and still shapes me today. I have volunteered at hospitals, at science parks, at tutoring

centers, at GLBT centers, at women's shelters, in courthouses, and at animal rescue facilities, and each time I leave with a tiny hint of what it's like to be someone other than myself. Once you're out of school, you mainly interact with the people you choose to interact with, and that can give you a pretty narrow worldview. It's good to diversify the kinds of people you're around, whatever that means to you. Volunteering has helped me gain a sense of the world's hugeness and of my own tiny place in it. It is incredibly difficult to hold on to your self-centered little universe when you're working with people or animals who rely on your free time. I also like volunteering because it's not something I'm doing for money—it's something I'm doing to gain experience I wouldn't have otherwise. You may think that you're too busy to volunteer, but I promise you that, just like working out or having a creative outlet, devoting your time to someone other than yourself is hugely important in keeping yourself centered. Also, you get the bonus of feeling good about yourself for donating your time to others. And listen, this is not even slightly the reason why you should volunteer, but imagine how it'll feel the first time someone at a party asks you, "What have you been up to?" and you respond, "Volunteering at _____! It's amazing." It's a pretty lovely and destinctive feeling, another that hasn't yet been named.

Tool: Reality Show

We've discussed this tool previously, when we were assessing our lives to see what changes needed to be made. I won't repeat myself too much here, but basically, if you're in a situation that feels vaguely upsetting, take a breath, take a minute, and mentally back yourself out of it. Then, replay the situation while imagining there are cameras mounted on the walls—dispassionate, divorced from emotion, cold, always-seeing cameras—recording everything. What would the cameras see? How would they assess the situation? Try to look at the situation with the cameras' perspective—with new eyes.

One of the relationship issues we'll discuss later is the assumption that someone who cares about you should just *know* when you're upset. Taking the perspective of a camera can help identify for you the huge difference between communicating that you're upset and falsely believing that you're communicating that you're upset.

Tool: Focusing on the Positives

Focusing on the positives can be hard, and it definitely can feel cheesy, but it's quite important all the same. First, think about all the horrible, sexist, racist, hate-filled stuff that can happen out there. Now, imagine that you spent a lot of time just focusing on those negatives.

Psychology calls this magical idea *confirmation bias*—that once you decide on a belief, you will pay attention only to things that confirm your belief, and automatically discount anything that doesn't confirm your belief. I encourage you to keep that in mind as you read the news and scan Twitter; try to be objective and even-handed in your beliefs as much as humanly possible.

THERAPY TERM alert

But for the people who feel they have to bear witness to all the terrible things in the world, suffering in their overwhelming fountain of knowledge doesn't actually stop that stuff from happening—it just bogs them down in the hugeness of it all, and then they're unable to do anything. They can become paralyzed with the pain, and that's not useful to anyone.

While we don't want to discount the negatives, we need to balance our perspective to include positive stuff as well, and that means focusing on positives. It's important to actively seek out examples of positive, lovely things, because they're all happening too—they just get less media coverage. And the thing is, the more you focus on good stuff, the more good stuff you'll remember, which makes for a much more positive worldview. And that can make it easier to see the bad stuff in our personal lives in a different light. Every bad experience can be a teacher; every bad day you have can help you appreciate the good days more. I'm not expecting you to immediately name all the excellent things about a breakup that just happened; I'm simply telling you that looking for lessons learned is as important as feeling the pain of a bad experience.

Super You Tool Category: Bigger Picture

To define this section of the Super You Toolbag I have to define also what it's not. While it's kind of like "spirituality," that's not exactly what I'm referring to. I'm angling toward the feeling that you're connected to a larger community—but I'm not talking about the social benefits of community. Instead, I mean the organized, ritualistic, soothing power of a community. And while many people accomplish this through religion, religion isn't for everyone. There are parts of religion, however—rituals, prayer, quiet meditation—that *are* incredibly useful for everyone.

Tool: Creating and Maintaining Rituals

I am a bit of a fanatic about ritual. There is a history of obsessive-compulsive disorder in my family—not the cute kind where you have to have your shoes lined up a certain way, but the debilitating kind, where you cannot leave the house because the dozens of tasks associated with leaving are too exhausting. I find that ritual is one of the truly bright spots of this harrowing disorder. Having ritual in your life keeps you centered, grounding your relationships and helping you understand your place in this world.

For children in particular, the parameters of their life are set up by other people—and though these parameters can be annoying at times, it can also be somewhat comforting to know what to expect, and what's expected, in any given situation. In my childhood, dinnertime had a ritual to it. Sundays had rituals. When I first became an adult and went to college, free to eat meals as I liked, spend my money as I liked, go to bed whenever, and go to church (or not), I experienced an immense feeling of joy and wonder at my newfound freedom, followed by a weird emptiness. I felt unmoored, unanchored, and somewhat scared. So I started creating rituals in my own little life and with my roommates to help restore some of the parameters that had been so soothing and reliable.

Rituals can involve many types of things: playing Dungeons & Dragons on Sunday, having brunch with friends, craft night, regular chat conversations, Tuesday FaceTime appointments with

your parents, date nights. Essentially, they're a series of actions assigned a special meaning. A ritual can be as tiny as cranking up good music while drinking a Coke Zero at the end of a long day. All that matters is, in your head and heart, that combination of actions has meaning to you.

Rituals can also function as a shortcut for complex emotional exchanges. I have a friend who, when experiencing a bout of depression, will email me a number from 1 to 10 to rate how she's feeling that day, to which I will respond with encouragement or sympathy. The long explanation of this ritual is that it's a way for me to check in with a friend who is struggling, it's a way for my friend to reach out for help if she's feeling especially down, and it reinforces that we matter to each other—but all she has to do to trigger my support is give me a number. Another ritual is that, when my husband and I are separated for days at a time, we text each other what we eat for each meal. In this way, we feel reconnected by some sort of code of our own.

The important thing for rituals is that you (1) make them clear and simple, (2) communicate them to the person you want to ritual it up with (if it's not a solo ritual), and (3) enact them regularly. Elaborating on items (1) and (2): don't create rituals so complicated that you're left feeling like a failure when they're too hard to keep up with, and don't expect the others you're including to automatically know what you're doing. Communication is key.

Tool: Meditating/Praying

Though this tool is similar to the journaling tool in the perspective tool category, I've included it here because, to me, this tool is really just journaling without paper while thinking specifically of one's place in the universe. Wow, that sounds ridiculous. For those of you who are down with praying or meditating but think journaling is corny, this is for you—and for those of you who think prayer and meditation are corny, try journaling. Considering yourself and your relationship to the universe is a practice that has incredible emotional and physical benefits, so whatever label you need to make it work for you, go for it. I also recommend watching the show *Cosmos* for inspiration here—the new version, with the wonderful Neil deGrasse Tyson.

Super You Tool Category: Social Support

Everyone needs a social support system. Of course, we all need different things from our social supports, absolutely, but we all need some social aspect to our lives that we can lean on, when times are tough or when we just feel like hanging out. I think a lot of us take our friendships as a given, but, just like romantic relationships, they deserve greater attention in two ways: one, we should evaluate our friendships for how well they're working for us, and two, we should work to maintain them. We'll talk more about friendships in chapter 10, but for now, let's go over some tools.

Tool: Identifying the Social Supports in Your Life

Every few months it's a good idea to take stock of the friendships you have. How strong are they? How much do you trust each friend, and is that a reasonable amount of trust? Do you have any friendships that are toxic and need some adjusting? Is there anyone in your life you feel yourself growing distant from whom you would like to reconnect with? For each friendship, what "friendship services" are you providing her, and what "friendship services" is she providing you? While it can feel somewhat tawdry to quantify friendships in this way, note that, selfishly, every friendship *is* supposed to bring you something positive. If it doesn't, why is it still a friendship? Being friends with someone because she needs you isn't a good enough reason, even if you really like feeling needed.

When I was a therapist and starting to experience burnout, I talked with my own therapist about keeping myself emotionally healthy using the metaphor of baking a cake. I like cake a great deal, so this was a useful analogy for me. Essentially, what you have to offer the world, socially, is delicious cake. You have a cake, which you can slice up and offer to whomever you like—it is yours to share. However, to do this you need to hang out with people who, in turn, provide you with the ingredients needed to make the cake. So if you're serving your friends your lovingly made cake but they aren't giving you flour, milk, sugar, and eggs in return, you'll soon run out of cake. Every relationship you're in should be a two-way street of caring and giving and gossiping—and if it's not, it's time for you to rethink the friendship, and decide whether perhaps your relationship should be downgraded to a warm acquaintanceship, or once-a-year check-ins. You only have so much cake to go around. Good solid relationships produce cake forever.

For bonus points, you can also go through your friends individually and parse out the kinds of support they offer you. This may seem a bit creepy, so you can skip this step if you like, but I started realizing how some of my friends are wonderfully intense and want to talk about feelings, and then some who make me laugh harder than anyone, and so on. This is not to say that you then seek out your friends only for what they can provide you—it's more of a personalized assessment of each relationship, appreciating what it is that each friend offers. I may want to know in advance that, if I'm pondering life after death and go to Pete to discuss it with him, he may respond by doing a humor bit and making coffee come out of my nose, which may not be super useful to me at the moment. Don't expect more from your friends than they have to offer, and don't set up friendships where you are continually having to over-extend yourself socially.

Tool: Focusing on a Friend

This tool could also go into the perspective category, but sometimes when I'm drowning in my own petty bullshit, what helps me is to focus 100 percent on someone I care about. Of course, you need his cooperation with such efforts, but, say, digging into a friend's dating life when I'm stressed about myself helps both my friend and me, as it reminds me that there's more to the world than just me.

Tool: Requesting Support

Asking for help is one of the toughest things to do. It can make you feel vulnerable, weak, or just plain weird—but it's also the stuff that close relationships are made of. What is a friend if you can't be vulnerable with her?

In my younger days, when I sought attention from a friend or a boyfriend, I greatly exaggerated what was happening with me, stirring myself into a faux crisis out of fear that my mundane worries weren't enough to warrant needing support. Have you done this? This exaggeration wasn't something I did consciously—it was just how the words came out. In looking back, I see it was my way of protecting myself from seeming dumb in front of a friend—if the issue was huge (albeit fake), I could get the support I needed without feeling stupid about my concerns and fears.

But let me tell you this now: if you're struggling with something, whatever it is, that's enough to warrant reaching out to a friend. So practice reaching out *and* being completely honest. Here's how you do it.

You: Hey _____, I'm having kind of a rough day and feeling wonky. Can we hang out sometime soon? I need some support.

That's it. Practice it in a mirror. Say it to a friend. It can be additionally helpful to have some sort of an idea of the support you want. For me, support falls under a few distinct categories:

⚡ Listening

⚡ Listening and empathizing

⚡ Listening and solution-plotting

- 🌀 Listening and gloom-and-dooming alongside you

- 🌀 Distracting you from your troubles

- 🌀 Giving a pep talk

- 🌀 Showing care and affection

Giving your friend a sense of where you fall in this list can be really important. As any human can tell you, for the times when you just want to be heard (listening), but your friend starts telling you how to fix your problems (solution-plotting), you'll want to punch that well-meaning person in his well-meaning face. So when you need support, scan this list and consider what kind of support would work best for you, and communicate *that*. People can't read your mind—even people who love you very much.

Super You Tool Category: Emergency

Sometimes none of this fun "self-exploration" and "meaningful habits" stuff works whatsoever, and you still find yourself in a bit of an emotional crisis. No matter how old you get or how evolved you become, this will always be the case. So when you don't have time to be a marvelous and human hurricane of emotions, what tools does your Super You reach for when the shit hits the fan?

Tool: Calming Down

We've talked a bit about getting emotional distance from yourself so that you can evaluate situations a bit more objectively. This step

is nearly impossible to do when you're very angry or upset. Some people refer to this level of upset as seeing red or getting tunnel vision or feeling as if they're underwater; I simply refer to it as being "in it." When my husband comes home after a long day and I find him sitting on the couch staring at the wall, I always ask, "Oh, are you in it right now?" If I'm right, I know that all he has the capacity for at that point is just to nod and reach for the Xbox controller.

That's his technique. My suggestions for calming down are to take a moment to isolate yourself physically to whatever degree you can. I usually stop responding to other people and start focusing on breathing, similar to what we talked about in developing Mega Awareness. Inhale for a count of seven, hold your breath for a count of seven, and exhale for a count of seven. Several rounds of this breathing help to relax you physiologically. If your breath feels shallow or you don't feel like it's working, place your hand on your stomach. For the relaxation benefit of true deep breathing, you need to use your diaphragm—you'll know you're doing it right if your abdomen expands as you inhale—so it can help to have your hand on your stomach. This calms me down faster than anything.

Tool: Distracting Yourself

Once you're feeling a bit calmer, it's time to get more distance. Finding mundane things to occupy your brain is a terrific, simple way to emotionally back out from whatever hole you find yourself in. I learned a trick a few years ago when feeling panicky of writing down all fifty states; if you're especially good with geography, try naming countries or the capitals or some other information. This trick takes up brain space but has no emotional weight, so it's nice and distracting. Another self-distraction option I use is forcing myself to notice tiny details about the environment I'm in. What is the pattern in the floor? Is the tabletop clean or does it have crumbs on it? Take in the room you're in as if for the first time. Notice and absorb every detail. Ask yourself weird questions about it. When's the last time the corners of the ceiling were cleaned? How does one even clean the corners of the ceiling? Has anyone died in this room? What's the name of this color of paint? (There's a fantastic book called *On Looking* where the author takes different types of "experts"—from a child to a geologist—on the same walk around a block in Manhattan to show how everyone looks at things differently. This was incredibly eye-opening to me—to realize how much detail I ignore on a daily basis.) These are my best tools. Come up with a few ways to distract yourself that you can turn to when you need them.

Tool: Relieving Stress Right Now

Let's say you've tried to distract yourself but your mind is still going a thousand miles a minute with no chance of slowing down. Here are a few other quick and easy things you can try to expend that stressy energy:

- 🗘 Dance really, really hard.

- 🗘 Jump in the air over and over as if you're listening to nineties hip-hop.

- 🗘 Paint or draw.

⚡ Shred pieces of paper slowly and methodically.

⚡ Take a "pool noodle" and smack it onto the surface of a pool over and over.

⚡ Cut an old T-shirt into strips (bonus: make something cool with the strips!).

⚡ Throw ice cubes at a building or a tree.

The point here is to do something that expends your physical energy in hopes of relieving some of your emotional energy.

These twenty basic tools should be a part of every Super You Toolbag. Here for you in easy times and difficult times, they can help keep you healthy and make you into a more centered, more badass human being. That's not to say there won't be days and moods and situations that no tools can contain—you are human, after all. For the next week, keep track of the number of Super You basic tools you use to get through each day. Aim for about three per day, if you can. If you want to do just the bare minimum, that's okay, but some people choose to do more and we encourage that, okay? (Note: this is an *Office Space* reference.)

Superpowers: Can You Leap Tall Buildings in a Single Bound?

uick, name everything you know about Superman!

He's able to leap tall buildings in a single bound. He has super strength. He's pretty noble. He (a.k.a. Henry Cavill) is also pretty ripped—probably how he manages all that super strength, single-building bounding and all that.

Now, could you do the same thing with your own Super You? Could you run through your superpowers and weaknesses as dispassionately, as objectively? My guess is that it might be hard for you. If I were Superman and someone asked what my strengths were, I might say something like:

Well, I guess I'm pretty good at leaping. Why do you ask? Did someone mention it? I just want to help people. I can't even be around Kryptonite though. I think it's because when I was young I was around Kryptonite and it was really harsh for me, so I like, kinda shut down when I'm around it now. It's so stupid. It's just Kryptonite. I don't know what's wrong with me—everyone else seems fine with it. It might be because I'm an alien who just looks human. Anyway, tell me about yourself!

Clearly, extolling my own virtues is not one of my superpowers. For years I'd simultaneously be ashamed of my weaknesses and downplay the hell out of my strengths. I had no objective distance to see how I actually was—but even if I could have seen myself objectively, I probably still would have had no pride in myself. But if you look at any "intro to superheroes" website or comic book, every superhero's powers and weaknesses are laid out so flatly, so objectively, that there's no arguing with them. They are what they are what they are. Batman is a lonely guy who uses his money and training to fight criminals. Spiderman is a sarcastic kid who's coming to grips with the powers bestowed upon him by a radioactive spider. And us? It's time for us to learn how to assess ourselves as if we were—ahem, I mean, *since* we're superheroes.

FUN SUPERHERO FACT!

Superman originally couldn't fly—hence the "leaping tall buildings in a single bound." But when they began making Superman cartoons in the 1940s, the animators complained that the leaping looked silly. The creators agreed, and Superman was upgraded to flying status.

How do we figure out what those best qualities, our superpowers, are? A few you might know right off the bat, since they're how you describe yourself in your online dating profile—being a good friend, having a sense of justice, being thoughtful—and these are all great because they sound great to strangers. They would be good qualities in anyone's personality, and should absolutely be included in your list of superpowers. But what about the ones that could belong only to you? The ones that make the person you are today, living in your skin and in the environment you're in, special? What quieter, less flashy strengths do you have that are often overlooked? And note: strengths are just the qualities you possess that help you be the best version of yourself right now. They energize you. They're the qualities that have led you to here and now in one piece, and they shift throughout your lifetime. They're also the qualities you've had to develop based on what you've accomplished and endured. There are some days when your thoughtfulness toward others is a strength, and some days—days that you need to circle the wagons and take care of yourself more—when thoughtfulness towards others doesn't serve you as well. The same is true with assertiveness, or positivity, or being a good friend. What's most important about your superpowers is that you realize that *you have them*. That you have positive qualities. You have qualities that make you unique and help you be the best version of yourself right now.

But the sad thing is that many people don't know they have superpowers. I meet so many people determined to self-deprecate into a hole in the ground, refusing to believe that they have anything good going for them, or that they have anything to offer. I've actually had this conversation with a near stranger in a bathroom:

Near stranger: But I don't have any good qualities.

Me: I'm guessing that's not true. At the very least, you are humble, and that is a lovely quality.

Why do we have such a hard time talking about our own superpowers? Maybe we think we're being braggarts if we discuss them. Maybe we've been raised to be humble to the point of self-deprecation. Maybe we're afraid people will disagree with what we see as our strengths.

Getting on Team Super You

If being able to recognize your positive qualities is hard for you, your first step is to get on Team Super You. You have to pull on the jersey of Team Super You and get on your own side. Instead of arguing with yourself (which we'll discuss in the next chapter), or doubting yourself, or undermining yourself, it is imperative that you be on your own team. What has helped me in the past, when I'm pushing myself into the depths of self-esteem hell while on the way to a meeting or something, is to picture a basketball stadium. On the court is me versus all my fears and concerns. In that scenario, who is sitting in the bleachers on my side of the stadium? Parents, friends, my cat, sure—but am *I* also on my side of the stadium? Am I fighting for myself to succeed and do well? Or am I on the other side of the stadium, cheering for the bad guys?

Even if I was faking it at first, I made a conscious effort to be sure I was standing on my own side of the stadium. Life is hard enough without there being one more detractor hollering at us from the other side. We are all alive, and engaged enough in our lives to be reading this book, so we all have qualities that have made us strong enough to get right here, right now. Sadly, not everyone has made it this far. Even more sadly, not everyone is reading this book. (I kid!) You make up an elite group, and being in that group, you absolutely have superpowers. Today, here and now, I want you to make a vow to yourself that you will, at least outwardly, rep your own Team Super You. You will think of yourself as an ally, as a friend, as a supporter.

Your next step, now that you're wearing a Super You jersey, is to take a step backward so you can catch a glimpse of yourself and your powers. I can't always be waiting for you in the women's bathroom, ready to have a deep talk with you! (Fun facts: One of the reasons I became a therapist was that, for as long as I could remember, I would get into extremely intense life talks with strangers in public bathrooms.) We've talked a few times about stepping back to evaluate ourselves, and it's time to use that technique again. Picture your life as a reality show, or picture yourself as the star of a show you're watching on TV—whatever works for you.

The Blockbuster Superpowers

From Team Super You's side of the gymnasium, take a few quiet minutes to yourself and think about your positive qualities. Refer back to "Realization 1: Who I Am Depends on a Lot of Factors" in Chapter 1 and revisit the qualities you learned about yourself either from taking the www.character.org personality strengths quiz or from my shorter list of questions. Write down your positive qualities, big or small. If you need help, think of yourself as a stranger you've recently met and interacted with. If you still need help, here are a few more questions

to ask yourself. (If you would feel comfortable getting some help from a friend for some of these, go for it.)

★ At work or in life, what kinds of tasks do I look forward to doing?

★ How would I describe myself on a dating profile?

★ I'm a guest on a morning talk show—how would the host describe me in his intro?

★ If I were a superhero, what qualities would the bad guys use to witheringly describe me?

★ What am I passionate about?

★ What are my best qualities, according to my coworkers?

★ What are my best qualities, according to my family?

★ What are my best qualities, according to my friends?

★ What are my best qualities, according to my romantic partner?

★ What do I do throughout my day that brings me joy?

★ What have I been proud of in my life?

★ What kind of situations do I thrive in that not everyone thrives in?

★ What qualities do I admire in the people who raised me? Did any of them transfer to me?

★ What qualities do I admire in others? Do any of those echo my own qualities?

★ What qualities do I like for people to notice in me?

Yes, these might seem a bit like Ms. America questions, but they're designed to help you home in on some of your best qualities: the qualities that serve you and make you strong.

The Less Obvious Superpowers

Now, let's move on to the host of positive qualities that are often dismissed or swept aside but that are just as important. For example, below are a few qualities that my friends possess that they probably wouldn't think of as being too important but which mean the world to me. To me, these qualities make my friends strong and amazing human beings to be around. And if some of these seem like weird superpowers, consider: the superhero Color Kid can change the color of anything, and Matter-Eater Lad can eat anything. So even real superheroes have some weird superpowers.

Some Qualities I Love in My Friends

↻ Being a good storyteller

↻ Being a hard worker

↻ Being able to complain to wait staff without seeming like a monster

↻ Being able to eat almost anything without complaining

↻ Being ambitious

↻ Being comfortable showing emotion

↻ Being interested in lots of different hobbies

↻ Being truly interested in other people

↻ Bringing the right amount of humor to a serious situation

↻ Having a quality I like to call "Fuck it, let's give it a try!"

↻ Knowing all the latest trends

↻ Knowing none of the latest trends

↻ Knowing which celebrities are dating

↻ Looking at things in a truly original way, and sharing that
viewpoint equally originally

↻ Not being afraid of conflict

↻ Not taking bad moods out on other people

↻ Remembering people's birthdays

↻ Staying calm in crises

↻ Thinking deeply before responding when asked a question

Do any of these ring true for you? If so, write them down! If you're
still having trouble coming up with superpowers, think of times in
your life—however long ago—that you've felt proud of yourself,
and explore why you were proud. Those qualities, whatever they

were, are still with you. This is also an excellent activity to do with a friend, especially when you're having one of those cornball "Let's talk about real shit" get-togethers. Tell your friend what you think his or her strengths are, and ask for some strengths in return. You might notice that you and your friends share strengths—shared superpowers are often what keep people invested in each other. Everyone leaves happy.

If you're still having trouble, or just want to find more positive qualities in yourself, let's dig around in your past and see what we can find. If you'll recall, in chapter 1 we talked about looking back at your life and defining the identities you created along the way—even naming them. Let's go back and take another look at those identities and see what superpowers we can find that are still with us today—and, beyond that, what gifts our past selves have given us that have helped usher us to where we are today. I'll show you what I mean with a few of my defined identities.

Clever Girl. This first identity I constructed was young and intoxicated with the idea that her intelligence could win her praise, so she wasn't afraid to be clever. I consider her cleverness, and her pride in her cleverness, an important superpower that I've kept with me, whether or not I'm using it.

Monster Girl. At this age, I was painfully and acutely aware of my size. I drew incorrect conclusions about that awareness, assuming everyone thought I stuck out as much as I thought I did. Though my intense, exclusion-of-everything-else focus on other people's reactions to me wasn't used wonderfully back then, this is a strength that carried me through grad school and my career as a therapist—with the adjustment that I broadened my focus to include reactions beyond reactions to me. For example, I can always tell if a couple has just been fighting in the moments before I run into them. I can usually tell if someone is preoccupied, and when to ask about it. I thank my overly attentive focus on others for this.

Freak Girl: At this age I was angry. Soooo angry. The anger I felt toward myself for so long was spilling out of me, and there was power in that anger. It helped motivate me—maybe not always in the right direction, but being able to aim my anger in the correct direction has been a key step in becoming my Super You. I learned to have anger as the Freak Girl.

Punk Rock Stepford Wife: Oy, this girl. This is a tough one to find strengths in, so let's work it out together. When I was a Punk Rock Stepford Wife, I had a wall up that would make the Great Wall of China jealous. I was impenetrable, a smiling, fishnets-clad cool girl, because I was too scared to let anyone see the real me. None of this is fantastic. Clearly, at that point in time I couldn't have handled being myself around boys, so I am grateful to have had such intense protection at the time. I needed the protection, and my psyche provided it for me. It might as well have been a magnetic force field keeping the bad guys away from my weak and confused heart. What an amazing superpower that is!

To sum up, here are the superpowers I've collected from this: cleverness, hyper-observance of others' emotional states, motivating anger, and a protective force field around my heart. Not bad, huh? I could go on and on, but I think you see my point. Your Super You is merely a step in the evolution of you as a person. None of these identities was perfect for me—they all had serious problems—but they each served a valuable purpose. So instead of throwing the baby out with the bathwater, it's time we start acknowledging the gifts our past identities have given us and realize how we can use their strengths now. Each of these identities was part of the journey of becoming who I am now, and they will continue to be part of the journey of becoming who I want to be. Were I a superhero, these strengths would be applauded and used against bad guys. But because I am me, I have spent many years downplaying and refusing to acknowledge their value. But no more.

Now, it's important to note that your superpowers or strengths are not always the things that you are "good at."

Positive psychology—which is a framework of thinking about human functioning that focuses on the characteristics of a fulfilled and satisfactory life, rather than just focusing on what is wrong—has something to say about the difference. In positive psychology, both *strengths* and *competencies* enable your best performance, but whereas your *strengths'* best performance energizes you, your *competencies* yield no similar enjoyment. So, you may be fantastic at responding to emails quickly and efficiently, but if you're just doing it because you're terrified of a full in-box, this is not one of your strengths; it's merely a competency. However, if you get a genuine thrill from giving information to people, answering their questions, and solving issues quickly over email, then this for you would be a strength. Make sense?

Our superpowers are large and small, world-changing and impossibly specific, weird and common, useful and rarely employed. Once you've made them official by writing them in your notebook, it's time to accept the strengths you have without bemoaning the ones you don't. We have to meet ourselves where we are; it does no one any good if we constantly yell at ourselves from the finish line miles away. You may not be good at small talk at parties—who cares? We can't live our lives focusing on the things we don't have—because that's how to make an empty life. Accept your superpowers. Accept what makes you *you*. Keep your list of super-powers with you for a bit, and just take a glance at them every once in a while. You might even find it necessary to stare into the mirror, hands on your hips, and say:

> **I am [your name here]! I am [shout out your strengths in as superheroey a fashion as possible]! In brightest day, in blackest night, no maladaptive thought patterns or life choices shall escape my sight! To those who aren't supportive of me being a badass Super You—beware my power!**

Note: this is an adaptation of Green Lantern's oath, and a weird one at that. I'm a big fan of repeating things like this into a mirror; it's something I learned in dance classes. At first you feel very weird confronting yourself doing something new and potentially silly, but if you keep looking yourself in the eye and really seeing yourself, the mirror becomes your ally. Then it's not so silly anymore. You learn to look *yourself* in the eye, and it feels more official.

We Know Our Strengths: So Now What?

Once we know our superpowers, what do we do with that information? Other than shouting our strengths to ourselves in the mirror for a self-esteem boost, what good does knowing about our super-powers bring us? Well, Superman knows that if a bad guy needs to be assaulted with a sarcastic one-liner and physically wrapped up and left dangling from the side of a building, that task might be better left to Spiderman. In knowing himself, Superman knows how he is most useful and how he is less useful. He learns to utilize his contribution appropriately. When we know our superpowers, we have a greater sense of what our jobs are in life, so to speak. So let's say one of your superpowers is helping people feel socially comfortable; then, when a new employee joins your team at work, you might volunteer to help acclimate him or her to the office. Or, you might not sign up for the office softball team if your superpowers do not include organized sports. Having an inventory of the ways in which you are proficient, and the proficiencies that bring you joy—versus the proficiencies that do not bring you joy, can help your day-to-day life both make more sense and be more meaningful. Once you've created your list of strengths with objectivity and rationality, I encourage you to see yourself as a Swiss army knife—and to see the world as a collection of tiny strings to be cut or tiny screws to be tightened. You've essentially created a toolbox for yourself that you can consult when problems arise.

For years, I resisted the fact that I am an incredibly organized person. All the signs have always been there: I've been organizing my stuffed animals since childhood, I looked forward more to buying school supplies every fall than I looked forward to Christmas, and I volunteered for every secretary job in every club I was forced to join. In my fantasy world, I am a freewheeling, loose, "anything could happen" kind of girl, but in reality, I am always punctual, I am always organized, and my assignments are always turned in on time. Not only does being organized scratch an itch that I didn't know I had, but it genuinely (and dorkily) brings me joy to organize something that is chaotic. Realizing this strength opened me up to job opportunities I didn't previously think I'd be into, like producing stand-up comedy. So not only do I get the little boost of listing the strengths that make me the best version of myself, I also know to look for opportunities to use those strengths—as well as to avoid the opportunities that don't employ them.

Now, let's take a brief diversion to talk about superpowers I wish I had, and then we'll dig into weaknesses.

Superpowers I Wish I Had

- ⚡ I wish I had the ability to pick the dish off the menu that would satisfy me the most. I constantly have eater's remorse.

- ⚡ I am terrible at wrapping up small-talk conversations at parties, and will often keep those conversations going for way longer than necessary out of not knowing how to get out of them. (I'm talking crying at a party over dead relatives with a bare acquaintance.) I wish I could gracefully exit small talk.

- ⚡ It would be great to be able to talk about myself in a positive way in public without sweating profusely.

- ⚡ Actually, it would be great just not sweat profusely. Would that even count as a superpower?

- ⚡ I wish I had the power to see myself as my husband sees me. He thinks I'm beautiful. I wish I could see what that looks like.

- ⚡ I would love to have the ability to know how much further I could go on the amount of gas in my tank. I irrationally hate getting gas, although I love the smell of gas.

- ⚡ I would love to never again compare my own success to others' success. I want the power to greet every accomplishment of another human being, regardless if we're in the same field or not, with genuine pleasure and enthusiasm—and never with a scowl or scathing comment that just masks my jealousy.

 Even though I fully embrace and love my past for all the gifts it's given me, I sometimes wish I had the ability to start a day with a different past being my experience. It's not that I wish I'd never been diagnosed with a serious illness, or that I wish I'd never been fat. I'm glad for both of those things, and wouldn't delete them from my experience. I just would like to know temporarily what it would feel like *not* to have had those experiences.

 I wish my cat and I could talk, although that would be more her superpower than my own. I wish I had the ability to understand my cat's attempts at communication. Just my cat, though; I don't want to be Dr. Dolittle.

 I wish I could take a person who is being ignorant and small-minded and a jackass and make her experience life as a member of the group she is hating on. I wish I could Freaky Friday people, basically, but for social awareness reasons rather than just hijinks.

 I would love it if social interactions with friends, acquaintances, audience members, and family members didn't exhaust me terribly.

 I would love to fly, obviously.

↯ I wish I had absolute and utter confidence in my work, at all times, rather than sometimes downplaying myself around people who I feel are more talented.

↯ I wish my fingertips contained just a smidge of hair product, to be used in times of flyaways.

CHAPTER

Weaknesses: Embracing Them, Working with Them, Protecting Them

et me get this out of the way first: none of becoming a Super You is about eliminating every perceived weakness you have. Not at all. Creating a Super You isn't about eradicating all weaknesses; it's about learning to recognize them for what they are—part of you—and finding ways to work with them. Some weaknesses deserve to be cradled and considered part of the charming package that is you, some weaknesses can be improved upon for your overall health, and some weaknesses can be reframed and made useful to you. As no one is perfect, no one is without flaws. But instead of hiding those flaws and making apologies for them, let's treat them as superheroes do: just another thing about us. Superhero weaknesses make them more relatable to us mere humans, and show us how even the best of us have to find a way to work through our weak spots. Our human weaknesses can become a more useful, more beloved part of us if we start looking at them more objectively.

After saying all that, I want to add that I don't even really like the term "weaknesses"; but it works within the superhero universe, and so here we are.

It is absolutely your choice whether or not you strive for improvement—and when I use the word "improvement," in no way do I mean "optimal emotional health." In fact, you don't even have to be healthy all the time. What we're looking for is an overall push toward healthy behaviors and attitudes. But within that scope, of course you'll still have days when you dwell on negatives, when you make terrible choices, and when you hold on to your weaknesses like a kid with a blankie. It takes all of these days to make a person, and a life.

Let's break down personal weaknesses into two distinct categories: less-than-stellar qualities we can improve with some modifications in thinking and behavior, and less-than-stellar qualities we cannot change that we therefore need to protect and understand and sometimes baby. Most of us have a pretty good idea of what our weaknesses are, but if you're having trouble, think back to fights you've had with significant others or friends, think back to times that you've felt terrible and guilty, think back to the mistakes you make over and over, making sure that you're focusing on yourself and not on the other party, and I bet you'll unearth a few things. The big surprise here is realizing that most of the weaknesses you'll discover can likely be improved upon to some degree *if* you choose to. Again, it's also absolutely your option to see your weaknesses laid bare before you and think, "You know what? I'm keeping these a bit longer." This is your Super You.

And as for the weaknesses we'll be discussing here, obviously and unfortunately I can't address them all, so instead I'm going to present and break down a few very common ones. If you're feeling confused or overwhelmed by any of your weaknesses, note that they might be best addressed with a therapist one-on-one.

Weaknesses We Can Change

Let's start with weaknesses that can be improved upon. To me, this would be a quality within yourself that has grown out of maladaptive circumstances or out of habit—it's something you know isn't great for you, but it feels so automatic it's hard to know how to stop.

WEIRDEST SUPERHERO WEAKNESSES

The Human Torch's Achilles' heel was asbestos—long before it was discovered that asbestos is a carcinogen for human humans, too. He was ahead of the curve.

Wonder Woman was originally weak against men binding her bracelets together. A quote from that comic: "When an Amazon girl permits a man to chain her bracelets of submission together she becomes weak as other women in a man-ruled world!"

If Thor lets go of his hammer for sixty seconds, he becomes a human man and his hammer turns into a walking stick.

Weaknesses We Can Change: Sneaky Self-Destructive Behaviors

I have friends who will rail on about how drug addicts ruin their lives with their unhealthy behavior, and then not eat until dinnertime because they're swamped at work. Not only do they not make the connection between the two unhealthy habits, but they fail to see their behavior as anything but noble, the badge of a hard worker. Of course, while hazardous substance abuse is a bit more severe than workaholism, don't for a second think that intense overwork doesn't jeopardize your health. Self-destructive behavior comes in many forms—but when it's for the greater good, like burning yourself out at work, yes, it punishes you, but it also makes you look like a superstar for working so hard. Watch out for that sneaky trap.

I was self-destructive for years, first in a pretty obvious, after-school special kind of way, and later in this more sneaky way. I didn't feel worthy of good treatment, so out of hatred of my body I put myself in dangerous situations and harmed myself in as many ways as I could. I was casual with my health and well-being. I kept people around me who were cruel to me because I was lonely. The more obvious self-destructive behaviors of people in this mindset might include:

- Picking fights with people who care about you out of wanting to release anger

- Substance abuse (not just use, but abuse)

- Unsafe sexual promiscuity

When I grew up a bit and went to graduate school, I proudly announced myself "cured" of my self-destructive habits because I no longer did risky things that made my friends shake their heads and proclaim I was nuts. During this time I had regular sixteen-hour days—classes, internship, two jobs—for which I perfected the art of eating while driving. I chose to work constantly rather than take on loans and long-term debt, and I took on extra responsibilities because I wanted to get as much out of the experience as I could. But these choices quickly surpassed "useful" and drove deep into self-destructive territory. The truth is that graduate school itself is self-destructive—it just has a positive goal. Some of these less obvious self-destructive behaviors include:

- Getting into Twitter fights with strangers

- Hooking up with lots of partners in a way that makes you feel small

- Not giving yourself any downtime

Then, when I graduated and found my first real job, I still burned the candle at both ends, mostly out of feeling as if it was the only way to be an effective adult. My effectiveness had to come at the cost of my health. At some point I realized I needed to do more work on myself: I needed to address *why* I felt the need to harm myself physically and emotionally, regardless of the cause. For me, self-destructive behaviors boiled down to feeling like I needed to apologize for my existence, and offering myself up as a sacrifice and an apology.

So how about you? Let's say you consistently put other people's needs ahead of your own. Now, if confronted about such behavior, you might say: "But I have to live like this—if I don't take care of this stuff no one will." Or: "Yeah, but I'm not hurting anyone but myself!" Unless you're working toward a goal with an end in sight, like a website launch or a degree, responses like these are a sign you need to make some changes. No life should consistently burn out so that the rest of the world can run smoothly.

If you're not sure whether you're exhibiting self-destructive behaviors, take a moment with your notebook and list the kinds of things you do regularly. Then, focus on them one at a time: are there any things there that you'd object to your best friend/lover/parent/child doing?

Once you start to see any self-destructive behaviors in yourself, it's time for that good old two-pronged approach to change: internal observation and external change. Internally, start asking yourself a few questions about your self-destructive behaviors.

★ Does this behavior happen because you fear stopping it would hurt other people?

★ Does this behavior happen because you want to help achieve a group goal?

★ Does this behavior (handily) keep you from confronting other parts of your life that you'd rather not address?

★ Does this behavior make you feel needed by others?

★ Does this behavior make you feel worthy?

★ Is this behavior, and its effects, something you feel you deserve?

The Hidden Benefits of Self-Destructive Behaviors

Next let's dig into the darker, more hidden benefits of self-destructive behavior. Yes, working until 11:00 every night gets stuff done and makes you look like a hero at work—but what else is it doing? Are you so swamped that you don't have time to date or nurture intimate friendships? Or let's say you are dating, but you date men who don't have their shit together. Sure, making all the relationship decisions means you're in charge of the relationship—but what else does it mean? Is it a relief to know that the child-man won't leave you because he literally can't exist without you? (Note: this was me for most of my twenties.)

Now, while it's a bummer to identify self-destructive behaviors, it can also be somewhat of a comfort to realize that almost all of our behaviors, even the self-destructive ones, aid and assist us in some manner. But, in the same way that burning down a house in order to get rid of a spider in the kitchen destroys more than the spider, our self-destructive behaviors often serve their purpose while creating a host of new, possibly worse problems. The good news is that understanding in what ways these behaviors are trying to help is a good step in learning how to alter them.

Sneaky Self-Destructive Behaviors: The External Fix

While you're considering that clumsy oaf of self-destruction and how it's trying to help with its big dumb hands, let's start making some external changes to help us get out of our rut. I find the key here is to start slowly, and one great way to do that is with an exchange. The exchange is a great technique for phasing out

unhealthy behavior and replacing it with healthy behavior. Essentially, for every unhealthy behavior that you can't yet give up, add one healthy behavior. Here's what I mean.

In my first real job after grad school I worked at a residential facility, which meant that my clients lived on campus whereas I got to go home. I felt very guilty about this. I would stay until 9:00 PM some nights because someone always needed me, and I didn't want to leave when I was needed! (Bonus: I love feeling needed.) So I made a deal with myself: for every hour I stayed late, I would have to exercise for twenty minutes. That way, staying three hours late meant that I got home at 9:00 and then had to go on a walk until 10:00. I'd be exhausted and miserable at the beginning of my walk, but then I'd be tired and calm by the end of it. So, if I chose to stay late, the exercise helped negate the effects of working too long—and if I didn't want my day to end at 10:00, then I had greater incentive to leave work earlier. Basically, the beauty of this technique is that the only way to get out of doing the healthy behavior is to stop doing the unhealthy behavior that "necessitated" it.

So now, how can we apply this approach for you? Here are some unhealthy/healthy behavior combos that might be useful:

- ⚡ For every time you hang out with a friend who is not supportive, make a date with a friend who is supportive.

- ⚡ For every meal you eat in a rush, plan a leisurely meal in recompense.

- ⚡ For every drink you drink to unwind, exercise for twenty minutes.

Write down in your notebook a few unhealthy/self-destructive behaviors you're having trouble giving up. If you need help finding healthy behaviors to trade them for, refer back to Chapter 5 for suggestions. We all know Super You is a strong, tough creature, but she has enough to deal with from external forces—let's help her not destroy herself from the inside out.

Weaknesses We Can Change: Expectations Without Communication

We all have preferences in how we want the people in our lives to treat us, whether or not we're even aware of them. For years I expected everyone I got into a relationship with, platonic or romantic, to come into it having already memorized my owner's manual. (Not that such a manual exists, and not that I wanted the other person to own me in any way, obviously, but you get the metaphor.) This is where I'm somewhat envious of superheroes, because everyone knows everything about them. Everyone knows not to bring up the topic of parents around Batman. Everyone knows not to bring Kryptonite around Superman. Wonder Woman doesn't have to explain her invisible jet to anyone. But alas, we are not superheroes, and we have no manuals.

But I expected others to know all my preferences simply based on the fact that we were in a relationship together. See if this sounds familiar to you: you get together with the love of your life (or of right now) after a long, terrible day, and all you want is to be babied and snuggled. But said love of your life has also had a long and crazy day, and starts excitedly telling you about it as soon as you both sit down. As he's talking and gesticulating wildly, a voice in your head

asks, "Is he going to even ask me about my day?" You dramatically sigh while listening to him and nodding, and the voice pipes up again: "Can't he tell I'm sitting over here miserable, while he just keeps going on and on about how Seth Rogen tweeted at him?" followed by the dreaded, "If he doesn't at least ask me how I'm doing in the next minute I'm going to be soooo pissed." And of course, the next step is working yourself into a lather of anger over something your one-and-only had no idea was happening. You were expecting psychic perception of a normal human being with no extrasensory powers. So you essentially set up a test that no one could ever pass: in truth, they are destined to fail. Does this sound familiar? (We'll return to this scenario in a later chapter.)

This was one of the biggest weaknesses of my Super You. I can't tell you how many times I've gotten caught in this trap—I essentially used to live in this trap. When it came to my close friends, my family, and the men I've dated, rather than helping them understand the blueprint of me, I'd create a dream scenario of how things should be—and then watch as no one ever came close to it. I justified this behavior by thinking, "Well, this is someone who's supposed to know me well. I shouldn't have to verbalize when I'm having a bad day." And while it's true that gradually, through trial and error, we learn the moods of the people around us, the possibilities of behavior are too infinite for us ever to know how to respond perfectly. Here's the truth: it's your job to know how you like to be handled under duress, and it's your job to communicate those desires. It is not a qualification of caring about someone to be able to read his or her mind.

The Hidden Benefits of Expectations Without Communication

If we've learned that all behaviors, even the maladaptive ones, have some sort of benefit for us, even if they're kinda creepy and gross, what on Earth do we get out of not communicating our wants while still expecting those wants to be met? What do we get out of deliberately setting up others to fail in our eyes?

For me it was a combination of things. As I've mentioned, I'm southern, and there's a very real pull within me never to seem too demanding—never to bother anyone, really. This may be a fairly universal feeling for women; it's certainly something I share with my mother. When I lived in New York, the first time my parents visited me I wanted to go all out and show them all the sights, but I was too poor to afford cabs everywhere. So I ran them all over Manhattan, and when I asked if they wanted to take a break, they'd say, "No, of course not, we're fine!" Eventually I wanted a break, and suggested we rest in a park, and as soon as we did my mother said, "Good gracious, I thought we'd never stop. I just need a minute off my feet!" She hadn't wanted to seem like she was pausing the fun—but that came at the expense of her physical comfort. She's a fantastic mother, and of course I'd have been willing to break whenever she wanted. Experiencing this with her helped me to see the ways I do the same thing, that part of the reason I don't communicate my needs and wants is that I want to be easygoing. To my mind, I should be happy just to be in a relationship, so making demands on how to be treated within that relationship would be too selfish.

Returning to why I didn't ask for attention at the end of that bad day: perhaps I was worried that I'd risk seeming too vulnerable by needing emotional support from another person. Real relationships

are full of squirmy, risking-your-coolness moments, and for a long time I wasn't ready to accept that. Or maybe, instead of all that, I just didn't have any good outlets for my anger, and relished the idea of expressing anger to someone close to me. Having a boyfriend who didn't know how to comfort me confirmed my belief that the world was always going to be messed up and I'd always end up feeling lousy because of it. While this might sound nihilistic, this was how I felt before my Super You days. In fact, sadistically and gleefully anticipating being angry with someone for messing up yet again is another terrible new emotion we don't have a name for. But name or no name, it absolutely exists.

Expectations Without Communication: The External Fix

If you find yourself guilty of expecting psychic behavior from those around you, regardless of your reasons for falling victim to this common Super You weakness, there are a few things you can do. But be warned: they involve showing vulnerability. Think back to the reality show technique we discussed previously. If someone in your life doesn't have access to your talking head segments (so that means literally everyone, unless you actually have a reality show), it is incredibly important for you to communicate what you feel and what you need—for you to essentially show her your talking head segments. And if you haven't yet figured out what you're feeling and what you need, then it's even more likely that the other person isn't going to be able to figure it out either.

So, if you find yourself getting frustrated because you're not getting what you want from the other person, stop and ask yourself what the ideal behavior would be she could do right now. Check in with yourself, as we talked about in Chapter 5. Once you've figured out the ideal response to how you're feeling, take a step backward and ask yourself why *that* behavior is what you need. What is going on within you that would make a hug/a quick romp/dumping your woes out the thing that would help you feel better? Then your job is to communicate thus:

**Hey _____, I'm feeling pretty _____ today.
I would like you to _____. It would
make me feel so much better.**

SOME REASONABLE, CONCRETE REQUESTS

→ Could you give me a backrub?

→ Listen to me complain.

→ Let's get dessert somewhere.

→ Can you do the dishes?

SOME UNREASONABLE, VAGUE REQUESTS

→ Stop being stupid.

→ Just understand me.

→ Quit your job and stay at home.

→ Take care of everything.

Also, when you communicate what you want from the other person, make sure the request is both *reasonable* and *concrete*.

The unreasonable requests are unreasonable because either they're not realistic ("Quit your job and stay at home") or they're so vague no one would know how to fulfill them ("Just understand me"). Plus, unreasonable requests can force the other person to translate what something like "understanding you" actually means. Be aware that making this request in no way guarantees you'll get what you want, because—say it with me—you can only control yourself. But asking, rather than expecting, is way more likely to get you what you want.

Will this whole process be hard to do at first? Absolutely. Will you grumble that it takes out all the fun if you ask for it? Absolutely. But life is not an adorable romcom movie where two people's souls come together with such ease and precision that they each anticipate the other's needs. This is life, and it's beautiful and messy and confusing.

I have two quick things to add here. One, it is absolutely okay to be a little needy sometimes in a relationship. Everyone has times—with parents, friends, lovers, coworkers—when they take turns leaning on each other. It's a natural part of being in a relationship, and it should be a two-way street. And two, if you find that your calm requests for reasonable, concrete attention are consistently ignored outright or met with laughter or scorn, that's a pretty good sign that the relationship is not worth your time and effort.

Weaknesses We Can Change: Negative Self-Talk

Have you heard of *negative self-talk*? If not, allow me to introduce you to something you might have been doing for a long time.

THERAPY TERM *alert*

Negative self-talk is that little voice inside your head that tells you you're not good enough, you're not pretty enough, everyone hates you, and you're going to look stupid. It's the poisonous, repetitive inner voice that makes you doubt yourself in horrific ways, and the more vulnerable you feel, the louder it gets. I don't know where negative self-talk comes from, but I also don't know that it matters. Maybe it's our culture or our parents. Maybe it's mental illness, just one that *everyone* has. Maybe it's Laura, the most popular girl in your middle school who used to tease you. All I know is that, at some point when I was very young, my negative self-talk started whispering in my ear and never stopped.

When I was very little, I was convinced that the cartoon mice on my bedsheets would come to life and bite me in my sleep. I tried desperately to sleep so as not to touch any of them, which literally tied me in knots. Try explaining that to your parents; I assure you, they'll think you're a basket case. As I got a bit older, I was plagued with constant, intrusive thoughts about the devil, and how I'd somehow created an accidental alliance with him. Eventually, rather than just scaring me, my negative self-talk started attacking me directly. So I had thoughts about being too big, and how no boy would want to be with someone bigger than him; of how I wasn't worth anything, how I was stupid and should take up less space. This led to fantasies about my fat being a suit that I could zip off. Later, when I was dating, my self-talk would whisper to me that my boyfriend was cheating on me. Eventually, in my twenties, the voice settled on constantly yelling at me about my career and how it wasn't going well enough. Basically, negative self-talk is a ridiculously obnoxious, passive-aggressive person who seems to exist just to torment you.

The Hidden Benefits of Negative Self-Talk

Remember how I said that all behaviors, even the maladaptive ones, have some sort of benefit for us? Well, guess what? There are no hidden benefits of negative self-talk.

So then what? How do we deal with such a toxic inner critic? Easy: we turn it into a creepy villain. As a Super You, you are destined to have a villain or two in your life; negative self-talk is simply the villain that worms its way into your head and tells you all the reasons why you're not a Super You. But to turn your negative self-talk into a villain that you can then fight involves naming your negative self-talker, perhaps even coming up with a backstory for him/her/it...

> **Born out of the fires of hell, gas station employee for several years: miserable and obsessed with making you miserable too. She doesn't even wash her hands after a visit to the bathroom!**

Note that by doing this we're not elevating our negative self-talk—in naming it we're separating it from ourselves, shrinking it down, perceiving it as the nuisance it is. You know how sometimes in a public place there'll be this one jerk on a cell phone talking way louder than necessary, so that everyone is treated to his scintillating conversation about mortgages or monster trucks? You know how eventually the sound of his voice goes from the only thing you can hear to a Charlie Brown/*Peanuts* teacher wah-wah that you register only as white noise? That's what you have to do with negative self-talk, or with Mega Rhonda, which is what I named my negative self-talk.

> **Here to bug the shit out of you... it's Mega Rhonda!**

Because here's what we forget about Mega Rhonda, or whichever negative self-talk villain we're facing: *it isn't speaking the truth.* It is, in fact, inaccurate. Believing our own negative self-talk is a totally natural inclination, because we want to believe that anything that comes out of our brains is somehow a deep, gospel truth about ourselves—but this just simply isn't the case. Not everything your mind cooks up is genius, and just because the call is coming from inside the house doesn't mean it has insight that you don't have. It's just Mega Rhonda, off work from the gas station, worming her way into your brain and trying to bring you down again. And though the negative self-talk spiel she gives may seem tailored to you, it's actually not about you. It doesn't need analyzing, it doesn't need "grain of salting"—it just needs to be told to shut the fuck up, and it needs to be ignored. If this seems like a daunting task, think about how you'd respond to Mega Rhonda if she said all those horrible things to your best friend, little sister, child, partner, or parent. You'd deal with her immediately, right? You wouldn't think, "Well, maybe you're right, Mega Rhonda," right? This is the same respect you owe yourself. You're on Team Super You, after all.

Negative Self-Talk: The External Fix

So it's time to start practicing this incredibly simple but hard-to-master technique. Today. When you hear your Mega Rhonda whispering negative stuff into your ear, realize that it's coming from your personal villain, and tell it to shut up. Have I demurely murmured "Shut up" in an elevator on the way to a job interview? Sure. Have I addressed Mega Rhonda unkindly in a mirror in a dressing

room at a store? Oh yeah. I absolutely think that an essential key to everyone's self-esteem is based on how well you're able to tell your villain to cram it. Eventually, you will notice the volume of your Mega Rhonda gradually diminishing. It may never stop, but your brain will adjust to the idea that the negative self-talk is just noise, that it doesn't speak your essential truths.

Are any of you asking, "How can I tell the difference between negative self-talk and actual, helpful warnings?" Well, that's a great question. And while, yes, some of the voices in our heads can be extremely useful to us, there is a big difference between instincts and negative self-talk. Negative self-talk is unequivocally negative and often irrational. It'll use words like *never, always, disgusting, permanent*—you know, words that leave no room for hope or improvement. Instincts are the little voices accompanied by our skin crawling or by a pit of weirdness in the belly. Instincts tell us that we're in an unsafe situation, or that our health is failing, or that our bodies need something from us. Not listening to these sorts of helpful warnings is not the same as not listening to a steady stream of insults and degradation. They are two separate voices entirely, and only one of them says things like "should," "can't," and "Go ahead humiliate yourself, see if I care." Only negative self-talk isn't accompanied by physical sensations. So listen to your instincts, and tell Mega Rhonda to shut up. If you do it consistently enough, her voice will fade to a sad, raspy, little whisper that tickles your ear every once in a while and makes you feel just pity.

Weaknesses We Can Change: Hating

Next up: hating. I'm not talking about hating the main characters in your life; I'm talking about hating strangers, hating the minor characters in your backstory. Whom do you hate? And more importantly, who is worthy of your hatred? Because here's the thing about hating: it takes a great deal of energy. I'm not going to use a tired analogy about the number of muscles it takes to smile and frown, but it is true that the amount of energy it takes to hate someone is often equal to the amount of energy it takes to care about someone—hate just involves more of a burning sensation. I would have said a few years ago that I have no enemies whatsoever, because I'm a grown-up, but the fun thing about the Internet is that it gives us such a wide array of people to hate, and such a wide variety of ways to hate them. You may hate someone on Twitter for her politics, you may hate someone you know personally for always posting about his awesome social life, you may hate someone for the essays she writes on the website you want to write for, you may hate someone for his success, or you may gleefully still hate someone named Laura who teased you in middle school, happy to learn about the nightmare her life has become. I once spent a lot of time and energy going through a woman's Instagram profile and critiquing each image just because she threw a really cool birthday party and didn't invite me.

The Hidden Benefits of Hating

Here's a pretty basic lesson about hate: hating someone else almost always means that you have some unfinished business within yourself to attend to. Just as criticizing someone else often means that you are critiquing your own qualities that you are less than proud of. Think about it: If you hate someone for having a successful career, aren't you actually feeling somewhat unsteady about your own trajectory? Or if you hate someone for being pretty, and say catty things about her to level the playing field, aren't you actually addressing insecurities about your own appearance? If you hate someone's amazing-looking social life on social media (I call it Instajealousy), isn't that really about your lack of focus on your own social life? Or, similarly, if you hate an attractive person for being in your partner's life, you're probably actually addressing your insecurities with the relationship. I mean, if you feel successful and beautiful and secure in your relationship, what's the reason to worry about where others may fall in those categories? The point is, whenever you hate someone for something, try to look beyond the person and the hate and identify the issue that's pestering you.

This subject affects an awful lot of us, so I have a lot to say about it. And yeah, it's easy to hate someone for being racist/sexist/homophobic—I totally get that—but isn't it more that you're upset with your lack of control over the world? Those others don't deserve any of your energy, not even hate. And if you find yourself deeply hating a stranger for tiny offenses like not flushing a public toilet or parking weirdly, it's usually a sign that you have some misdirected anger in your life. Daily events might deserve your momentary annoyance—but if you find yourself focusing on them for too long, it's definitely not about the annoyance; it's about a deeper unmet need inside of you.

Hating: The External Fix

Though hate can sometimes be galvanizing, hate-based motivation is more rare than you'd think. More often, hate paralyzes us, keeping us from doing anything to improve our situation.

In my case, hate kept me from looking inward, because I was too busy plotting the demise of Kim, that slutty girl at work that all the guys fawn over. Basically, I had a problem of hating attractive women—for years. First, I refused to admit they were attractive. I also convinced myself that attractive women were slutty and "unfeminist." And I could sometimes be heard insisting they'd probably had traumatic pasts they were trying to bury with their primping. But not only did all that hate get me nowhere, I ended up much more stressed-out about my own appearance. I didn't trust women, and I had few female friends. I was a mess.

At some point, though, I made a conscious decision to take all the energy I was using to reject women around me to start embracing them instead, even if it didn't feel natural at first. I cannot possibly express how helpful this has been in my life. Acknowledging other women's attractiveness, and reaching out to get to know women I would have previously scoffed at, has been a bonanza for me. I've become more secure in my own looks, I've become more secure in my marriage, I've made absolutely amazing friends, and I've learned a million makeup and clothing tips. Let's be clear: it's not that my immediate thoughts have changed 100 percent. Sometimes when I see a gorgeous woman at a party I still have a knee-jerk reaction: "Look how short that skirt is, come on now!" But instead of spending the party seething—"How dare she dress sexually at a party!?"—I walk up to her and introduce myself. I make small talk. Essentially,

I force myself to confront myself. I'm not suggesting that pretty women at parties just exist for me to further my emotional well-being, but where's the harm in furthering myself *while* making small talk, something we're supposed to do at parties? Sometimes the woman is awesome and we click; sometimes we don't. Either way, she's a human being, and no longer just a representation of my failings and my sausage-like legs. She doesn't deserve that bullshit, and I have too much to do to fill my spirit with hate.

Now, with all this I've been talking about times when the hate is coming from you; this equanimity stuff can be harder to pull off when the hate is coming *at* you. When confronted with systemic hate or ignorance that makes my blood boil, as much as I may disagree with the person spouting that hate, I've found it helpful to do a few things. First, I try to understand what underlies that person's beliefs. You may learn that the Joe (or Josephine) spouting racist stuff online is just someone who grew up in a fairly homogenized town and is afraid of change. That doesn't excuse the racism, of course, but it does explain a bit where he's coming from. Let your emotions shift from hate, which can leave you powerless, to pity and

FUN FACT ABOUT LOS ANGELES

In Los Angeles, porn actresses are just everywhere, and they are some of the most fun and interesting women to talk to, women I would have missed out on if I were still in hate mode. They are naked and sexy for a living, and they also have hilarious stories about scenes gone wrong, lovely stories about relationships, and horrifying stories about how people talk to them. Get to know a porn star if you can.

sadness, because there is power there for you. Next, I ask myself what my hatred of that racist person accomplishes. Does it change her views? Does it eradicate racism? Nope. Instead of spending your energy on hate, spend it on a charity or organization that you believe injects good into the world. Spend that energy volunteering, or marching, or spreading factual information; if you're a writer, spend it on creating characters that push people's perceptions of what "those kinds of people" are like. When you cancel out your hate by doing something productive, not only will your energy be better spent, but you'll get to witness how your positive injections can counteract those toxic negatives. There will always be something terrible happening in the world, unfortunately, and your hatred will not make it go away. So when you feel hate bubbling up, first take a look within yourself to see if there's anything you can address inside to fight the hate. If not, take a look in a more positive direction to see if that doesn't help. (Note: I am aware that as a white woman, I don't get to tell anyone how to react to racism. There are mere suggestions for reframing terrible things.)

Weaknesses We Cannot Change

As I said back at the beginning of this chapter, there are two types of weaknesses: those we can adjust and therefore could improve, and those we can't adjust and therefore should protect. What's the difference? Great question. I'm still trying to work that out myself, and there are no real set-in-stone rules about this, but for now we're talking about maladaptive habits that you've learned over time (changeable) versus lifelong personality traits (unchangeable). We could also consider the weaknesses you cannot change as actually weaknesses you *will* not change—but it's a moot point. More important than the difference between the two is learning how to fit the weaknesses you aren't actively working to change into the beautiful puzzle that is you.

Step one of this puzzle-fitting concerns how you classify yourself in relation to those unchangeable weaknesses. Think about it this way: Superman's weakness is Kryptonite, right? And yet, he doesn't call himself Kryptonite Man. Well, you may say, how stupid would that be? You'd just be advertising your weak points to strangers. And yet, so many of us define ourselves by our weaknesses rather than by our superpowers. In fact, many of us walk around weakness first, apologizing for ourselves right out of the gate.

I've met people who, within the first few seconds of being introduced, will tell me they're bipolar, or OCD, or fat, or alcoholic—and when I've asked them why that information comes with their introduction, they'll say, "I just don't like to be fake," or "I want you to know what you're dealing with." But leading with what you consider to be your faults isn't being more honest—it's just showing your "weak" hand, or shoving your complex identity into the weakness cubbyhole. Conversely, protecting what you consider to be your faults isn't being fake—it's simply opting not to promote your faults to headliner status. We all contain positive and negative qualities; the negative ones don't deserve any more attention than the positive ones. When we advertise our faults first, we usually do it in a bid to test others, to see if they'll be willing to stick by us even though we're problematic, or to give them an out before we get too attached. But this is not how a Super You operates. The goal here is to be accepting and accommodating and gentle to our weaknesses—and not to deem them our most defining personality traits.

Let's discuss a few common unchangeable weaknesses and how a Super You can best protect them.

Weaknesses We Cannot Change: Being a Control Freak/Wanting to Feel Needed

I put these two qualities together because for me, personally, they are connected. They may not be connected for all of you, but I've yet to meet anyone who struggles with one and not the other. As I mentioned in Chapter 3, I've been a control freak for most of my life. I've run a stand-up show in Los Angeles for the past five years, and everyone knows that the show always starts on time. Even when I was a teenage social outcast, my piercings and tendency to wear shirts that said ENJOY SATAN were my attempts to control how people felt about me—maybe you didn't like me, but you were going to not like me for the reasons I chose, not for the reasons you chose.

So what can we control freaks do? I don't want to change my control freak nature, because it serves me incredibly well in my work. I just want to use it only when necessary, and keep it safely tucked inside me the rest of the time. Basically, I treat my control freak nature as Daenerys Targaryen's dragons—I love them and am proud of them, but I realize that they should be unleashed only on special occasions. (That was a *Game of Thrones* reference.) So in situations where it wouldn't be appropriate to unleash the dragons, like planning a social outing or dealing with plumbers in my house, I purposely bite my tongue. I'm good at planning trips for movies and dinner, but that doesn't mean other people aren't also. Whenever I feel like I want to step in and take over, I repeat, silently to myself,

"There are a million good ways to do something." If things go poorly, that's because things sometimes go poorly—it isn't proof that your way would have been better. Besides, my friends all remember much more the time we walked two miles to a restaurant that was closed than the times we had an easy, successful brunch. I wish I had a better trick to offer you, but honestly, forcing myself just to be quiet and let other people take over has been the best technique I have for this. By accepting the plan that comes together, I end up enjoying it just as much, or even more, because it isn't my sole responsibility.

Weaknesses We Cannot Change: Needing to Feel Needed

Now let's talk about how we handle being a control freak in a relationship when we really just want to feel needed. (We'll talk more about relationships in chapter 10.) For now, suffice it to say that when I yearned to make myself indispensable to the men I dated, I sought out men who already seemed like they were barely making it out of the house with matching shoes on. Some of the more villainous men that my Super You faced exploited this particular weakness in me, getting me to basically run their lives, and for a time it was a gross but mutually beneficial agreement. He got a maid/mother, I got a guarantee that he would stick around. After getting myself a good therapist, I gained the strength (to be honest, I was faking the strength at first) to start dating a man who was headstrong and fairly driven. He didn't need me to pick him up or make him dinner—he was willing to do all that—and it terrified me. I was constantly afraid that he'd leave me, so I responded by

GET TO KNOW EMILY'S CONTROL FREAKNESS

My control freakness, to the best of my self-exploration, isn't about thinking I'm always right—it's more of a fun cocktail of some of the darker corners of my personality. Some of this has been covered in chapter 3, but there's more ickiness to behold! First, I have some trust issues. It takes a lot for me to trust other people. If I'm working with you in a professional capacity and if I don't know you well, I'll probably assume you can't be trusted with complex tasks. This has both served me well and made me incredibly overworked. Also, as previously mentioned, I like feeling needed. Especially in personal relationships. In some ways, this is not as much a weakness as a human quality: as social beings, we all want to feel needed. For some, however, there is comfort in the idea that if you do literally everything for a friend or a boss or a romantic partner, you'll in effect be indispensable, and others won't leave you. You'll be necessary, like oxygen! But please hear me now, dear reader: in relationships, each person should function as vitamins for the other person, not oxygen. It took me years to realize that it's actually much more romantic to have someone stick around because he wants to be with me, rather than because he has to or he won't be able to pay bills. Basically, since I didn't consider myself worthy of someone's love, friendship, or attention, I thought if I made myself useful the relationship would last longer. Beyond my need to feel needed, I also have a lovely martyr complex going on, and it goes like this: if I do *everything*, then I'm the most put-upon person around, and I can throw that back in your face when you question me. Perfection can't possibly be expected from someone who is taking care of literally everything, can it?

inserting myself into his day-to-day functioning as much as I could, trying to stake a claim in this territory. It was sad to behold. Slowly I realized that this quality in myself, this need to feel needed, was only hurting Super Me. It wasn't bringing me anything helpful: the men still left me, or we just settled into the ugly grooves of an unhappy couple that doesn't find joy in each other.

I made a vow that, from then on, any guy I dated would have to function completely on his own without me. I forced myself to stop doing things for the men I was interested in, even if it was extremely hard for me. I continually told myself that, if he left me for not helping him do laundry, he was doing me a favor. I also did some work within myself on what I really got out of relationships, and realized that the perfectly normal need to feel needed could be met outside of romantic relationships. So I started volunteering with organizations that did desperately need me (or anyone, really) in order to keep functioning. I started applying my need to be needed to myself. And once I got into a healthy relationship, I let it be okay that every once in a while he needed my help with something. I even allowed myself to need him too. All of these things helped to tame the dragons. I couldn't have achieved this without working on myself, which included forcing myself to stop doing things the way I always had. There's no magic to this. It's just effort and exploration.

Weaknesses We Cannot Change: Shyness/Introversion/ Social Awkwardness

I don't think of shyness as a quality to fix. The only reason to alter any quality is if it's hampering your day-to-day life and bothering you. There's a difference between people who are just shy in large groups and people who are riddled with anxiety at the thought of social interaction. And unfortunately for those of you who feel that anxiety, unless you're a Buddhist monk with a lifetime vow of silence, being social is a part of all our lives. Plus, I think shyness has been demonized enough in our society, so I'm not adding to that chorus whatsoever. There's a fantastic book called *Quiet: The Power of Introverts in a World That Can't Stop Talking* by Susan Cain that addresses the value of being shy; I highly recommend it if this topic speaks to you. I also recommend it because I'm not going to get too in-depth on introversion and shyness here—I'm just covering the basics.

I happen to know the secret to being outgoing at parties, and I'm going to get in trouble for revealing it: most of us are faking it. An "extrovert" is someone who derives energy from social interactions. That is definitely not the case with me—nor is it the case with several of my outgoing friends. Social interactions exhaust me; I need time to myself afterward to recharge. A really intense party can even make me physically ill the next day, but that expense of energy is often worth it to me. To the outside world I may look like a social butterfly, but it takes effort, and sometimes it takes faking that effort. I sometimes feel awkward in conversations at parties, and I'm usually terrified I'll have nothing to say, or that I'll say something ridiculous. In fact, I hate weird silences among new acquaintances so much that I'll usually keep a weird story on hand just to dole out at awkward moments.

So if going to parties exhausts you, please keep in mind that many of us feel the same—we just try to pretend otherwise. This is probably why Irish Goodbyes, or Ghosting, was invented—so we can leave without saying goodbye, since we can't handle one awkward moment more.

But what do you do if your shyness and social awkwardness are keeping you from enjoying life? What do you do if you've been like this your whole life but wish things were different? How do we, as Super Yous, properly support and protect this vulnerable part of our nature, one that can take us down like Kryptonite? How do we strike a balance in pushing ourselves to grow a bit while still understanding this is just how we are? I think the best compromise lies in a duo-combo: finding a comfortable place to exist socially, from which we can regularly (or occasionally) push ourselves to try new tricks.

FUN FACTOID THAT CAN BE RANDOMLY BROUGHT UP DURING WEIRD SILENCES AT MOST PARTIES

Wonder Woman was created by an American psychologist named William Moulton Marston who also invented components of the modern-day polygraph test. One of Wonder Woman's primary weapons is the Lasso of Truth. Hmmm . . . Also, he based the character on two women: his wife, and the woman he and his wife had a romantic relationship with. Hot stuff!

Shyness Tip I: Becoming More Comfortable in Social Spaces

Finding a comfortable place to exist socially simply means recognizing ways that you're already social that *aren't uncomfortable* for you. This could include anything as small as going to a crowded café and sitting among the people for a few hours. It could mean hanging out with people one-on-one, or planning your own event with just the people you aren't weirded out by. It could mean movie outings, where the small talk is (hopefully) limited to just before and after the movie. It could mean researching things you're passionate about and finding where people who share your passion gather in your town. It could also mean being incredibly social in an online setting full of like-minded people—with a caveat: I caution you about subsisting *solely* on interaction where you don't share the same space with your, shall we say, *interacteur*. You may not think the people in your real life get you at all, and maybe they don't, but spending too much time socializing online only makes you less capable of socializing offline.

In my early teenage years in the early nineties I did all of my dating exclusively online, on Internet bulletin boards. Bulletin boards functioned like articles on a website, basically. Someone would post a paragraph-long post about a topic, and then everyone would respond in individual notes that cascaded from the original post. There were also chat rooms where groups of people could all type at each other at the same time. That's all we had back then, folks, but at the time it served me well. When online, I was divorced from my physical form, which I hated and was convinced everyone else hated, so I blossomed into a bit of a femme fatale on the Nine Inch Nails BBs (bulletin boards). I was witty, I was funny, I was cool, and

I was bold. And, thanks to the nascent technology (modems were super slow), rather than just stumbling around and blurting out weird stuff, I had time to think through my responses, successfully projecting into cyberspace the awesome girl I wished I were. (I've been plotting the Super You concept for years.) The problem was that I was only projecting and not making any moves to reach that projection. My online flirting just confirmed for me that this was something I could *only* do online, so instead of making me wittier in person with the guys at my high school, it drove me further into a little self-doubting shell. It took a bad experience of meeting an online boyfriend in real life—after weeks of typing how we'd definitely have sex and/or get engaged, we were both sucked into the black hole awkwardness of it all and barely spoke—to firm up my decision that I'd rather take my chances with the guys that I could talk to in person.

Shyness Tip 2: Pushing Yourself Socially

Which brings us to an important part of finding a comfortable place for your social life: pushing yourself socially just an eensy bit every now and then. We do this by trying new behaviors, faking our proficiency if we have to. This might involve taking a class with strangers, where you're forced to interact with new people, but you don't have to worry about embarrassing yourself with anyone you know. Or you could take a chance asking a new friend to hang out one-on-one, something that's both exhilarating and a little bit scary. Pushing yourself could involve, if you can believe it, volunteering. At the place where I currently volunteer, an animal shelter, I interact

with a wonderful mix of older men and women and teenage girls. Previously I'd never have thought I could make more than two minutes of small talk with any of them, but instead we gossip about the cats for hours on end, treating them as our very own soap opera. It's been really eye-opening for me to find a comfortable place, socially, in an environment that I didn't think could yield such a thing.

Now, some of the new things you'll try might feel a little like fakery at first. As I mentioned earlier, fakery is a part of many people's social lives—not necessarily to their detriment, and often to their advantage. Consider: if Superman were protecting himself, he probably wouldn't walk into a party going, "What's up guys? Hope there's no Kryptonite here. Where's the cheese plate?" We can think about shyness or social awkwardness similarly. If you're shy, when you arrive at a party you can enter as quietly as you like, but be sure to greet the first person you know with eye contact and a firm handshake. There's no need to announce that you're socially awkward—that can just ratchet up the awkwardness. If there's a lull in conversation, don't feel the need to jump in immediately, and don't feel weird about it—just let it sit for a moment. And it's okay to people watch if you're standing alone. Treat your conversations at parties as crop dusting: get in, sprinkle some socialness, and then get out of there. And note, while I can cheerily pop off advice like that, I'm personally really bad at social crop dusting—I get way too in there. And while I don't mind having intense conversations at parties, it would be nice to have another option. So, make a little conversation, and when it runs out, have a great, preplanned parting line—"Well, it was nice to talk to you. I'm going to go check out the snack bar/bar/bathroom/inside of the house"—and then gracefully exit. The great thing about this technique is you can keep moving, have several small conversations, hightail it out of there if you're feeling uncomfortable, and still look like a social butterfly!

This combination of both finding comfortable spaces and pushing yourself slightly is a great way to keep true to who you are—which can be as awkward or weird as you wanna be—while not handicapping yourself in public. Because we all have to exist in public.

Weaknesses We Cannot Change: Impostor Syndrome

A close cousin to negative self-talk, Impostor Syndrome is a bit more specific and harder to battle, and, if my anecdotal research among successful friends is to be believed, it affects women more than men. It's the belief that, no matter what you accomplish, you still expect to be uncovered as a fraud eventually and sent back down to the minor leagues where you belong. You never internalize your accomplishments as your own doing, instead attributing the success to outside factors like luck ("I just happened to be in the right place at the right time!"), people being nice to you ("They gave me this award because they felt sorry for me not having any awards"), or faking your way through it ("I can't believe I got all that done; I don't know what I'm doing!"). Now, as you know, I'm a big fan of faking confidence or skills until you can grow into them as your own. My argument is that performing the actions of a confident person yields the same result. The disconnect people with Impostor Syndrome have is that, though they're indeed performing the actions of a confident person, they're never able to realize they're actually competent. And that's the problem. Faking it is supposed to be a temporary phase, but a lot of us don't know how

to stop faking and start existing—or, we don't believe we deserve that existence.

I suffer from this a bit personally. I started out my career in a very specific field, therapy; I was highly trained, and I felt pretty confident. My education was the buoy I clung to when applying for

A QUICK RANT ABOUT SUCCESS

I could go into a long rant here about how women are still expected not to make too much of a fuss in their respective fields, and how research has shown that even very successful women sometimes attribute their success to ridiculous things like "luck" or "supportive coworkers" or "magic"—but I'll try not to yell for too long. Whereas men are often raised with the idea that everything they do is golden, women are often raised with the idea that they'd better not let on that anything they do is golden, lest they be seen as pushy braggart bitches. Plus, sometimes we fear that if we don't do our work perfectly, we'll be letting our gender down—not to mention confirming for everyone else what we've known from the start: we're not cut out for this. So we stay silent and under the radar. It's a lose-lose that a lot of us internalize for various reasons, be they familial or cultural. Fortunately, I'm convinced that mindset isn't going to stick around.

So pull up a chair and let me tell you a few things. It's okay for you to take up space. It's okay for you to put yourself out there requesting work if you feel you can do it adequately. It's okay for you to get rejected. It's okay for you to succeed and be happy about that success. It's also okay for you to fail. Failing doesn't mean you're a failure, and it certainly doesn't mean that women are failures. And besides, come tomorrow, you'll probably have another success to add to your wall.

jobs, my proof that I knew what I was doing. I framed that proof and hung it on my wall. Then I stopped being a therapist and started writing and producing comedy shows, where there are no papers to frame and display to help legitimize what you do. In the first few email pitches I sent to editors asking to write for their sites, I felt apologetic for even disturbing them. "I am not a real writer," I'd think before hitting SEND, "and I'm taking them away from the real writers emailing them." But I sent them anyway, and when I got positive responses back I was amazed and astounded. Years later—years filled with rejections and successes—I have learned this important lesson: no one really knows what he or she is doing. The difference between the people who go for it and the people who don't? The people who go for it just ignore the fact that they don't know what they're doing.

There's no real cure for Impostor Syndrome other than recognizing it in yourself and calling it out. Once a year or so I'll look back at what I've done that year, job-wise, and ask myself what skills I've gained from all that work. I force myself to take stock of what I've internalized from each job I've done, and I write it down in my notebook so I can refer to it when I'm feeling unsure.

We can also just keep at it. I was in a room with a bunch of writers/performers recently, male and female, all of us pitching ideas for a project. The goal of such a gathering is essentially to make the other people laugh. I was somewhat intimidated and didn't speak much, which you probably know by now is hard for me. But a male friend of mine spoke up quite a bit, with ideas that sometimes worked and sometimes didn't. Afterward I pulled him aside to ask how he had the confidence to pitch so easily. "That one joke got, like, nothing!" I said, half teasing him to hide my genuine interest

in his confidence. "Sure," he responded, "they didn't like that one. But I knew they'd like something eventually."

Oh. So that's what that looks like.

Weaknesses We Cannot Change: Mental Illness

It feels weird to put mental illness in the category of unchangeable weaknesses that must be protected and managed, but I wasn't sure where else to put it.

Of course, in my professional life I've seen mental illness in hundreds of forms, and, as is likely the case for many therapists, my personal life has had its share as well. Indeed, my impetus for becoming a therapist was in part growing up with family members who suffered mightily from various disorders. So let me speak to you now with my therapist hat on: if you believe you are suffering from mental illness and have not yet sought out treatment, this book is not the answer for you *yet*. Working on your self-esteem and becoming your Super You is less of a priority than getting your thoughts and moods more stabilized. Depression, severe anxiety, obsessive-compulsive disorder, any disorder with psychotic features, and personality disorders are extremely taxing and disruptive; if you suffer from any of those, you'll want your symptoms managed a bit before you try to work on your self-esteem. Besides, dealing with active and oppressive mental illness while trying to work on your self-esteem is like Spiderman trying to stop jaywalkers while Green Goblin is terrorizing the city. First Spiderman must prioritize dealing with Green Goblin; he can deal with the jaywalkers later.

Of course, we don't always realize we have a Green Goblin situation going on. If you're finding that nothing in this book is working to help you feel better, that you're having trouble with day-to-day functions and find yourself feeling off without any real rationale, I highly encourage you to seek treatment. Find a good therapist, discuss options for medication if that feels appropriate, and involve your closest friends and family. The National Institute of Mental Health has a pretty good website with information about disorders and how to get help. Please be aware that looking up information on mental illness can sometimes lead you to believe that you have every disorder, so do research with a grain of salt, and find yourself a therapist that you feel comfortable with. It takes a group effort to treat mental illness, and that effort involves *you* reaching out for support, taking steps forward, falling backward—as is pretty much inevitable—and then getting up and doing it all over again.

The best part is, when you've reached a point where you're feeling stable, and are no longer in day-to-day crisis, your Super You will be waiting for you.

Amazingly, there are some incredibly positive qualities that can come from mental illness, and I don't just mean how paranoia can keep us safe from ne'er-do-wells, though it can. Depression can help us to slow down and ruminate, staying for a while in our emotions. (Obviously, for such sufferers this can become too much of a good thing.) Depressed people have been found to be more adept at analytical thinking, especially examining larger problems and breaking them down into smaller parts. Anxiety and OCD tendencies are a fantastic aid in life organization and are one of the reasons we can keep on top of many tasks at once, getting everything in place just in time for curtain call.

MENTAL ILLNESS IN COMIC BOOKS: AN APOLOGY

As you can probably guess, in most comic books mental illness has not been treated with sensitivity or even with basic understanding. Because they're so full of secret identities, comic books often give characters "multiple personality disorder"—something we now call dissociative identity disorder, which happens to be very rare.

One example of this is Jack Ryder, a character in the Batman universe, who is a political pundit by day but by night dresses up as the Joker, calls himself the Creeper, and injects himself with drugs to make him stronger. Unfortunately the drugs also make him psychotic, and he starts believing he and the Creeper are two different people.

Erica Fortune, also known as Spellbinder, has a superpower of traveling through different dimensions. At some point the stress of experiencing other dimensions makes her lose her marbles, and when she returns to our dimension she kills her family because she's insane.

I've come to see how anxious and intrusive thoughts—like how I make deals with myself that I'll stop fretting about something if "X" happens; I told you about that, right?—are part of a continuum of behaviors.

For me, the key was learning that my anxious thoughts don't mean that I'm somehow more observant about the world around me, or god forbid, psychic. I do my best to accept the gift of being detail-oriented while dismissing the self-beliefs that often come with anxious thoughts. In the same way, you can recast your weaknesses as superpowers for your Super You—like how Spiderman's superpowers mean that it's somewhat hard for him to date girls like a regular teenager. Again, I don't mean to downplay or trivialize mental illness, and it's not that I wouldn't love to lose the intrusive thoughts that keep me awake at 4:00 AM about how I'm not going to enough museums—even at the cost of my attention to detail. What I do mean is, in assessing the parts of ourselves we don't think we can change, we can work to recontextualize qualities we've up until now seen as weaknesses.

To help with that, here are some tips for people coping with mental illness.

Mental Illness Tip 1: Getting Treatment

To help destigmatize mental illness a bit, let's instead think of it as asthma. If you have asthma, you might take a daily pill or inhaler and carry an acute inhaler to use as needed; you might also see a doctor every few months. And that makes sense, right? If you have an ailment that calls for some kind of attention, taking care of it makes sense. So, whatever your disorder may be, make active maintenance and treatment of it part of your routine, whether that means medication, a semi-regular therapist, or a support group. Make it like brushing your teeth.

Mental Illness Tip 2: Knowing Your Triggers

If you have asthma and you know that hot weather can set off attacks, then when it's hot out you know to be ready. Or if running for a train makes you grab for your inhaler, then you'll want to leave

yourself plenty of time to get to the station. I'll bet there are triggers that can similarly cause your disorder to flare up, be they certain times of year, certain situations, or certain people who can bring it on. Take stock of yourself: list your triggers so you know what you're working with.

Mental Illness Tip 3: Having Action Plans Ready

Once you know what your triggers are, you can set about determining great plans for when they kick in. If I feel a panic attack coming on, I like to write down all fifty states to distract and calm myself—and because I've planned this in advance, I know what to turn to when I need it. If you feel the big bad sads creeping up on you, have DVDs at the ready that always comfort and energize you. And when you need someone, know which people you can call for support.

It's important to remember: even though mental illness can happen to you, it *isn't* you. It's part of you, absolutely, but it isn't all you are. It's simply a chronic condition, which calls for regular treatment—rather than an acute condition like an infection, which requires just one dose of treatment. So, whatever your situation, know what your particular deal is, and know what to do with it when it arrives.

Your weaknesses are yours, whatever you decide to do with them. Own them, get to know them, figure out which ones you can change and which ones you'll keep around out of necessity or affection. We've gone too long keeping our own darkness in the dark—it's time to bring our weaknesses to the light, noting their importance without making them the most important thing about us.

Cheap Armor and Weapons: What Outmoded "Protection" Are You Hiding Behind?

et's take stock of things so far. We've discussed how to become more aware of who we are right now and how to use that to become the Super You we want to be. We've talked about the external and internal changes, big and small, that will make that Super You a reality. We've talked about the superpowers and less-than-super weaknesses that we can either use to our advantage or protect and nurture properly. Now it's time to talk about where our similarities to actual comic book superheroes end—other than the fact that they're fictional and we are not. Our commonalities with comic book superheroes end with the super gear.

One of my favorite things about superhero movies is nerding out over all the cool new equipment that's trotted out. Our protagonist goes to meet his/her head of development, usually played by Morgan Freeman or Judi Dench, tirelessly working in a lab cooking up some cool new gear that our heroes can call upon in times of need. Shoes that can also punch a guy in the face? Heck yeah. A cell phone that can tell you where the closest bomb is? I mean, Wonder Woman literally has an invisible jet. How do you even design something like that? How does she know where it is? As a kid, when playing superheroes with other kids, I always preferred playing the inventor role to the ass-kicking role, although the best I could come up with when playing such games was a coat that also functioned as a sleeping bag. Don't knock it—it would have been very handy in cold climates. And the Dark Knight is constantly looking for new ways to protect himself, and new ways to inflict pain on others... for the good of society, of course. Lighter armor. The ability to spy on cell phone conversations. A flying Batmobile. Does Super You need this stuff as well?

In my opinion, no. Not in the long run. Weapons, armor, and intense technology look cool in movies and comic books, but for those of us building our own personal superheroes, that stuff is just a distraction from being ourselves. And where we're going, we won't need it. Some of us, in our early Super You phases, might have used some simplistic weaponry and armor to protect our psyches, our feelings, our vulnerable parts. Some of our early Super You prototypes had weapons that fired so hot they kept people from wanting to get close to us. Our armor was so fierce and strong that it kept people from penetrating our tough outer layers and getting to the soft gushy parts inside. And as we discussed before, protecting parts of ourselves that we feel uncomfortable revealing to the world, like our shyness or any emotional issues, is totally understandable and necessary. The problem is, when we forget to take that armor off, keeping people from ever being able to truly get to know us (read: hurt us). But we shouldn't be ashamed of using weapons or armor to protect ourselves in the past. Just as with any other coping mechanism, we were doing the best we could with what we had in front of us. While weapons and armor might be incredibly useful to fictional superheroes, for a Super You, they are just a method for keeping us isolated, emotionally and sometimes physically.

Now, please hear me: there are times in life when armor is necessary. There are times when it's necessary to isolate yourself, to circle the wagons and push people away. So when I talk about psyche weapons and armor, I am not speaking of the day, week, or month that you're feeling so vulnerable and stressed and overworked that you need to shut yourself off from the rest of the world and fully immerse yourself in yourself. That, to me, is a healthy choice, and one we discussed in chapter 5. I'm talking about what happens when you make protecting yourself from the rest of the world a daily practice that's been going on so long you forgot what it felt like to have fresh air on your skin. I'm talking about when shoving people away from you with various high-tech methods starts to feel normal.

The problem with emotional armor and weaponry is that it really isn't built for long-term use—it breaks easily under pressure and leaves you more vulnerable than before. So before we continue, let's first acknowledge the important role that these cheap armor and weapons have served for you in the past. As you're reading this chapter, perhaps take a moment to thank your armor and weaponry for doing the best job they could to protect you over the years.

Thank them for working so hard to keep you safe from the perils of reality—and let them know they're officially retiring from duty. They're getting too old for this shit.

And while you're hearing me, let's keep hearing me: there is such a thing as healthy self-protection. I am not suggesting that you go skipping into the world tra-la-la trusting everyone and leaving your car doors unlocked. Being naive doesn't serve anyone. I am suggesting that we all proceed through our lives with both open hearts *and* open eyes. A Super You that has been properly building herself and stepping slowly into the best version of herself doesn't need extra protection or weaponry. She is able to evaluate people based on how they present themselves, and make decisions on how to interact with them accordingly. Her superheroness is enough for most days.

DUMBEST SUPERHERO WEAPONS

Stone Boy can turn himself into stone, but then he can't move.

Madame Fatal can dress up like an old woman, and be really convincing.

Dazzler converts music into light, because light is great at fighting bad guys.

If you're not sure about the difference between healthy self-protection and unhealthy self-protection, take a look at the chart below and ask yourself, honestly, what needs your armor and weapons are serving you.

How to Tell If You're Employing Cheap Armor and Weaponry

UNHEALTHY SELF-PROTECTION	HEALTHY SELF-PROTECTION
Applies to every person in your life equally	Is only pulled out when people reveal themselves to be untrustworthy
Is focused on others	Focuses on you alone
Is permanent	Is limited to times of need
Keeps you exactly where you are, mentally and emotionally	Allows for growth and evolution, even within the protection
Is utilized out of fear of others	Is utilized out of love for yourself

If you suspect that you might be donning some of that cheap, black-market armor and weaponry that wouldn't protect Batman's little finger, keep reading. We'll be talking about both armor and weaponry. (Some could have gone in either category, but I had to put them somewhere.) As always, this list isn't exhaustive; it's just meant to help you identify ways you may be perpetuating unhealthy self-protection.

Most Commonly Used Types of Armor

Self-Deprecation

Perhaps you've seen this in other people, and maybe even in yourself: the constant need to refer to yourself as ugly, incompetent, or stupid. The need to bring yourself down in other people's eyes. Self-deprecation can be incredibly charming and funny when used sparingly, but for the most part it's deployed as some sort of suppressive fire of the ego. Self-deprecation tells people they can't possibly think more poorly of you than you do yourself. It's an act of humility when no humility is called for. And it's lame.

"But Emily!" I hear you saying. "It's not like I'm doing this on purpose!" And certainly, you are not, I understand that. But this entire process of becoming a Super You is about upping our self-awareness and intentionality—questioning the thoughts and behaviors in ourselves that have become automatic, and evaluating how helpful they are to who we are and who we want to be. And self-deprecation is definitely autopilot behavior.

So if this is an issue for you, it's time to start focusing on it and shedding it—slowly. And if it hurts you to hear other people say negative things about you, I'm here to tell you it's equally hurtful when you say them yourself, maybe even more so.

It's not a natural inclination to think the best way of presenting yourself is to lower expectations; it's just a coping mechanism. In military terms, I like to think of self-deprecation as pretending to be dead on the battlefield—you're protecting yourself by demonstrating you're not a threat, essentially by harming yourself before anyone else gets a chance to. From a strictly strategic standpoint, self-deprecation is a genius suit of armor. But if we're firmly on Team Super You, which we are at this point (even if we've been dragged kicking and screaming), self-deprecation doesn't have any place in our lives. So let's thank it for managing the world's expectations of us, and then let's take off that armor.

The best way to stop self-deprecating, unfortunately, is just to stop. And while we're doing some work in this book on recognizing and appreciating our strengths, unfortunately we don't have time for our minds and hearts to catch up to our mouths. This is one of those external changes we just have to do. I have four tips for becoming aware of self-deprecation and learning to stop it.

Tip 1: The Rubber Band

Wear a rubber band on your wrist. When you catch yourself saying something self-deprecating, snap the rubber band. Don't snap it enough to hurt; the sensation should just be surprising enough to call you out on your behavior. (Use this method for lots of bad habits that you may want to take off autopilot.)

Tip 2: Breathing

In situations when you know your self-deprecation comes out—such as meeting new people, being the center of attention, being praised, or interacting with strangers—before you respond, stop and take one deep breath. While you are breathing, tell yourself that you're on Team Super You, and that you cannot respond with anything that would upset Team Super You or hurt their chances at the play-offs. No one will notice the deep breath, but you will notice the difference it makes.

Tip 3: Enlisting a Team Member

If you're still having trouble with recognizing your own self-deprecation, call on a buddy/spouse/parent/coworker to help you. This is great because explaining to someone else what self-deprecation is can actually make you more aware of it yourself, and also because

knowing that your behavior is being watched ends up affecting your behavior anyway. Ask your buddy to alert you with a predetermined signal or word that you've self-deprecated again. This can help you keep track of the things you're saying, and what environment you say them in. Keep working toward self-awareness.

Tip 4: Saying Thank You

This is a simple one: when you're offered a compliment, say thank you. It feels like a small thing, but it's not. The women in my family have never ever been able to take a compliment—I chalk it up to our being demure and charming southern belles. These days we have a rule in our family: any compliment can have only one response, and that response is thank you. No making excuses about why your skirt they like is hideous, no explaining that you don't actually deserve credit for the art you created. Just thank you. This tip has been incredibly helpful for me, and is (I hope) helpful to my female family members, who now sigh at me before semi-shouting "Thank You" when I admire their earrings.

Self-Sabotage

Self-sabotage is what you're dealing with when the universe consistently seems as if it's out to get you, but when what's really out to get you is... you, disguised as the universe. It's a wily beast that has brought down many a superhero. So why do I call it a type of armor? Why isn't it just a poor way of interacting with the world? What is it, even? Like a bacterial infection, self-sabotage can present itself in many different ways, all with the same basic function: inadvertently ruining your chances. It's considered armor here because your self-saboteur psyche is protecting you from failing by not letting you attempt at all. What your psyche doesn't realize is that you need to attempt *and* fail every once in a while if you are to grow at all. Let me tell you a couple of stories.

Paula the Putter-Offer

My friend Paula loves writing so much she has a part-time job so she can devote the rest of her time to writing. But even with all that time she sets aside, she often has trouble getting started. Then one day Paula finds out about a talk show that's hiring writers. To be considered for the job, she needs to submit a collection of writing prompts within ten days. Paula's too overwhelmed for the first couple of days even to look at the writing prompts. When she finally does, she thinks, "Okay, I think I can do this," and starts reading and taking notes in the margins. She then realizes that her house is unbelievably filthy—and that she'd be able to write much better if she just cleaned it a bit. Two more days go by. Paula finds incredibly logical reasons for not really starting until two days before the prompts are due. She completes the writing "audition" in a rush and a panic—and doesn't do her best work. She submits it with an apology saying she wished she'd had more time to work on it. Paula doesn't get hired.

Romanov the Romantic

My friend Romanov is a romantic, and really wants to be in a relationship. He has a pretty clear idea of what his ideal relationship

would look like, and he's not willing to settle for less. He wants a girl who has her own career but is also very invested in his success; he wants a girl who cooks and plays video games and also likes to cosplay. He wants a girl who had a bit of a rough upbringing so he can help her understand what good relationships look like. He wants a girl who won't want to stay over too often but who also can drop anything and stay over if necessary without needing to feed her cat or walk her dog or air her cockatoo. Romanov goes into every first date with this complicated, intense rubric in his head and heart. Needless to say, no girl fits into the box he's created for his "girlfriend." When each new girl disappoints him, as they all will inevitably do, he breaks it off. When I ask Romanov what went wrong, he shakes his head sadly, looking off into the middle distance. "It just didn't work out with Angelique Ravensborn. Such a shame."

Both Paula and Romanov are self-saboteurs, but with different methodologies. While Paula is passionate about writing, she's also terrified she's not actually good at writing. Dreams that stay dreams never have the ability to disappoint you. By keeping her goals at arm's length, Paula never has to find out if she wouldn't succeed as a writer. Because that would be the worst thing to happen: if she's not good at writing, what on Earth would she aspire to?

Romanov, however, just doesn't actually want to be in a relationship—but he hasn't told himself that yet. Parts of him know, but his brain/parents/society keep telling him otherwise. If the thing you want is so bogged down with criteria that *must be fulfilled* or else, it's time to take another look at whether or not you actually want that thing at all, as it would be wise for Paula and Romanov to do. Paula looks for reasons not to attempt her goal; Romanov makes his goal too complicated to achieve. Both are protecting themselves from experiencing the thing they say they want, because, for various reasons, the thing they want scares them.

But here's the thing: that fear is totally normal. Since fear is meant to signal potential danger to our bodies and minds, it's a healthy reaction, especially to intensely desired goals and dreams. But fear can also be a false flag, warning us only of potential danger to our egos. Sadly, these warnings can look very similar. Your ego wants to believe it's constantly in danger, but it's amazing how much an ego can actually handle. Many of us listen to our egos a bit too much, protecting ourselves from the incredibly normal, healthy step of self-evolution: rejection. So, to save the universe the effort of rejecting them, self-saboteurs reject themselves—and as an added bonus they get to remain victims. It's a tidy little package.

Learning to diagnose yourself as a self-saboteur is tough, as your ego will work to protect you from such knowledge. (Fixing it is even harder, which is why I often recommend such work be done with a therapist rather than on your own. But we can cover some of the baby steps here.)

You might be a self-saboteur if you keep missing out on opportunities in your life for weird reasons, like Paula and her house-must-be-clean-before-I-write requirement. Or maybe you keep realizing that an opportunity you were excited about at first might not be that great after all.

If you're finding yourself screwing up opportunities before you even get a chance to attempt them, it's time to ask yourself two questions.

Self-Saboteur Question 1

What do I want here? What do I really want here?

Answers could include: "To be in an honest, caring relationship," or "To get a job in the _____ industry," or "To get a raise," or "To make a close friend." Keep digging until you get to an answer that rings true.

Self-Saboteur Question 2

Will _____ help me get what I want? Is it serving some other purpose?

Answers could include: "This is keeping me from being open to actual healthy relationships," or "This goal is too low/too high for me at this stage," or "While this is getting me attention, it's not necessarily accomplishing my purported goals."

Remember: It's okay to be afraid of success. It's okay not to want to be in a relationship. It's *not* okay to keep deluding yourself regarding what you want and don't want. And while realizing you're afraid of success won't immediately solve the problem, it will help you shift your focus to what's underneath: *why* you're afraid of success. You can't prevail over your enemies if you don't know who they are.

Being "Too _____" for Other People

This one holds a special place in my heart. I've spent many years attempting to puncture this particular armor on men I've dated. For years I sought out dudes who thought they were too smart, too badass, too mysterious, or too magical (really) for the general population. I'd find them at parties, sitting in a corner, scowling at everyone, and I'd set out to make them like me, so that I'd be the one thing they didn't hate in the world. I wanted to be that one special thing immune from their scorn. Then I'd proceed to be just as smart or badass or mysterious or magical as the scowly guy in the corner so I could be his unicorn/dragon/beacon of hope. Each new relationship like this would last until I got tired of being the only person he could really relate to.

The truth is that believing you're too specialized to interact with regular people is usually a way of hiding your vulnerability in social situations. It's an impressive suit of armor: you get to hide behind your noble quality, feeling superior and not interacting with others. Excellent deal! But this armor also keeps you from forging connections with the people outside your tiny "acceptable" range—and connections with people who *aren't* like us are very important.

So if this has been an issue for you, take comfort: you are artistic/smart/funny/weird, and that makes you incredibly special. But you are not too artistic/smart/funny/weird to make connections with other people. The connections you form with others despite not having a lot in common are just as important as the people with whom you can discuss deep feminist theory for hours on end. So have some small talk at the ready that you can slide into almost any interaction—about news or mysterious phenomena or how weird things got their names. You don't have to get along with everyone, but it sure would be smart to try—for your own good. You're wonderful, but you're not better than anyone else. A Super You doesn't need armor like that.

Not Trusting Others

The "I've been hurt before so I have trust issues" armor is the most common type I've seen, in friends and clients alike. It's usually donned when someone we trusted betrays that trust, and it can be both incredibly protective and well-meaning. The problem is that it can outlast its welcome, isolating you from all relationships rather than just helping you ward off the sketchy ones.

I'll be the first to admit that relationships can be terrifying. In a real relationship, you put your cards on the table, you make yourself vulnerable, and you ask another person to take in all the things that make you "you," holding them, cautiously and sweetly, within his heart. That's a big ask. What if, once he sees who you are, all vulnerable and squishy, he rejects you? He could even see and appreciate who you are and still do something mean to you. He may hurt your feelings and apologize and hurt you again. Or he may keep your heart safe within his heart forever. That's what being in a relationship is—experiencing, in another person, all of the shades of the human behavior rainbow.

However, the problem comes when we interpret the scenario of one relationship as how *all* relationships function. For example, we might think that the completely normal ups and downs of a relationship mean that *all* relationships are painful. Or maybe we were hurt by someone who was casual with our heart, so we decide *everyone* will be casual with our heart. If that's how we think, then we'll look for protection from future pain, but a suit of armor that refuses to allow trust to be built just ensures that every relationship we're in will end because there's no "connection." It doesn't matter when the hurt occurred—I've met people who are still keeping suitors at arm's length because of a breakup they experienced in high school. What matters is that, when we judge people, we need to be sure we're judging *their* behavior, not the behavior of those who came before them.

SUPER YOU MISSION CHECK-IN!

It's time to check in with the list of Super You Missions you created earlier. How's it coming? Have subsequent chapters caused you to rethink what you want to accomplish? Are you keeping up with making small changes in your everyday schedule?

Okay, now back to your regularly scheduled book.

I am not advocating we blindly trust everyone we forge a relationship with. I'm instead advocating that we judge people individually, and give them the opportunity to earn trust and our hearts—while at the same time keeping our eyes open for red flags. It's the difference between emotional profiling and actual emotional detective work. We'll talk a bit more about building trust in chapter 10, because it's important to relearn how to trust someone without wearing protective armor.

For any type of armor you may have been employing, sit down and get to know it. Thank it for its service. Let it know you appreciate it for protecting you all this time, but you think you're ready to stand on your own now, and so it's time for it to skedaddle.

Most Commonly Used Weapons
Sarcasm

Sarcasm, you say? Are we considering sarcasm a weapon that pushes people away from us? Absolutely we are. Sarcasm certainly has its place, and can make for extremely hilarious interactions with others, conveying with wit and charm and wry humor just how you see the world. It can be devastatingly sexy. However, if sarcasm is your only method of communication, it can also be very isolating. I think of sarcasm as a bit like tear gas—it fills a room and burns people's eyes. And though sarcasm communicates to the world that you're untouchable and unflappable, I often find that sarcastic people are in fact extremely sensitive, and have learned to employ sarcasm in order to keep others at a safe distance.

Of course, I am speaking of myself. I cry over dog food commercials; if people I care about are in conflict, I'll start crying before I can choke out any reassuring words. If someone says something insulting to me, I'll carry it in my heart for weeks, turning it over and over, trying to deduce meaning from it, trying to make it okay. So sarcastic tear gas was my weapon of choice for many years. If I make some witty jabs, others will think I'm tough and won't try to mess with me—and won't ever know I'm a crier at heart. Human behavior is hilarious when viewed from afar, huh? I refused to be vulnerable in any way, and then wondered why I wasn't making any real friendships. Perhaps for that period of my life I couldn't handle real friendships, but at the time I couldn't admit any of this to myself. I just realized that, even though I had a ton of acquaintances, there were very few people I could be vulnerable with.

Sarcasm, like perfume (here's where the tear gas analogy breaks down), is best used sparingly. If you find yourself spraying sarcasm to everyone and everywhere, it's time to take a step back and ask yourself why you work to keep others at bay.

Passive-Aggression

Passive-aggression could go into either the armor or weapon category. Being passive-aggressive—demonstrating hostility indirectly—protects you from the terrible awkwardness of having to be direct with another person. It saves you from being honest about your feelings. It's a somewhat painless way to get across displeasure or concern without seeming concerned. But passive-aggression is a weapon, because it inflicts damage on others instead of using more effective means of communication. Essentially, passive-aggression is the sniper rifle of the emotional weaponry world.

There are four universally accepted styles of communication: passive, assertive, aggressive, and passive-aggressive. (Note that, though all four have their strong points, in America assertive communication is generally considered the most effective.) To convey the distinctions among all four styles, let's say you were trying to communicate to someone that she'd broken in front of you in line at the bank.

> **Passive Pete:** [*heavy sigh*]
>
> **Assertive Abigail:** Hey man, there's a line of people waiting here. Could you move to the back?
>
> **Aggressive Aaron:** What the hell? You broke in line!

Passive-Aggressive Penny: [*fakes a phone call*] Hi! I'll be a little late. This jerk just broke in line.

All four people here were attempting to communicate displeasure to the line breaker. Since for most of us confronting a stranger can be fairly awkward, we'd rather not have to deal with it; the same goes for confronting a loved one. The beauty of passive-aggression is that it avoids the awkwardness of initiating conflict—by not actually initiating it. So you don't express your displeasure that someone didn't show up on time—that would be awkward. Instead, you make a joke about how dinner is cold because *somebody* was late. No problem, right? And when your partner asks if anything is wrong and there is *totally* something wrong, instead of delving into the treacherous territory of "Yes, something's wrong," you can avoid all that and say, "No, I'm fine"—followed by thirty minutes of seething, silent glares. Perfect.

Conflict is a healthy part of any relationship, and successfully wading through small conflicts is a fantastic way to both deepen a relationship and develop your conflict-resolution skills. Passive-aggression cheats us of that. Plus, it's just a nasty habit to get into. Some of my passive-aggressive pals have defended their actions by saying, "But I *am* communicating that I'm irritated, just in a different way!", but I call "bullshit" on that. No real Super You needs to take aim, at a friend or a stranger, so casually and so secretively. It's not the other person's job to scan and assess hostile comments for the intended message buried within. The onus is on us, as Super Yous, to communicate calmly and clearly our displeasure with something. It's on us to request different behaviors (if necessary) in a reasonable manner, especially since being reasonable can only increase the likelihood of improving the situation.

We'll talk about conflict resolution a bit more in Chapter 10, but I can offer a taster for now. If you have a tendency to break out the Passive-Aggressive Sniper Rifle, when you next get irritated with someone, take a deep breath and ask yourself a few questions. What are you angry about? What has this person done that's bothered you? Is your expectation of behavior reasonable, or is it a "should" that you're imposing on someone else? (Note that, if your expectation of behavior is not reasonable—and I realize it's tricky here to determine what is unreasonable—you should probably deal with your anger on your own.) How can you communicate your displeasure to this other person in an assertive, healthy way? If the offense is not worth calling out in an open, honest way, then perhaps the offense is not as offensive as you thought.

Brutal Honesty

Oy, brutal honesty, you are my least favorite of the common weapons. Nothing blows away and keeps away the people in your life better than regularly "telling it like it is." I mean, you're just trying to warn peeps of impending danger, right? You speak bald truth so as to prevent others from getting hurt worse later on. As such, brutal honesty is a fantastic weapon: it allows you to injure the people around you while maintaining a martyr-like truth-teller position that no one can touch. I consider brutal honesty the drone attack of the emotional arsenal, deployed from a safe distance.

Here's some brutal honesty about brutal honesty: its intent is very rarely to help. Most of the time, brutal honesty is wielded to make the recipient feel wrong and small while making the truth-teller

right and large—in a word, superior. But brutal honesty types aren't any better at assessing and navigating human behavior than the rest of us—they just think they have magical powers, and want others to feel inferior to those powers. "Telling it like it is" is neither healthy nor useful; it's simply a weapon that some people wield so they can avoid focusing on themselves. Why? It could be so they can feel a sense of control about the universe that is lacking. But as we Super Yous know, you cannot control anyone but yourself.

Of course, honesty can be a good thing every once in a blue moon, if it's a loving honesty. If you care for someone you want good things for, and you have information she may not have—let's say someone you love is caught up in a harmful pattern she cannot see—it can be appropriate to offer some kindly observation. But note that such occasions come up extremely rarely in life. Take it from me: speaking as a person with lots of dramatic friends and a therapist background, there has, amazingly, been only one time when I felt the need to dole out some difficult honesty. It was for a friend who was in a terribly dysfunctional relationship. After years of hearing about it limping along, sadly, I felt it might be time to gently introduce the idea that perhaps it wasn't an ideal relationship. It was a heart-wrenching, gut-wrenching conversation. I said my piece and then backed off, determined not to dictate to her again. And it sucked. Also, they're still together. So now, even though I wanted to be helpful, and carefully thought out how to wield my brutal honesty, it didn't change a thing: my truth-telling is just a lame thing that floats around between us. I am at peace that I said my piece, but it was a difficult decision, and one that didn't net the result I'd hoped for.

Here's a handy chart to help you determine whether the truths you dole out are of the loving or the brutal variety.

BRUTAL HONESTY	LOVING HONESTY
Makes only the truth-teller feel good	Is difficult for both speaker and recipient
Assumes stupidity of the recipient	Understands that the recipient is intelligent and can make the best decisions about his/her life
Isn't necessarily vital for the recipient to know	Is vital that the recipient know
Is usually expressed spontaneously	Is usually expressed after a great deal of thought
Is said out of irritation with the other person	Is offered out of concern for the other's well-being

So if honesty is one of your things, make sure you're not wielding it in an effort to hurt others while distracting yourself from yourself. You may be one of those rare birds who can keep it real without hurting others, but it's more likely that you just need to focus on the truths of yourself a bit more.

Since we're all works-in-progress, if you find yourself employing any of the above weapons or armor, please do not be ashamed. I assure you that we have *all*, out of the need to protect ourselves, meddled with unsavory powers. The point is that Super You gets bogged down by sad little tricks like these, and so it's better to learn to recognize them and then ditch them when you can. Keep your heart and mind open to the intentions of your behavior—and to the intentions behind those intentions. Keep evolving, and keep shedding that cheap shit.

CHAPTER

From the Annals of Time: Constructing Your Origin Story

'm a bit of a storyteller. The before, during, and after of any event is important to me—and important in how I present to others the things that happen in my life. I take pleasure in unwrapping a series of events, in building to a climax, in ending with something silly or bittersweet. I cannot explain to you a weird thing that happened at dinner in under three minutes—context is essential to my understanding of myself, and how I communicate with others.

For example, I can tell you that I once shot a squirrel in my apartment, but without you knowing the context of my sobbing while doing so, the squirrel being horrifically injured and stuck in my bathroom, no one else being able to take care of it, and the fact that it's haunted me ever since, you might just think I'm an animal abuser. I don't exist in a bubble, untouched by what I've been through, what's happening around me, where I've been, and where I am now. All those events combine to make the person I am today—to forge my identity. (Here we return to this important topic from chapter 1.) But identity goes beyond just the events that make up a person's life: it also includes how we think about and talk about those events. Identity is part of the story we tell others of who we are.

I love reality TV. I'm particularly partial to competition shows, where plucky weirdos from all corners converge to cry on camera and try to win some "Best in _____" prize that will be irrelevant come next season. As I said, I love reality TV, and yet I'm well aware that it contributes to the distortion of some weird quirks in how we present ourselves to others. And yes, I have uttered the sentence "I don't think she's here for the right reasons" several times in my life, and once in reference to a cat, but that's not even what I'm talking about. Reality show contestants come perfectly packaged with a sympathetic backstory—I lost my parents! I am really poor and this is my only shot! I have ADHD!—that they parrot endlessly to the camera, to each other, and to the judges. It becomes the mantra, the thing they overcome to win, or the thing that's pulling them down when they're not doing well. Knowing that a singing competition contestant is in a lot of debt and was in an abusive relationship doesn't mean that you know that person, and it certainly doesn't make her a good singer—and yet, that's considered her "story," the key to understanding her.

This got me thinking: how many of us do this sort of thing to ourselves? Like Kryptonite Man, how many of us present our personalities as the sum of our faults and sticky pasts, as helpless ships tossed around in an ocean of nuttiness? What happens if we internalize those negative (albeit compelling) stories about ourselves? Do the rest of us also create origin stories for ourselves? For those who do, how do those stories serve us?

When I started working with clients years ago, I wasn't most interested in the actual facts that brought them into my office; I cared more about their telling of those facts. Learning someone was abused by a caregiver doesn't tell me the whole story. Look at the differences in how caregiver abuse can be experienced: "I was abused by my dad and it tortures me every single day." Or "My dad would beat all of us kids if we got out of line, but it was a different time back then!" Knowing how the abuse affects the person is, to me, more important than just the fact on its own. Though there are certainly some commonalities in similar experiences, those experiences have a unique significance for each person. The unique significance of our experience shapes how we think of ourselves. Remember, we all actively construct our identities at all points in time, whether we like it or not. We *are* our origin stories: the stories of who we were that led us to who and where we are now.

Who's Writing Your Origin Story?

There are two questions we have to ask ourselves: (1) are we in control of the origin story we're constructing for ourselves? and (2) what purpose does our origin story serve? In my therapy office I've had mothers explain they're not good at parenting because their own parents abused them. I've had kids tell me they're bad because their mothers have told them they're bad. I've heard grown men say they're bad in relationships because they were dumped in the eleventh grade. How sad it is and suffocating it is to have your future mapped out by other people, or by things that happened years ago. How sad to have your story told by other people. How sad it is that we allow others to write our origin stories for us—that we internalize others' views of us instead of constructing our own. Because we aren't just good kids, bad employees, weird classmates, supermoms, lonely girls, or gorgeous perfect princesses. We aren't what we've been called, good or bad, throughout our lives. But some of us spend our lives trying to fulfill a role that was handed to us by someone else. Bosses, parents, exes, friends: they can all tell the story of you—but would their version be faithful to who you are?

Living with intention, which we've learned is a vital part of being a Super You, includes taking ownership of your origin story. It means exploring how you present yourself, identifying both the ways it serves you and the ways it hinders you. It means breaking that whole origin story down and starting from scratch so that you can properly honor the things you've gone through without being beholden to them.

Remember that exercise we did back at the beginning of this book: describing yourself in three different ways, depending on whom you are presenting yourself to? Each description was accurate, and yet each was different too. Given that we have many iterations, each different and truthful, we have just as many options in how we think about what makes us who we are—and in choosing how we present ourselves to the world.

When I realized that *I* got to be in charge of my own origin story, I was terrified and overwhelmed. It's tough to piece together how you're the sum of your individual parts! And the process gave me more power over my history than I thought I deserved. But what I realized in slowly taking ownership of my origin story is that we are a sum of the good things and bad things that have happened to us—but *we* get to choose the significance of those events.

Having a worthy origin story is one of the final pieces to creating your own Super You. She-Hulk, a.k.a. Jennifer Walters, certainly understood this. Jennifer Walters was the daughter of Sheriff William Morris Walters. One day, a mob boss shot Jennifer in retaliation for something the sheriff had done. Jennifer needed a blood transfusion, and the only person who matched her blood type was her cousin, Bruce Banner, a.k.a. the Hulk. The transfusion saved her life—and also made her into She-Hulk. So, like her cousin, when she got angry she hulked-out and fought bad guys. Now, some women might not be so thrilled about being shot and then made into a monster. But Jennifer, rather than being upset about her new life, decided to embrace its confidence and badassness—and elected to be She-Hulk full-time, something not even Bruce Banner could handle.

Need another example of an origin story that could go either way? Think about it: according to all the comics and movies, Bruce Wayne—Batman for those of you who haven't been paying attention—had to watch his parents being murdered in front of him when he was a very young boy. This would be enough to emotionally traumatize anyone, and if you met a miserable, homeless, alcoholic adult man who told you this story, you'd probably say, "Oh, that's horrifying. I totally understand how you've ended up this way." But that didn't happen to Bruce Wayne. Oh no. Instead, he decided to focus on making sure no one else would have to experience what he did. And yes, he focused on bats too, perhaps too much. He poured every single ounce of his grief and anger and sadness into training himself to become the most badass crime fighter around. So, look again at just two of the options that could result from little Bruce Wayne's origin story: miserable, homeless, alcoholic, or Batman! The things that happened in our lives could serve as our excuses for why we're not fulfilled with our lives—or they can serve as our inspiration to keep striving for better lives.

Now sure, Bruce Wayne and Jennifer Walters are fictional characters, and even as superheroes they have their own issues: she created a psychological block that kept her from being human; he's a friendless, secretive workaholic. No one is suggesting that either is a model for good mental health. Neither is anyone suggesting we put a sunny and false veneer on our pasts. In no way do I mean to make light of anyone's traumas, or to dismiss them entirely; on the contrary. I am looking for us to take charge of how we think about our life stories, processing and honoring the traumas without letting them be all that defines us. Put it this way: if our pasts were photographs, I'd be looking for us to change the Instagram filter we view them through.

Let me give you an example, using myself. My husband, when we first met, described me as "a real mess on paper." I found this hilarious. On paper, I do look like a real mess—but I don't think of myself as being a mess whatsoever. I think of myself as having character. To show you what I mean, I'm going to list the many events in my life that I consider to be important to who I am today, and then I am going to give you two versions of my origin story. Pay attention, because you'll be doing this too in a little bit.

Emily's List of Important Events That Made Her Who She Is Today

Emily...

⚡ Was raised in rural North Carolina by her parents (still married!)

⚡ Saw *E.T.* many times as a child and developed a fear of aliens

⚡ Had many family members who were mentally ill

⚡ Stepped on an earthworm as a kid

⚡ Thought about the devil way too much over one summer

⚡ Was placed in classes for the "academically gifted" at the age of nine

⚡ Experienced a growth spurt at a young age and towered over her fellow classmates

⚡ Felt a lot of self-loathing about her size

⚡ Gained a lot of weight

⚡ Experimented with drugs and got a bunch of piercings

⚡ Started dating at around fifteen, and was popular with boys

⚡ Had an older sister who was "traditionally" gorgeous, so decided to be actively ugly

⚡ Discovered industrial music in high school and became a goth kid

⚡ Did well in school

- Got suspended several times for "behavioral issues"

- Hung out with "bad kids" and spent a lot of time in seedy neighborhoods

- Studied psychology in college

- Had her first serious boyfriend at the end of her undergrad years

- Went to graduate school to study couples and family counseling

- Married first serious boyfriend

- Earned a master's degree and started working as a therapist for teenage boys

- Moved to Chicago with husband

- Started seeing a therapist

- Started exercising and lost some weight

- Requested and was granted a divorce

- Started burlesque dancing classes, made female friends

- Moved in with a stranger found on Craigslist; repopulated her life with new stuff

- Had serious boyfriend after divorce

- Became incredibly sick with pneumonia-like symptoms

- Was hospitalized for a month and diagnosed with chronic inflammatory disease

- Learned how to take care of her body after her diagnosis

- Eloped with her boyfriend

- Moved to NYC with her husband for his career

- Quit being a therapist; started freelance writing

- Moved to Los Angeles with her husband for both of their careers

- Started running a stand-up show in L.A. and writing full-time

- Appeared on TV for the first time

- Wrote a book (hi!)

Emily's Origin Story, Version 1

I grew up around a lot of mental illness in my immediate family. I was a fat kid, and much taller than the other kids in class, and that made me feel incredibly isolated and alone. I dealt with the pain by getting really into goth/industrial music and being a rebellious punk rock teenager, which led to some self-destructive behaviors. I was promiscuous because I didn't care much for myself. I got a college degree, and got married at a young age— too young. I got a master's degree in therapy. My husband got into a PhD program in another state, and once we moved there, our marriage fell apart. After we got divorced I became skinnier and met a new guy. I was still having some self-destructive behaviors. I got sick and kept refusing to take time to get better; eventually I got so sick that I had to be hospitalized. My vital signs were so unstable that I couldn't be trusted to breathe on my own, so I was put in a medically induced coma and spent a month in the hospital, during which time I was diagnosed with a rare chronic inflammatory disorder. The experience shook me up so much that I no longer felt like I could be a good therapist, so I quit and started over as a writer and comedy producer. I married the new guy and moved to New York so he could focus on his career. (I usually feel so grateful that a guy wants to be with me that I'll go anywhere he wants to go.) After a few years of being unsuccessful in New York, I moved to Los Angeles with my husband because he got a job there. Five years after leaving the mental health field, I finally became able to support myself in a new career.

Emily's Origin Story, Version 2

I grew up in a stable household in the South, with a close-knit family that had a lot of mental illness. Because of that, I became incredibly attuned to people's emotional states. I was taller than most of the kids in my class and had trouble fitting in as a result, which led to me embracing more "alt" and "rebellious" friends and pastimes. I found a group of friends that was supportive and "got me," and felt like I fit in. I had an active social and dating life. I had a lot of anger and learned to channel it into the music I loved, and into writing, which was my favorite hobby. I got an undergraduate degree in psychology, paid for by my parents, and got engaged to a wonderful man. We got married on the cheap; I used the money my parents gave me for a wedding to instead pay for a graduate degree in couples and family counseling. After working in the field for several years, my husband got into a PhD program in Chicago, and we moved there together. Soon after, it became clear that our relationship was not fulfilling, and I had some work to do on myself. I put myself into therapy; later my husband and I divorced, amicably. I continued working as a therapist and fell in love with a new man. I used lessons from my first marriage and from what I learned in therapy to approach the relationship in a healthy way. I became incredibly and mysteriously ill, and after several doctor visits was admitted to a hospital, where I would stay for a month, intubated for ten days. I was diagnosed with a very rare genetic condition that had been afflicting me for years, and would require me to monitor myself and keep myself healthy so as not to experience more episodes. This, combined with the fear that I could have died in the hospital, helped to change my outlook on life. I started focusing on self-care and really listening to myself. I continued to write as a way to express myself, and started rethinking my career path as a therapist. I married my boyfriend, and together we moved to New York, to tackle our dreams together. We struggled financially but loved our time in such a wild, opportunity-filled city. I started writing and producing comedy shows. I learned that my identity wasn't wrapped up in being a therapist, but in being myself, whatever job I was doing. My husband got a job in Los Angeles, and when we moved there, I started working full-time as a writer and a producer.

By the way, both of these versions would make pretty lame superhero origin stories. There are no radioactive powers or weird aliens involved at all (except for E.T.). But separate from that: does the difference between the two stories make sense to you? Just like you, I contain multitudes. I'm a mess on paper, but I'm also a girl that has done very well in school, a girl that found a group of friends and learned to express her anger and frustration through goth music and black clothing, and a girl who started writing as a means to stop feeling so lonely and pent-up and ended up making a career out of it. And you may simplify this down to "Okay, sure, you can talk about yourself either in rosy terms or in realistic terms," but that completely misses the point. This isn't just about having a "glass half full" versus a "glass half empty" attitude—this is about realizing that the story you construct about how you came to be *matters*. And further, the story you tell yourself about how you came to be isn't just a rehashing of things that have happened to you; it's another way to create your identity. It's another way to present yourself, to yourself and to the world, as either a superhero or a victim. I fought to reframe myself and my past, and I continue to fight that battle. And while that reframing is a battle worth fighting, it's something many of us don't even realize is possible—let alone important.

Our pasts are why we're here today. It would be wonderful if we could define ourselves based on just the lovely good things that have happened to us—but those lovely good things are only half of the story, and they're not the part that so many of us get stuck on. We are the product of everything that's happened to us. So let's start talking about the bad stuff.

Step I to Writing a Super You Origin Story: Understand Your Relationship to the Bad Things That Have Happened to You

I meet people, professionally and personally, who have survived some truly horrifying things. Their bravery and resilience in the face of such horror are inspiring and awe-inducing. I have also met people who have survived some not-so-horrifying things. Their resilience inspires me too. All pain is relative, and it is absolutely not my call, or anyone else's, to decide what was traumatic to you. As I mentioned, I am still mildly terrified of aliens because I saw the movie *E.T.* when I was way too young. Our parents took us to see it several times the summer it was in theaters, and at night, E.T. would come to my bedroom window and croak at me in that creepy voice. Honestly, he was a disgusting little creation, right? The point is that even though it doesn't seem like a huge deal to other people, my fear of E.T. was very real to me.

What traumas, big or small, have you experienced that have stayed with you? What negative things have shaped who you are and how you act and react to your world?

"Wait, Are You Telling Me I Just Need to Get Over My Traumas?"

Let me reiterate that this is not a discussion of "you need to just get over it" when it comes to painful things that have happened to you. That's just another level of victim-blaming, which disgusts me. Whatever your relationship to your traumas is, that is exactly where you should be right now, because that is where you are. You are not expected to relate to your traumas in any specific way. We respond to bad experiences differently, and we are affected by them differently, and all versions are valid. What I'm interested in is how *you* feel about your relationship with your traumas. Is it a torturous relationship? Does it color every interaction you have? Is it the silent but enormous elephant in the room? Is it a little bird on your shoulder, content but ever-present? An embarrassment that you'd rather not deal with?

Basically, it comes down to this: are you comfortable with the relationship you have to painful things in your past, or would you like it to change? All I want to do is help you evolve the relationship you have with your traumas—*if* that is something you feel ready for. Learning to evaluate and recalibrate how you relate to your past traumas, and where they fit in your own origin story, is a vital part of becoming a Super You.

So let's say we're going to give this a try. How do you figure out what your relationship with your past negative experiences actually is? How do you determine how much of your current identity construction—your origin story—should include certain events from your past? While there's no exact science to this, below are a few questions to help you try to figure out how you relate to a trauma from your past. (Keep in mind that there's a big difference between trauma from your distant past and trauma from your immediate past. Any recent traumatic events deserve specialized care and processing and crisis work—which I hope you will seek personalized treatment for.)

What we're considering now is the stuff you've been hanging on to for years. So, with your trusty notebook to serve you, pick a trauma from your distant past—maybe start with a smaller one—that you're possibly willing to reconsider. The crucial step here is to think about the *objective facts* of the trauma and your *relationship* to the trauma as two completely different entities.

★ Do you ever think,
   "If _____ hadn't happened, I'd be able to . . . ?"

★ How many of your day-to-day fears can be traced back to that event?

★ Is this event something you consider important for new friends to know about you?

★ How often do you think about this event that happened to you?

★ Have your thoughts and feelings about this event changed over time?

★ Do you have a wide array of conflicting feelings when you think about it?

★ Does this event influence how you date?

★ Does this event influence your confidence level at work, in public, or with friends?

★ Have you given yourself permission to do something because this particular thing happened to you?

★ Have you denied yourself permission to do something because this particular thing happened to you?

★ Is this event something you feel like everyone can see just by looking at you?

Now, let's consider how we relate to our traumas with another exercise, using this analogy that our relationship to our traumas is similar to our relationship to certain types of people. In fact, think of them as characters. For example, let's say you caught your mom cheating on your dad when you were a child. And your relationship to this event is that you feel it's always there, and you can't do anything about it—but you hope if you just ignore it it'll go away. In the table below you'll find a character that fits the bill: Wendy, the roommate you hate who's *always* home. Again, this is not meant to make light of serious events in our lives by comparing them to annoying roommates. The point of this exercise is to help us understand (1) there are different ways we can feel about the events of our lives, (2) those feelings exist separately from the event itself, and (3) those feelings can change over time. I simply present this framework as one possible means of helping us conceptually separate ourselves from our traumas.

The table below includes just a few of the many different types of relationships that traumatic events can represent. If this analogy feels ridiculous to you, feel free to ignore it—I'm merely trying to present some examples of the multiple ways we as humans can relate to the things that have happened to us. So if you're having trouble understanding how much a past trauma is affecting your day-to-day life now, see whether any of the character manifestations of those traumas below seem familiar to you. (I'll explain more about how this can be helpful later.)

Trauma Relationships

TYPE OF RELATIONSHIP YOUR TRAUMA MIMICS	HOW IT COULD MANIFEST INSIDE YOU	HOW IT COULD MANIFEST OUTSIDE OF YOU
DAMON—THE OVERBEARING, CREEPY GUEST AT YOUR PARTY	You feel overwhelmed, freaked-out, and unable to get away.	You shut down, interacting less with everyone
RICKY—THE STRANGER HARASSING YOU FOR SPARE CHANGE ON THE SUBWAY	You feel unsafe. You wonder why other people don't do anything about the situation.	You don't feel comfortable interacting with strangers on the subway. You may even start avoiding it.
FIDO—THE DOG THAT BITES YOU	You thought dogs were awesome. Do you now have to rethink the awesomeness of dogs? Everything hurts.	You start being afraid of all dogs. You'll do anything to keep them away from you.
MR. SMITH—THE BOSS WHO DOESN'T TRUST YOU AND QUESTIONS YOU CONSTANTLY	You go back and forth wondering: Are you really that bad? Or does the fault lie with Mr. Smith?	You're more tentative, less confident. You question all your thoughts and actions.
TERRY—THE NEW PERSON YOU'RE DATING WHOM YOU'RE UNHEALTHILY MIND-MELDING AND NESTING WITH	You start wondering where you end and Terry begins. You forget what it was like to have your own opinions. Plus, how Terry feels about you is now how *you* feel about you.	You don't introduce yourself as *you* anymore, but as one half of a pair. You feel as if you don't exist without Terry.
ANGELINA—THE FAMOUS PERSON YOU MET ONCE	You really want people to know you've met Angelina; that meeting validates your existence.	Within five minutes of meeting new people you tell them about how you met Angelina.

GINA—THE COWORKER WHO EMBARRASSES YOU; YOU HANG OUT WITH HER ONLY WHEN YOU'RE ALONE	You feel deeply ashamed, and would prefer to hide that you even know Gina, but she's always there.	You spend most of your time trying to pretend you don't know Gina, to the extent that you even lie about her.
MARCUS—THE FRIEND WHO IS CONSTANTLY NEGGING YOU	You feel bad about yourself, because of the negative things Marcus says about you *and* because you keep hanging out with him.	You question whether maybe Marcus is right— perhaps to the extent of avoiding other people. This makes you feel lonely.
WENDY—THE ROOMMATE YOU HATE WHO IS *ALWAYS* HOME; YOU FEEL ALL YOU CAN DO ABOUT HER IS DESPERATELY TRY TO IGNORE HER	You know Wendy's there, but you think if you ignore her she'll eventually go away.	The efforts you need to take to keep away from Wendy tie you in knots. You no longer invite your friends over, and they don't know why.
DANNY—THE FRIEND YOU'VE OUTGROWN	You no longer feel like the two of you are in sync. You don't get anything out of the relationship, but you feel bad letting your friend go.	You find yourself going through the motions with Danny without enjoying your interactions.
MORGAN—THE FRIEND YOU FIGHT WITH CONSTANTLY BUT STILL APPRECIATE	You sometimes wonder if you'd be better off not knowing each other, but that can't be helped—you already know each other.	You come to a decision to agree to disagree on certain topics; otherwise, you co-exist peaceably, side by side.
EDGAR—THE GROSS FAMILY MEMBER WHO SOMETIMES SAYS OFF-COLOR STUFF BUT IS ALSO WEIRDLY WISE	You definitely chafe at that weird, inappropriate thing Edgar said, but he is family.	You think of Edgar as family, like it or not. You can handle the weirdness and discomfort he throws at you here and there.

The concept of thinking about our traumas this way is loosely based on the Cass Identity Model, which is a theory of gay and lesbian identity development. That model's structure has a clear progression: from being confused and questioning one's sexual identity (confusion), to wondering what the implications of being gay would mean in one's life (comparison), to realizing that one is not alone and seeking out other gays or lesbians (tolerance), to accepting one's sexual orientation (acceptance), to feeling an over-whelming need to make one's self-discovery the most prominent thing about oneself (pride), to finally integrating being gay into your personality—so that it's part of who you are, but it's not the *only* thing you are (synthesis).

Because I find this progression a helpful construct, I've designed the "Trauma Relationships" table above so that it reflects a progression *if* the idea of progression works for you. In other words, you could think of top-row "Damon" as being the most upsetting and overwhelming way you could feel about your event (and thus Damon is your most disturbing trauma relationship) and think of bottom-row "Edgar" as being your least disturbing trauma relationship. So if, for example, you've been cheated on, my hope is that you would go from feeling shut-down, overwhelmed, and miserable; to thinking that everyone will cheat on you; to avoiding relationships; to at some point thinking of being cheated on as a miserable experience that you learned from without it being a defining characteristic of who you are. So, ideally, the traumas we've experienced in the past, though they may start out as Damon, eventually become Edgar, our kinda gross and lame family member who occasionally doles out wisdom, even if it's wrapped in a thin veneer of inappropriateness. Ideally we learn to make Edgar small in our minds, to keep him from ruining our good time at the Christmas party, but we also don't forget that he's part of who we are. In other words, while we never forget him, we don't let him overwhelm us either.

I hope that all made sense—but if not, let's try it with an example. If you were to take a fairly familiar experience like "being cheated on" and ask several people to pick which character example above best defines how they feel/have felt about being cheated on, you'd get several different answers. Hell, you'd get several different answers from me, just from my own life, because I've been cheated

on several times. One time, my boyfriend cheating on me became an Angelina to me—a life-defining moment that I told everyone about within moments of meeting him/her. In a weird way, I boasted about how blatantly he cheated, and how much it had devastated me. I wore his betrayal as my bizarro badge of honor. I had fully crafted stories, full of laughs and "poor me" moments, about the moment when he asked me, in a coffee shop at 2:00 AM, "You didn't think we were dating, did you?" I'd trot out this tale for laughs in the hope that it'd make me feel less stupid for having trusted him, and probably too because at that time it worked for me to feel like the victim. This cheating, by a guy I'd been seeing for about four months, became a big part of who I was—and it certainly was my reason for not trusting guys.

Later on in a different relationship, I thought I was being cheated on again, but I didn't want to accept that it might be true. This time I related to the experience as if it were Wendy, the horrible room-mate I desperately wanted to ignore, even though trying to keep my distance from her tied me in knots, like I was playing Twister every minute of the day. Basically, I had suspected the cheating had been happening for a while, and I had all the evidence I needed, but my brain wouldn't let me fully accept it. I guess I thought that if I kept ignoring it the problem would take care of itself. Spoiler alert: it didn't. But anyway, the point is: both reactions, and both ways of relating to being cheated on—Angelina and Wendy—were totally valid. It's just that neither was super healthy for me.

To return for a moment to the progression thing: you might notice that Wendy's row in the table is lower than Angelina's. And you could definitely consider that thinking of being cheated on as an annoying roommate is a progression from thinking of the cheating as a tabloid-worthy story to tell at parties. I personally like thinking about processing a traumatic event as progressing through stages of acceptance. But it's also perfectly okay to be wherever you are, without thinking about progression at all.

The key is identifying if how you're relating to your past traumas is *acceptable* to you. That means (1) finding yourself on the chart above, and (2) determining if you're okay with where you are. Do you recognize yourself in the table? How do you feel about what you see? Are your traumas taking up too much of your heart, mind, and spirit? Do you wear your past as the face you present to the world? Does it affect every single interaction you have? Are traumas keeping you from forming healthy new relationships, or from being fully satisfied with your life? And if your relationship to your traumas is not acceptable to you, is there a way we could change that relationship? I hope you will explore these questions and more, and that you will find this construct helpful, as I do.

Step 2 to Writing a Super You Origin Story: Changing Our Relationship with the Bad Stuff

Let's get real: this is a tough battle. Even the absolute best version of yourself, the most super of Super Yous, is never on "Edgar" terms with *all* of her past traumas. (Check out the "Trauma Relationships" table above if you don't know what I mean by "Edgar" terms.) Some traumas take a lifetime to accept and synthesize, whereas others just need a little nudge. I'd love to think that a few nudges will serve your purpose just fine, but I also know that's kind of unrealistic. So if this chapter stirs up things for you, and nudges aren't enough, I

highly recommend that you continue doing this work with a therapist. As much as I would love to work with you all individually, I am not an omnipresent therapist being. And though this book is my closest approximation to being that, it consists of words on a page that cannot tailor themselves specifically to you. If you've experienced a lot of trauma, or recent trauma, or are having a tough time parsing your relationship with those traumas, a therapist who can sit down with you individually is the best bet for processing tough stuff. I also suggest you continue reading this book and writing out for yourself what you get out of it—you might find what you learn about yourself very helpful in determining what to share with a therapist. And I just want to add that deciding to seek therapy need not be reserved for only "I'm feeling horrible and have to talk to someone before I explode!" situations. Seeing a therapist can be beneficial at many stages in life, helping you evolve and grow and improve yourself on your own terms.

What If You Don't Want to Change?

Exploring rough stuff is complicated. It's also not black or white—there are hundreds of completely understandable and natural shades of gray to our relationship with our traumas, and many of those grays can be squirmy to talk about. When I worked with clients on this stuff in the past, I was often told they didn't want to change how they thought and felt about being cheated on, or being assaulted, or having their parents divorce. Not wanting to change how you think and feel about something painful is completely normal—even if that change would lessen the pain. Changes, even if they're positive, can be overwhelming and upsetting; for someone who experienced something overwhelming and upsetting, it can be much easier to keep things as they are. And while it may not feel good, keeping the pain in the forefront of your mind is at least a known quantity. A known misery can sometimes be preferable to an unknown, especially if you're feeling fragile. And it can be confusing if something that's been taking up space in your heart and mind changes its shape or size; that change can leave you feeling hollow. Please know that you don't have to change.

I'd like to add that thinking about changing how you feel about something traumatic has absolutely nothing to do with forgiveness. I am *not* saying that if you learn to forgive you'll be able to forget—I have no tricks for forgetting. I *am* saying that it's possible to feel less pained about the bad things that have happened to us, whatever those things are.

So let's say the thought of changing how you think and feel about a traumatic event doesn't appeal to you. That's completely fine and understandable. But if you're also not satisfied with the amount of space that event is taking up in your heart and mind, I would challenge you to explore *why* you're not ready for that change. Returning to my life as an example: why, after I was first cheated on, was I not ready to go from a place of "being afraid to commit to other relationships because I didn't trust anyone" to "letting new relationships earn trust slowly slowly slowly, staying wary but also a bit hopeful"? Answers to the question "Why aren't you ready to change?" could easily include:

🌀 I'm angry, and I want to stay angry.

🌀 This event has become part of my identity; I don't know who I'd be if I changed how I felt about it.

⚡ I will feel guilty if I change how I feel about this.

⚡ This has become my reason for keeping myself isolated from others.

⚡ The fact that I experienced this thing brings me attention. I don't know if I deserve attention otherwise.

⚡ Change sucks. Change is scary.

Exploring why we hang on to stuff that feels detrimental to us requires another therapy term: secondary gains. *Secondary gains* are, simply put, the benefits of *not* solving a problem. For example: you have a flat tire (ugh), but you also don't want to go to work (hmm), so instead of changing the tire, you call work to say you can't come in because of car trouble (Eureka!). I know it's reductionist to think of changing how you relate to a past trauma as a problem to solve, but the fact remains that sometimes there are benefits to holding on to our traumas.

When traumatic things happen to us, we may feel powerless. And many times there can be a weird comfort in feeling powerless—it can be somewhat of a relief not to have to be in charge. I am in no way suggesting that people are happy with the traumas they've experienced. I am recommending that we—as the superheroes we are becoming—consider digging deep in order to at least understand our *motivations*. Part of living with intention, thank goodness, is having the right not to make changes, even if you see the benefit of making changes. So learning why you don't want to make change doesn't mean making that change is your required next step; far from it. My only wish for you is that you understand the motivations and fears behind not making changes. Later on, if you ever get tired of your current relationship with your trauma, if at some point it's served you as well as it can, I will still be here (in book form), and face-to-face therapists will still be available to you. This is on your time.

The Pain Funeral

For those of you with a trauma or two you'd like to move a bit along in your psyche, it's time to have a pain funeral. This is an activity I have done with teenagers, adults, families, groups, friends, and everything in between. It's been done while stifling giggles and it's been done while sobbing, and both were lovely to behold. The point of the pain funeral is (1) to come to an understanding of what a particular event has to teach you, (2) to acknowledge those lessons, and then (3) to lay it to rest.

In effect a pain funeral is making a conscious effort to dismiss the aspects of a traumatic event that aren't serving you well—the fear, the misery, the grief. But note: this is not about pretending the event didn't happen, or about diminishing that event's significance in your life. It's about regaining your power over the event. If someone or something in your past left you feeling miserable, powerless, upset, or scared, and you still feel this months or even years down the line, that trauma is taking up some prime real estate in your psyche. So when you are ready to let go of the bullshit baggage that was heaped upon you, then it's time to pack it six feet under.

That trauma doesn't deserve this much of your time and heart and mind.

The first real step of a pain funeral is to get mad. To get angry at all that you've lost out on by being held captive by this traumatic event. To be furious that any person or any thing ever got to control how you feel. I mean this seriously, even in situations where no harm was ever intended to anyone. Even if your trauma is that a loved one died, I say, fuck death for taking that loved one away from you, for bringing you the pain of missing him/her. Or maybe you were cheated on. Well, fuck that person for being such a shit, and for causing you to be less trusting of other people. Your parents didn't show you love? Fuck them for being a terrible blueprint for all the relationships you might have in life. You experienced a serious illness? Well, fuck that illness for making you terrified to push yourself physically. Whatever your traumatic event is, write down every "fuck you for _____" you can possibly think of. Spend some time with this; allow yourself to feel all the anger you have over this.

Next comes the silver lining: learning what we can from what happened to us. Now, some people blanch at the idea of learning lessons from a terrible event. And that makes sense; some feel that learning such lessons means they must have done something to invite the event in the first place. I'm here to tell you that that's *not* how it goes. It's more about the fact that we can learn—about ourselves, about the world—from every experience, bad or good; it just so happens that there's often more to be learned from the bad stuff. Sure, it would have been great if we had not gone through something bad, but if we don't figure out how to move on from the experience, changed and improved, we're holding ourselves back, keeping ourselves victims, when we could be survivors. So can we try this out together?

Choosing whatever experience you want to learn from, sit down with it and ask yourself: What did it teach me? What positive thing have I come away with from going through such pain? Sometimes the answer will be: "I learned I have a good support network." Or, "I learned that my trust should be earned and not given out readily." Or, "I learned not to jump off a balcony for a laugh." Or, "I learned that I have it within me to survive horrible things." I'll repeat: the point here is *not* focusing on what you could have done differently to prevent the trauma. I may be into superheroes, but I'm not interested in time machines. The point here is, given that the trauma happened, which we can't change, what did you learn about yourself and the world as a result?

To follow are some examples, from my life and others', to give you a sense of how this could look.

Lucy

Lucy went through a bad breakup. The guy she'd been dating for two years—the guy she thought she was going to spend her life with—cheated on her. Multiple times. With different women. When she finally figured out what was going on, she confronted him and they broke up. She was devastated. She thought everything had been going great. For months she felt she was a bad judge of character, or at the very least was a bad judge of men. She was suspicious of any man who wanted to date her—essentially, she wouldn't trust any man. Eventually Lucy got into therapy; from that, and from talking through things with friends, she eventually came to the realization that her relationship hadn't been as picture-perfect as she thought. She had, in fact, ignored feelings of frustration and incompatibility with their relationship—in exchange for believing he was "the one."

Now, what could Lucy learn from this experience?

Lesson 1: Go into each relationship with an open heart and an open mind. And if you hear tiny pings in the back of your mind, pay attention to them. If maintaining the version of the relationship you've created in your head requires that you ignore those pings, then your subconscious is trying to tell you something; be sure to listen.

Lesson 2: This guy was not good to you. Not every guy will be like this guy.

Lesson 3: Trust should be earned, not immediately given. Withhold trust until people prove themselves worthy of it.

Emily

I became incredibly sick at the age of twenty-seven and had to be hospitalized for a full month. I was in a coma for ten days, and my survival was in question for most of those days. I was diagnosed with a rare condition. I was so weak when I was discharged that I had to sit down in the shower. I couldn't walk more than a block, I couldn't lift a jug of milk. As a girl who'd always made it a point to seem easy to be around, and who prided herself on being tough, I was absolutely horrified to find that I was now a "sick girl" that people clucked over. I was also horrified that I had almost died, and that I had ignored my body to the point that it had to shut down in order to get my attention. For at least a few years, I couldn't think about it without crying, and every doctor's appointment filled me with terror that I would be hospitalized again.

What lessons was I able to learn from this experience?

Lesson 1: The people who cared about me stuck by me while I was in a coma. Maybe it's okay for me to be vulnerable around them.

Lesson 2: I really need to pay attention to my body and take good care of it. I almost lost it.

Lesson 3: Nothing is scarier than almost dying. Remember that when you apply for jobs. Rejection is nothing compared to dying.

Dan

Dan was a chubby kid. He was made fun of for his weight throughout middle school and for most of high school. He's an adult now, and he keeps himself healthy with exercise and by eating well, but he still feels very body conscious.

What could Dan learn from this experience?

Lesson 1: Kids are complete terrified assholes who are desperate to find someone they think is even lower on the totem pole than they are. They don't deserve to be feared; at most they should be pitied.

Lesson 2: Your body is more than just a thing that makes you a target for bullies. It's also a piece of machinery that does your bidding. It's so much more than what the kids in school reduced it to.

Lesson 3: Being made fun of forces you to develop and rely on your own inner strength. It also fine-tunes your friendship-assessment skills as an adult.

Marianne

Marianne was sexually assaulted at a party she went to with friends. She'd wanted to meet a guy that night and did. She spent most of the night flirting with him and had a great conversation. Later that night when she entered the bathroom, he slipped in behind her. At first she was slightly charmed, but then he sexually assaulted her with his hand over her mouth. Upon leaving the bathroom she went home, numb, and then called friends, who took care of her for the next few days. She felt terrible about how she had flirted with him the whole night and wondered if she'd basically brought on the assault. Now it's been two years; with therapy and support, she's finally regaining her confidence in her interactions with others.

What did Marianne learn from this experience?

Lesson 1: No possible action is an invitation to be assaulted. This was not your fault. You do not seek out "bad" men.

A NOTE ABOUT THE DIFFERENCE BETWEEN UNDERSTANDING AND SELF-BLAMING

Before we move on, I want to make an important distinction between "understanding" something terrible that happened to you and "taking the blame" for something terrible that happened to you. As we talked about in earlier chapters, acting with intention and having an internal locus of control means that you believe your destiny is yours to shape, and that you'll take the reins and shape it. When terrible things happen to us that make us feel out of control, and as if our destiny is not ours to shape, an essential part of moving on is understanding what part we played in the experience, even if that part is simply "the person who learned she was strong enough to survive this." If it took something terrible for us to learn that we can survive something terrible, well, that sucks, but how can we apply that information going forward? How can we keep ourselves as safe as humanly possible, knowing that we can control only ourselves? Understanding the lessons that come from a trauma has absolutely nothing to do with taking the blame for that trauma. Understanding the lessons that come from a trauma is only something that can serve you as you continue your life, post-trauma. This is *especially* true in instances of physical or sexual assault, situations where victim-blaming is disgustingly prevalent. So while I encourage you to understand your part, please understand that, in many situations, "your part" only concerns how you can evolve and grow through such horror.

Lesson 2: You have fantastic friends who are very supportive of you.

Lesson 3: You are stronger than you realize. Much stronger. You survived something truly horrendous. You have a fire within you.

As you can see from these examples, sometimes the lessons you learn from traumatic events are about the world, and sometimes the lessons you learn are about yourself.

Okay, let's pause and review this stuff for a moment. We've discussed the benefits of holding a pain funeral. We've reviewed a few traumas actually experienced by some people, including myself. And we've emphasized (especially in the sidebar distinguishing "understanding" from "self-blaming") how all we're talking about here is ways to view the events of your life in as empowering a fashion as possible. So let's continue in that vein.

It is important for me, and a huge step in my journey of becoming a Super You, to feel I act and react to things that occur in my life with as much agency as possible in every situation. I no longer want to feel like I'm just a bucket that will hold whatever the universe throws at me. My illness is a genetic condition I was born with. I could do nothing about the fact that Adult-Onset Stills Disease (that's the sexy name of it) is written into my DNA. But does that mean I am meant to suffer? No, and thinking about it that way leaves me feeling helpless and frustrated. It's also true that my condition flares up when I'm under physical or emotional stress for extended periods of time. I can't change my DNA; but what I can do, going forward, is keep myself from being stressed-out so that my condition doesn't flare up. For me, that's the distinction that

keeps the reins in my hands. To describe this stance in superhero terms, if I were Batman, it'd be the difference between constantly mourning that my parents were killed in front of me and focusing my life on dressing up like a bat and making sure that doesn't happen to anyone else. Or if I were She-Hulk, it'd be lamenting that I received blood donated from a mutant versus choosing to be She-Hulk and doing something productive with my power every day.

So, thinking along those lines, consider a trauma from your past and ask yourself: "What can I take from this that will help me move on to a brighter, more intentional future—a future where I'm the superhero version of myself?"

Now, since we're throwing ourselves a pain funeral, the next logical step is to write a eulogy. This eulogy will serve to usher the trauma into its next stage of life, where it is less present in your heart and mind (whatever that means to you). This eulogy will detail all the pain the trauma caused you, every emotion it triggered, and how it has affected you overall. This may or may not include "fuck yous" as we discussed earlier. After you feel you've gotten out all that you have to say about the trauma, thank that trauma for the lessons it's taught you and explain what those lessons are. Because, though cheesy, it's nonetheless true: that which does not kill us makes us stronger. You wouldn't be who you are today without those traumas. The fact that you're still here means you won. You are victorious.

Now, let me share with you my parting words with my illness.

Emily's Eulogy for Adult-Onset Stills Disease

We are gathered here today to lay to rest my condition, diagnosed in 2007, that completely fucked up my world for quite some time.

I didn't know I was going to be hospitalized that day. I had been sick for a while, and that day was my third trip to the doctor in a week. I'd even left a milkshake in my car, convinced it'd be all nice and melty when I got out. Instead, I was whisked to the hospital in an ambulance, and everything changed. I have never felt so much physical pain in my life. I couldn't breathe, I couldn't get comfortable, and I was constantly poked and prodded and asked questions I didn't have the answer to. Without those answers, it was decided to put me in a medically induced coma, so a team of doctors could work to stabilize my vitals and figure out what was wrong with me. There was just darkness, punctuated by the sounds of my family and friends in my room. I wandered around inside myself for ten days, frightened and confused and in pain.

When I woke up, I was so overwhelmed and terrified that I couldn't process anything. All I knew was that I was suddenly extremely weak and sick. I was scared that I could have died. I was embarrassed that my boyfriend was seeing me so undone. I was mortified that I couldn't do anything for myself. I was angry that people kept giving me sad puppy-dog eyes. I was suffused with shock and cried for hours most days, and then became embarrassed and angry when people tried to comfort me. I was angry at my body for giving out on me.

It was only later that it dawned on me that I could feel grateful. Grateful to the hospital staff for saving my life. Grateful to my family for flying in to be with me. Grateful to my boyfriend and friends for sticking by me, even when it probably would have been easier just to let my family handle everything.

Thank you, Still's disease, you slippery little bitch of a disease. Thank you for teaching me that it's okay to rely on other people sometimes. Thank you for teaching me that I can be weak and the world won't end. Thank you for pushing me toward accepting my body in a way that had never occurred to me before: as a piece of machinery designed to move me around. Thank you for forcing me to befriend my body, after years of hating it, and thank you for forcing me to listen to it. Thank you for teaching me to be fearless, because after almost dying, very little scares me anymore. I wish I hadn't needed to be hospitalized to learn these lessons, but I'm happy to have learned them.

I am tired of living in fear that I'm going to be hospitalized again. I now understand that I can manage this disease by keeping myself healthy, and I feel empowered to keep myself healthy. I'm not going to be hospitalized again. I'm going to keep you where you belong, as a lesson I've learned and a reminder to be healthy.

Okay, so that was my eulogy. Now I encourage you to write your own when you're ready to. Then, after writing it, the next step will be to find a tangible, physical object, preferably a small one, to represent that trauma, as well as something to be that trauma's coffin. I find, weirdly, that wedding favor boxes make excellent pain coffins, although I recommend you not mention this fact when you're checking out at the craft store. Once you have your eulogy, your trauma object, and your coffin, find an appropriate spot for the funeral itself. You may want to invite friends or loved ones, or you may want to do this on your own—it's your call. Once you're there, dig a hole, bury the item in its coffin, and then read your eulogy.

It bears repeating: you're not burying the past; you're burying all the negative things about that past trauma. You're putting to bed the idea that the trauma does anything to harm you today, that it does anything other than making you a better person today. In other words, with the pain funeral I held for my medical condition, it wasn't as if I thought that in burying it I no longer have Still's disease in my DNA. I still have the condition—I'd just decided to change how I relate to my condition. I had buried all the negative ways I had related to it as things that belong to the past.

Step 3 to Writing a Super You Origin Story: Make a List, Check It Twice

Early in this chapter, I made a list of things that had happened in my life that seemed significant to me; now it's your turn. Since you have your handy-dandy Super You notebook already out—right?—let's start by making a list of every life event that has made you who you are. These events can be objectively huge (moving, parental divorce, car accident, graduation) or they can be smaller (discovering mastur-bation, the first time you were flirted with, passing a class that was tough for you). Since your notebook is private to you, I encourage you to be as honest with yourself as possible. As for my examples, for the purposes of this book I left out some of the clammier events of my life that I wanted to keep to myself, but I assure you that even just somewhat clammy events are on my private list. All the same, "Emi-ly's List of Important Events That Made Her Who She Is Today" is a pretty accurate list of things that stick out in my mind as significant, even if I'm not always sure why they're significant.

For instance, it took me until my early thirties to add some meaning to the very clear and disturbing memory I have of acci-dentally stepping on an earthworm with my bare foot at age three or four. I knew the memory was in there and wasn't leaving, but I didn't really know why. Upon maturity and reflection, I realized it might have been the first time I truly understood that I could affect other living creatures with my actions, sometimes in ways I didn't intend. I was shocked and hurt that I didn't see the earthworm, and I was disgusted at how its little body squished between my toes. It crushed me (like an earthworm under a toddler's foot) to think that I could hurt something without meaning to, but I had no way of understanding or even articulating these feelings. Looking back, perhaps this event started me on a pathway of being careful not to harm things if at all possible.

So basically, I'm saying think about it like this: Have you experienced anything that to you seemed huge, even if to others it seemed small? If so, can you figure out why it seemed so huge? How has it affected you?

So here we go. First, list every life event, starting from birth up until today, that you think might have shaped the person you are. Write them out as coldly and clinically as you can—and by that I mean if you let me look at your list, which obviously you won't, I'd want to feel neutrality radiating off it. I want this list to be the Switzerland of lists. Rather than *That rat bastard Aaron cheated on me with that skank Renee*, I'd want to see *Was cheated on by Aaron and had to find a new place to live*. It won't stay this cold and clinical, but it's a bit easier to start off this way. Once you think you're done, review it again to see if you can't find a few more items that belong on it.

Next, we'll want to scrutinize your list more closely. I want you to look for life events that you remembered enough to write down but whose significance escapes you. I don't believe that our memories are always geniuses, saving up all the potent stuff. I do believe that, for the most part, we keep things that seem important, we assign meaning to them, and then we restate that meaning to ourselves over and over. So if something has seemed important to your history but you're not sure why, ask yourself if you were different after this event in any even barely perceptible way. Ask yourself if you learned a lesson from that event. Ask yourself if that event laid out a blueprint for how you thereafter interacted with others or thought about authority. Keep digging. Even if you find just a kernel of meaning in a life event, write it down.

Of course, it's also perfectly acceptable for events to stay weird and random and not be assigned a deeper meaning. As much as I now believe that my earthworm encounter unlocked a door of "how Emily relates to the world," it could also be that I just remember how disgusting it was to step on an earthworm. I hope it's clear by now that actively constructing your identity and your origin story isn't an exact science.

Now, it's time to start reconstructing our story with a little more intentionality. First is getting rid of the passive action in our stories. As we talked about before, having (or trying to have) an internal locus of control means that we aren't just floating around in the universe, but instead actively controlling how we act and react to things. So I'd like you to review your list and circle any life event in which you were the passive recipient of whatever happened, good or bad. Passive voice statements can include: *I got dumped, University kicked me out, Got a scholarship at a faraway school, Grandmother passed away, Got a promotion, Got fat, I was raped,* or *Got hit by a car.* "But wait!" I can hear you screaming. "I'm not taking that bit out of my story—it's *Important!*" You're correct—it is important. I wouldn't dream of having your story exclude an important thing like this. (And note I didn't say "cross out" every passive action; I said "circle.") I just want us to restructure those passive voice statements so that, even if the event is something that just "happened," like a family member passing away, we're identifying your *reaction* to it, positive or negative.

So now, for every item on your list that you've circled, go back and rewrite it so that *you* are the one driving the action. Or, if that's not possible, rewrite it so you include your reaction to the event, positive or negative. In the table below you'll find active/reactive rewrites of the passive examples I named above.

Converting Passively Described Important Events into Active/Reactive Ones

PASSIVE	ACTIVE OR REACTIVE
Got dumped	I got dumped and responded by spiraling into drinking and casual sex for a few months. *or* I acted like a jerk in a relationship because I was afraid to initiate a breakup, until I was eventually dumped.
University kicked me out	I didn't study and partied a bunch, and as a result flunked out of university.
Got a scholarship to a faraway school	I busted my ass in high school and earned a scholarship so I could get out of my hometown.
Grandmother passed away	I lost my grandmother and went through a long period of depression.
Got a promotion	I worked really hard at work and earned a promotion.
Got fat	I wasn't exercising and ate only comfort foods and put on 30 pounds.
Was raped	I was sexually assaulted and spent the next year holed up in my apartment with friends, feeling afraid and ashamed and unhappy.
Got hit by a car	I was hit by a car and my parents flew out to take care of me for three weeks.

I hope that after doing this you will get a feeling for how important an internal locus of control is to becoming a Super You.

Step 4 to Writing a Super You Origin Story: Create Every Version (the Darkest Timeline)

Now that we have a list of important events that have made up your life, described only in active and reactive terms, I want you to comb through it to craft the origin story that paints you in the worst possible light. "What?" I can hear you saying. "You just forced me to actively grasp my internal locus of control with both hands!" Yes, I did, but hear me out. I'm asking you to write for yourself the equivalent of "Emily's Origin Story, Version 1" early in this chapter. The version of yourself that makes *you* look like a "mess on paper." It'd be the bio you'd submit if you were competing in a singing competition. In no longer than a paragraph, intentionally paint yourself in the worst light possible as a mostly passive participant of your life who does terrible shit when you do act.

Once it's written, I'd like you to read it aloud. Now, ask yourself how it would affect you to think of yourself this way every single day. This may be close to the story of yourself you already tell yourself and others, or it may not. But regardless, sit for a bit with the feeling of you being nothing but a lame sum of a bunch of random parts.

But don't sit with it too long, because your next task is to write the best, fakest, most gee-whiz golly ain't-life-grand whitewashed version of yourself. Like your first bio, it should include only real events, but it should make you sound damn near perfect. And if that means leaving some stuff out, that's fine. It should be your Ms. America bio. Once it's done, read that story aloud. Sit with that feeling as well.

Once you've done both exercises, and have two extreme versions of your story, it's time to write your *actual* Super You origin story. It will draw a little from the worst version of you, and it will draw a little from the best version of you. It will paint you as an active participant in your own life—responsible for your own decisions, whatever they may be. It will make you sound flawed and human and lovely, because that is what you are. And if you catch this version being too self-deprecating, go back and mine yourself for how you took a shitty lemon of an experience and made even just a drop of lemonade out of it. Know that your being alive and well enough to read this book means there is definitely lemonade to be celebrated in your life. Create a story for yourself that you mostly embrace, and even if you think some of it makes you sound better than you are, give it a try. Super Yous are smart enough to know that everyone needs good PR, and that includes how we talk to ourselves. Constructing an origin story that celebrates your success, your triumph in the face of failure and adversity, your stepping on earthworms, and everything in between is an important step in becoming the best version of yourself. It's an essential part of being on Team Super You. Plus, it's an essential tool. When the chips are down and your day is going terribly, you can always remind yourself of your origin story, which means celebrating what you've accomplished in order to get where you are now. Establish in your mind that you are a superhero among women, a creature with a fascinating past who has made the choice, again and again, to succeed and live and thrive.

CHAPTER 10

A Super You Among Regular Others: Being Out in the Universe

tocktaking time: look how far you've gotten! You've spent all this time getting yourself into a good place, figuring out what you need to do and creating healthy habits, and exploring yourself from the inside out. All of that is super—but what about the rest of it? How does being a Super You affect the other parts of your life? Is striving to become the best version of yourself something you can do amongst friends, while dating, and while working a full-time job? I certainly hope so, because it's not always feasible for you to take off several months to "figure things out." In reality, all your inner work has to be done within the context of both the life you're leading now and the people who are in it. So in this chapter we'll talk about some tricks for making those interactions as healthy as possible. And as I've mentioned before, I can't cover everything—entire books have been written on work relationships, interpersonal relationships, and romantic relationships—so I'll keep to the basics relevant to Super Yous.

Work

Motivating Yourself

I run a Tumblr where I answer anonymous questions from readers. The number one question I get concerns increasing motivation to complete life tasks like paying bills, doing chores, starting a new creative endeavor, or finishing work/school tasks. Given their contributions, it appears my readers are better at Tumblr than they are at chores and homework. I'm here to tell you there is no real magic to increasing your motivation. Like everything else involved with becoming a Super You, the solution is a combination of things. In this case, starting and sticking with tasks even when you're not motivated—even if they feel like a slog (behavioral changes, for example)—and adjusting how you think about what you're doing (as with internal exploration). My biggest trick is to break down any project into the smallest possible parts, list those distinct parts, and then set up a series of rewards for completing each tiny part. So if my project is doing laundry (something I hate), I break that down into (1) collecting all the dirty laundry, (2) washing and drying the laundry, and (3) putting everything away. And then when I've done the first bit, collecting the laundry, I reward myself with a celebrity gossip blog. After I've started the laundry, I reward myself with lunch. Finally, I put away the laundry while watching a TV show I've been looking forward to.

I do the same thing for bigger projects like writing this book, just with many more steps. For the long haul, I motivate myself by setting up rituals that, over time, I come to associate with buckling down to get the job done.

This is called *classical conditioning* (or *Pavlovian conditioning*), and it's all over Psych 101 courses. In the original experiment, Ivan Pavlov rang a bell and then presented dogs with food; as soon as the dogs perceived the food, they salivated. After just a few repetitions of this pairing, the dogs started salivating when they heard a bell, even if no food was presented.

THERAPY TERM *alert*

This kind of training works on humans too, so I did the same thing with writing. When I felt motivated and had an idea to write about, I'd sit at my desk with a cup of coffee and put on a play-list of high-energy instrumental music, and tap out my inspiration on the keyboard. After a number of times doing this only when I felt motivated, I tried sitting at my desk, with my coffee and my music, in hopes that my motivation would follow—and it did. Now, on most days, my brain expects writing to happen when I do the other parts of the ritual. Of course, even superheroes have days when they're just going through the motions, and that's okay too.

The upshot? If you can, create an environment where, ultimately, hard work is its only reward. If that's not possible, trick your brain with smaller rewards and rituals—and don't forget to savor the rewards.

What Do You Get Out of Your Job?

But often there's a wide gulf between creativity, fulfillment, and motivation and how you earn your living, so let's talk about what you do to make money. How do you feel about your job? Does it fulfill you? Do you feel passionate about what you do? Or do you just work to make money so you can live the rest of your life?

Even some superheroes needed to work in order to live. Clark Kent worked at the newspaper because he needed a job, but it also helped him keep an eye on news stories. Bruce Banner, a.k.a. the Incredible Hulk, was a scientist—but that was really just a way to explain how he got Hulky. A superhero's job is really being a superhero, but that's not the case with Super You—we still have to make a living. I was talking to my father recently about the idea of work. He worked at the same company for over twenty-five years before retiring. When I asked if he loved working there, he responded: "I got satisfaction out of working there, but that wasn't my life's purpose. My life started when I left the office every day." I found this to be a lovely statement; it's also a very different mindset from that of many under the age of forty. We all, myself included, expect work to be the thing that gets us out of bed in the morning. We expect every task to be magical and creatively fulfilling, our soul's call answered. And while some jobs can, overall, bring you that fulfillment, there is no job whose every task is a joy to behold. Every job, from being a movie star to writing to being a customer service consultant to running a comedy show, involves at least some menial tasks.

My father getting satisfaction out of his job epitomizes for me the difference between regular old you and Super You at work: understanding the difference between satisfaction and fulfillment.

When you look up these two words in a dictionary, they each use the other in their definition, which I find hilarious, but pay attention: whereas "satisfaction" is described as fulfillment of one's wishes, expectations, or needs, "fulfillment" is described as satisfaction as a result of *fully* developing one's character or abilities. So you can get satisfaction out of completing a jigsaw puzzle, but it's not going to complete you as a person, and that's okay. Jobs can bring us several different types of satisfaction.

Here are a few types of job satisfaction I've experienced:

- Developing mastery—getting really good at the tasks of a job

- Earning experience in a field you're interested in

- Earning money

- Feeling pleasure with tasks completed

- Gaining a social group

- Gaining prestige with a job that looks cool

- Getting all-around "this job is everything" fulfillment

- Getting paid to do your hobby

- Making a difference/helping a good cause

- Making other people happy

In my head, what we do for work at any point in our lives should hit at least one or two of these types of satisfaction—but very rarely will a job hit all of them. This is a fact of life we must learn to accept, just as we often must accept less-than-fulfilling jobs in order to pay

the rent. I was a telemarketer in college, and let me tell you, that was miserable—I essentially called alumni of our school and begged for money. That job earned me money and a fun little social network of fellow weirdos who didn't mind working odd hours, but little else. Later, I was a phone customer service rep for a company that did in-home appliance repairs. You'd think I would've been unhappy there, but I found an odd joy in helping people get their refrigerators repaired; plus, since I worked there long enough to become a trainer, the gig allowed me to develop mastery. I've been a lowly office floater in a women's resource center, which I loved because I was working for a good cause. I've had a cushy job managing a small private practice; that one I didn't enjoy because I didn't feel I was making a difference. I got a job at a hotel because I'd always thought it'd be fun to work at a hotel, but it turns out I hated working at a hotel. People are jerks at hotels, and the uniforms are often miserable wool things. I currently run a weekly stand-up show, which people think may be the most fun job on Earth, and yet most of my job is spent returning emails, setting up chairs, and dealing with customers.

Regardless of whether you're happy with the job you have now, realize that, while your job should serve a purpose in your life, that purpose might not be utter and complete fulfillment. It's okay for your job just to be how you make money. That simply means that certain important aspects of a healthy life—like your hobbies, or making a difference, or your social group—will need to come from other parts of your life. Work has become so all-encompassing these days that I think a lot of us figure it'd be easier if everything got taken care of in one fell swoop, but that mentality, that a job has to be perfect, just leads to more stress and anxiety than it's worth.

It's okay to have hobbies that don't become how you try to earn money—hobbies can be their own reward. I have a friend who loves playing guitar; he's so good at it he started giving guitar lessons. Guess what he now hates doing with his free time? If you guessed "playing guitar," you win!

So take a little survey of your job. Using the list of satisfaction types above, see how many ways your job satisfies you. (If your job is satisfying in a way not listed, let me know about it, because I'd be excited to hear it.) If your job's only satisfaction is earning money, it might be time to think of getting another job, one that ticks even just one more box. If getting another job isn't possible right now, let your job be just how you earn money and look for ways to bolster other parts of your life. You will most likely have many jobs throughout your life, and those jobs will satisfy you in many different ways. A Super You allows her job to be what it is, and seeks to add satisfaction if possible; if not, she seeks to add fulfillment to the rest of her life. Jobs will come and go—your life is yours for the long haul.

Romantic Relationships

The second most common question I get on my Tumblr concerns romantic relationships, and there are endless things to say about them. Endless ways to be in a relationship, endless ways to get lost in a relationship, and, like, five ways to get out of a relationship. There's a reason superheroes often can't handle dating, or date someone only for the extent of one movie. It can be tough to constantly fight crime and maintain a cover persona while also trying to get intimate with someone. Luckily a Super You, if she's able to

focus on herself healthily while also focusing on someone else, has a much easier time dating. Before I was a Super You, I forgot about this "focusing on myself healthily" part for much of my dating life. I fully believed, whether from my upbringing or the culture at large, that a romantic relationship should be the absolute centerpiece of my life. So I was disappointed to find that even making the other person my reason for being still didn't guarantee that I'd be happy in the relationship, that I'd be loved, or that it would fill my life the way I'd thought it would. Both that life experience with dating and my education in couples dynamics have gone into this list of tips for Super Yous who decide they can handle being in a relationship. So let's dig in.

Super You Dating Tip I: Make Sure You Can Date Yourself Before You Date Someone Else

Maintaining self-care is absolutely essential to Super Yous maintaining their Super You status, and yet a lot of us forget all about that when we get into a relationship. Think about the things you do for the other person when you start dating: you delve deep into your partner's wants and needs in this world; you listen to your partner's every inkling of a thought, transfixed and awestruck; you might provide nice back rubs and genital action; basically, you do nice things for your partner. But it's important to note that everything that makes you a good girlfriend applies to dating yourself, and keeping up with those self-care skills (remember chapter 5) is essential for maintaining yourself when you're in a relationship.

Don't stop dating yourself when you date someone else—a Super You has to juggle both relationships.

Part of my problem in earlier relationships was surrendering myself so completely to the other person that I expected him to do all the nice things I would normally do for myself: bubble baths, understanding my deepest thoughts, reading to me. You can slowly teach a partner how to take care of you, but even then, it's not the same as the necessary work of self-care, and it's setting you up for disappointment if you try. This leads to my next tip.

Super You Dating Tip 2: Don't Look for a Romantic Relationship to Fill All Your Holes [Insert sex joke here]

Relationships can be so rich and amazing and fulfilling: they can help you understand yourself in new ways, they can help you build intimacy with another person that you never thought possible, they are fun and challenging and beautiful and weird and can be life-altering. Since a lot of us are clear on what great things relationships can be, I want to remind you of a few things your romantic partner cannot be, which of course you also cannot be for your partner:

🌀 Assistant

🌀 Caretaker

🌀 Decision-maker

🌀 Doormat

🌀 Financier

- 🌀 Hobby

- 🌀 Moral compass

- 🌀 Parent

- 🌀 Social life

- 🌀 Therapist

Way back in the day, relationships were more business arrangements—as well as the means of creating more humans to work for family businesses—than they were romantic arrangements. No one expected one's spouse to be sexual partner, best friend, business partner, confidant, meal preparer, housekeeper, and everything else—that seemed ludicrous. I'm not saying this was an ideal setup; I just want to point out how crazy it is that, today, we assume that the person we choose to spend our life with will fulfill all our needs for the rest of our days. It's a tall order, and it partially explains why so many people are gun-shy about marriage.

I can see now that I made this end-all, be-all mistake with my first marriage. I cringe thinking about it now, but I remember feeling a sense of relief when I got married, relief that I wouldn't have to keep up with all my friends, that I wouldn't have to worry about paying the bills on my own anymore. I felt relieved that all the work (emotional, social, whatever) I'd been doing could stop—because now I had a man. I wanted my husband to be literally everything to me; and while I was willing also to be everything to him, neither of us had the tools we needed. That's because those tools don't exist. No one person can fill all the holes you have, and no one should be expected to. It's not your partner's job to be the parent or assistant or doormat that you never had, and going into a relationship with that expectation is unfair to both of you. Your friends are necessary. Your therapist is necessary. Your self-care is necessary. Your ability to manage a household is necessary.

You must, before dating someone, figure out what your "romantic partner" hole actually looks like. You may figure this out by trial and error, or by talking to friends. Let's say you decide you will seek someone who will treat you with respect, have sex with you, listen to your dreams, have his/her own dreams, and play with your hair. Once you've determined that, make sure that you only look for partners who fill that specific hole. Of course, it's good to be open to someone with additional qualities you didn't realize you wanted, but *do not* date someone who doesn't fill the hole at all.

This idea works both ways—it is absolutely not your job to fulfill every need your partner has, nor is it a good idea. But that can be tricky, because it can feel lovely to be necessary to your partner, making your relationship essential rather than just a romantic interlude. But while a lot of us like to feel necessary, ultimately this setup will only burn you out, likely making you resent your partner in the end. Comedian Sarah Silverman summed up this concept beautifully in an interview in *Glamour*: "I don't want to make a guy whole: I want him to come whole." Love has enough trouble on its own without being saddled down with unnecessary expectations.

Super You Dating Tip 3: Take a Romantic Hindsight Stroll

While I'm in a relationship, it's sometimes impossible for me to understand what I'm really getting out of it, but after it's over, suddenly the fog lifts and I can be like, "Oh shit, I was just dating that dude to seem more interesting!" To save the egos of the guys I've dated, I'm not going to go through each one, but just be aware that at one point I did date a member of a cult who was also a life-guard, who moved out of his parents' house only after he accidentally released a demon into his bedroom and needed to escape it. I'd hang out with him at the pool while he worked (from under an umbrella and many layers of clothing) and we'd talk about religion and music and everything else. He would sometimes try to practice his psychic abilities by guessing what I was thinking. If you've guessed I lied to make him feel more psychic, you guessed 100 percent correctly. I dated this dude because he was attractive, and because I realized it would make a hilarious story at some point. (If you hadn't realized, this was during my "intellectualizing feelings" phase.) And by the way, he's doing great these days—married with kids, which I'm sure he didn't see coming.

So let's try out this exercise, which I've found can be quite illuminating. Looking back at the relationships in your past, going as far back as you can remember, start examining them with some healthy emotional distance to figure out what you wanted out of each. It's completely okay for the answers to be as shallow as "I wanted to have sex" or as deep as "I wanted to spend my life with this person." Here are a few questions to help you figure this out. I hope you'll answer these questions—without judgment—in your trusty notebook:

★ Where were you, emotionally, when this relationship started?

★ What effect did you think this relationship would have on your parents?

★ What effect did you think this relationship would have on your friends?

★ What effect did you think this relationship would have on you?

★ Did you think this person was "the one"?

★ Had you gone through any life changes directly before this relationship started?

★ When this relationship started were you trying not to date, or were you seeking out a partner?

★ When this relationship started were you pretty satisfied in other areas of your life—friendships, work/school, etc.?

★ Was there an element of excitement to this person that made him/her particularly appealing? (Accents, weird jobs, cool history, bizarro hobbies all count here.)

Using these questions on my own relationships, I learned that often what I wanted was "to not be alone"—and while that want was technically fulfilled, it wasn't necessarily the best way to fall in love. I also often got into relationships because, like my cult-member lifeguard, my sense of adventure won out over my sense of romance. Did I actually think that dating a pseudo-psychic cult member was going to be a fulfilling relationship? No, not really. Again, there is no judgment here; it's perfectly fine to date someone for the story—all we're looking for here are patterns. Patterns could include: consistently expecting a guy to be "the one," dating only when you're in a fragile place emotionally, dating when you happen to have a couple of weeks free and expecting a guy to just fit into your life as is, or consistently dating for the story more than for your affection and interest in the guy himself. There's nothing specific you need to do with this information—it's only to serve you as you consider getting involved in relationships in the future.

Super You Dating Tip 4: Be in the Relationship You're In

If you take nothing else away from this section of the book, take this in: make sure you're dating the person in front of you. When you're interacting with the person you're dating, make sure that you're reacting only to that person's actions. While this might sound extremely obvious, it can go wrong in many different directions because we all have so many expectations for how romantic relationships *should* be. Focusing on these expectations, rather than focusing on reality, has ruined many a good relationship, and has sustained bad relationships for weeks, months, or years.

To explain what I mean about this, below I've collected a few of the types of relationship "villains" we sometimes conjure up that keep us from seeing the person actually in front of us. Obviously, these aren't the only possibilities, but they are a few of the more common ways we avoid being in the relationship we're actually in. When it comes to love, open eyes and open heart are really the only way to proceed.

The Fantasy

The Fantasy has become more prevalent since online dating has become the norm, but it's existed forever. The Fantasy is created when you develop a set of ideas about who a potential love interest is but then ignore any ways those ideas don't actually match the person. I've dated guys who tell me they're feminists, and I've taken that information and built around it a complete picture of an egalitarian, brilliant, gorgeous man, completely ignoring how the guy actually thinks of women as cute little objects to keep in his pocket. If you meet a man who tells you he's "broken" and "has a hard time connecting," listen to that information and evaluate his behavior toward you, rather than working to earn the trust and love of a gorgeous, damaged person. People who tell you they have a hard time connecting aren't giving you a challenge; they're giving you essential information about themselves. And pay close attention to how the person behaves. If you're being treated poorly, that treatment should carry more weight than anything they say.

If someone you meet has some of the characteristics of an established, beloved character, like a super cool movie character, try to realize that the person is *not* that movie character. If you come to love that person, make sure your love is for the actual person and not the character who's lived in your heart and mind for so long. (I call that one the Lloyd Dobbler Effect, and I've dated sensitive men in trench coats several times specifically because of him.) I once dated a guy and spent months waiting for him to go back to being the soft, sweet, lovely person he was on our *first date*. The real him was the guy I was seeing every day, but I was hung up on the fantasy. I have friends who have fallen in love with a person's online

THE *fantasy*

THE *pedestal*

THE *ghost*

THE *shoehorn*

persona, never noticing that the actual person behind the persona is quite a bit different. And look, as we've discussed: we all have personas that we put on in different social situations, and there's nothing wrong with that. As an adult, part of our job is to become more and more savvy about evaluating those personas, as well as the flawed, wonderful, weird humans beneath them. The onus isn't on others to make sure you're aware of exactly who they are; the onus is on us to try to understand other people—and decide if we want to be around them based on that understanding.

Confirmation bias is a fun term that applies to many things, including romantic partners. It's the tendency to seek out and process only the information that confirms your already-formed beliefs. It's the reason that racist people will always find support for their racism by reading the news, because the odds are that someone they feel racist toward has committed a crime. So if we go into a relationship believing the other person is a hardworking aspiring actor who likes to have fun, we have to be willing to adjust our mental picture of who that person is while also maintaining our respect and affection. This way, if the person turns out to be a pessimist drunk, we'll be able to adjust our assessment without clinging to the idea of him as a fun-time party guy who's just had a string of bad luck. We all change and evolve throughout our lives, in both positive and negative ways. I'm not saying you should leave if the change is negative. I'm just saying it's important to make sure we're dating the real person in front of us, and not a fantasy we've created.

THERAPY TERM alert

The Pedestal

The Pedestal is quite similar to the Fantasy, with one distinct difference: you believe your partner is absolutely perfect. So perfect, in fact, that he or she is untouchable. Untouchable is never good in a relationships, because relationships need to be touched. They need to be altered and examined and dealt with. They need to be malleable. Elevating someone to pedestal status is something people sometimes feel the need to do to honor and respect the person they're with, but it's not conducive to a real relationship. When a person is considered to be perfect in every way, the relationship isn't on even footing. Not only are you never good enough for the person on a pedestal, you aren't even really interacting as two mutually appreciative humans. Putting your partner on a pedestal essentially guarantees two things: that you won't be able to build any real intimacy, and that the person will disappoint you. No one can last on a pedestal. Everyone is flawed and will eventual show those flaws—and then you'll be left wondering what you've been worshipping the whole time. Don't treat a partner like gold. Treat a partner like a person you like and respect and also want to make out with. You can still behave chivalrously on occasion, but I want a real, touchable relationship with someone on my level.

The Ghost

My first husband and I had fairly separate leisure lives, which meant that relaxing around the house was often done alone. There is absolutely nothing wrong with this. We also happened to have very separate social lives, emotional lives, goals, and intimacy needs—and that was a problem. After I got divorced, I kept going back over my marriage, trying to figure out how it went wrong, what part I'd played in it, and how never to repeat it. Then later, a few months after my current husband and I got married, there was an evening when we'd both had a long day—I was on my computer, probably looking at pictures of cats, and he was playing a basketball video game. For about an hour we sat in silence in separate rooms of our apartment, and the silence was deafening to me. "It's happening again," I thought, panicky. I did that thing where you make little deals with yourself—"If he speaks to me within two minutes, then it means he still loves me and it's going to be fine"—and after doing that for way too long, I decided just to discuss it with him like an adult. "I'm worried about us developing separate lives and growing apart," I said seriously. He paused his video game and looked at me like I was a crazy person, and in our discussions that followed, I eventually learned a good lesson. My second husband is a completely different person than my first husband, my second marriage is completely different than my first, and I cannot treat the former as if he were the latter. I cannot isolate one aspect of a past relationship, compare and contrast it with my current relationship, and as a result make determinations about how the universe works. Every single person you date should be taken on his/her behavior alone, and not required to somehow know what you've been through with past partners and take care to be different. It's good for you to be aware of your own patterns in relationships; it's not good for you then to project those patterns onto every new partner. Creating a Ghost out of your partner doesn't just keep you from really connecting to that person; it also sets you up for failure time and time again.

The Shoehorn

We create Shoehorns when we set up expectations for a relationship before actually meeting the person we date. Most often, this happens when we decide it's time to settle down with the idea, conscious or unconscious, that the next person is going to be "the one." This will be the person we get serious about. It's time to give it a go, right? We're getting older! If you've ever been made into a Shoehorn by a person you're dating, you know how bizarre it can feel. How weird to have someone pre-decide he wants to marry you before dating you! What is this, an adorable romcom? But we need to be careful we aren't doing this either, and not go into relationships with a pre-conceived notion of what this relationship will mean. Every relationship is a blank slate, and shoehorning someone into the role of "future spouse" or "person who will save me from myself" won't magically create that person. All it does is set you up for failure.

Super You Dating Tip 5: Ask Yourself What You Want

This is a fantastic question to ask ourselves whether we're single or dating. If you're single: what do you actually want out of your next relationship? If you're dating: what do you actually want out of this particular relationship? What was missing in your life that you're hoping to get out of this/the next relationship? How do you want this/the next relationship to be different from your last one? What holes would this/the next relationship be filling? These are not easy questions. Sometimes we won't know what we want out of a relationship until long after it's over. And sometimes we won't necessarily love the answer. But living with intention means asking and answering even the tough questions.

Why? Because we pursue relationships for all kinds of selfish reasons, some of which have nothing to do with wanting to form intimate bonds with another person. I think that, quite often, we perhaps don't even want to be in a relationship—but because everything in our society pushes us to look for love, we temper that societal expectation by pursuing relationships we know deep down aren't sustainable. It's as if we shout to the universe: "See? I'm doing the thing I should be doing!" But we're really just going through the motions, dating people who don't deserve our time, and satisfying the expectations we feel are put upon us.

So, what are some reasons for wanting to be in a relationship? How about:

- I don't want to feel lonely.

- I want to date *someone*.

- I want to feel adored.

- I want to feel and show affection to someone.

- I want to have sex regularly.

- I want to keep up with my friends.

- I want to love someone.

- I want not to have to think about what I'm doing on a weekend.

- I want to share my awesome life with someone.

⚡ I want you in my life every day, however I can have you.

⚡ The other person wants to date me, and I want to make him/ her happy.

⚡ Winter is coming and I wanna cuddle on a couch.

As you can see, some of these wants are more noble than others, some are healthier than others, some are more *Game of Thrones* references than others, and some are more selfish than others. I used to base whether or not I would date a guy on all the following factors: if he wanted to date me. I figured that I wasn't good enough to snub anyone's advances, so if someone wanted me, I should make myself want him back. But almost every other reason for dating someone is perfectly legitimate; it's just important to make sure you're not making wedding plans with the person you're dating simply to avoid feeling lonely. Dig down, gently and sweetly question your intentions, and realize that you deserve to have *all* your wants met.

Other Relationships

Okay, enough talk about love. Though romantic relationships make up only about 1 percent of the many different types of relationships out there, they tend to take up more room in our hearts. But we have still more to cover.

Superheroes are often not fantastic at interpersonal skills, which is usually excused because they're focused on the greater good of crime-fighting. But we don't have that luxury. Super You still has to be around friends, acquaintances, coworkers, cashiers, cab drivers, parents, doctors, children, and that lady at the gym who's always trying to make small talk with you when you're clearly out of breath and listening to music. Since there are endless ways to interact with and react to the people you deal with every day, what follows are just a few thoughts on successfully existing among people in general when you're working hard to be the best version of yourself—and that means looking out for your own needs and growth while being respectful of others. For this entire book we've been thinking of Super You as the star of her own spin-off movie franchise, à la Thor or Captain America. Now it's time to realize that, to the rest of the world, we aren't the star of the movie—we're instead part of the Avengers, and have to cooperate appropriately.

Like the Avengers, who are made up of superheroes like the Hulk, Black Widow, and Iron Man, our lives are really a constellation of people who have their own strengths and are on their own journeys to improve and grow. Sometimes we collaborate, sometimes we fight, sometimes we work on our own in spin-off movies that can't afford to feature the others. But since it would be uncouth (and costly) to borrow the Avengers title, let's call your social circles the Badass Division. That sounds like a show ABC would put on the air next fall. "Badass Division: Divided They Fall, United They Badass." But I digress. Is your Badass Division movie full of people understanding each other's strengths and communicating clearly and so accomplishing awesome things? Or is it full of unclear motivations, miscommunication, and bad conflict resolution? It's that second description, full of fights and intrigue, that I'd rather watch on TV, but I'd rather *exist* on the show where people learn to work with each other effectively to solve problems and move through life. So let's talk about a few of the ways communicating with others can go wrong, and what we can do about it—with just a few handy pocket-sized tools to add to your toolbag.

Badass Division Tip: Don't Expect Psychic Behavior

We talked about this a bit in Chapter 7: having expectations without communicating them. Let's talk about it again—that's how important it is. What are the unspoken rules that guide your day-to-day life, your social interactions, how you react to strangers? We all, even if we're unaware of it, have our own expectations of how we want to be treated. What boundaries do you set with strangers, and how are they different from those with coworkers or close friends? Questions like "How should a person show love to you?" or "How should a person react when given a gift?" are a good place to start figuring out these unspoken rules. One important thing to note about "shoulds" is that they're not very effective; in fact, problems often arise when we expect other people to know our "shoulds." As Stuart Smalley—an *SNL* character from the nineties—used to say: "You're shoulding all over yourself!" Sitting down and asking yourself what the "shoulds" of your life are is a great way to figure out which "shoulds" are reasonable and which "shoulds" derive from long-held patterns and negative beliefs. Try it out.

If you're finding it difficult to come up with your "shoulds," I have two tips. One, you usually discover "shoulds" when they're broken—that's how unspoken they are. Two, I find that comparing my "shoulds" with my parents' "shoulds" has been instrumental in helping me figure out how we differ. For example, my mother says: "When I deliver food to neighbors, they should return the Tupperware to me." She is adamant about this fact, to the extent that she sees return or non-return of Tupperware as a deeper indication of your personality and worth. This is not to say that she's correct or incorrect; this is merely to say that, to her, hoarding Tupperware is a sign of a person who is greedy and possibly even terrible. (Did I mention I'm southern?) For me to keep this "should" would mean that I thought all my friends were terrible human beings, because it's very rare that my friends return my Ziploc plasticware—though that might be because I rarely deliver them home-cooked meals.

My parents also believe that "you should not advertise your accomplishments lest you be seen as a braggart." Unfortunately, that doesn't work in my line of business, where it's part of my job to pitch myself to people. My "should" in this area is an update of my parents' "should": "You should quietly and firmly allow your work to speak for itself. Your work should speak louder than you do."

So, basically, defining your "shoulds" in areas like romance, friendships, work, and parent interactions can help you gauge where you are in your life, and where you can stand to make some improvements to advocate for yourself a bit more. Expecting other people to know your "shoulds" is a trap members of the Badass Division, and really any Super You, often fall into. Let me set the scene.

> **You have a new coworker in the cubicle next to yours. During lunch, he has an extremely loud and personal conversation on his cell phone—every day. You want to destroy him, but instead you seethe and decide to hate him forever. He should know how rude he's being.**

> **Or:**

> **Your roommate always leaves her dirty dishes in the sink and only washes them days later; it makes you crazy. She should just know that you're supposed to do your dishes right after you eat, right? You come home from a long day to find your roommate sitting on the couch, eating, and you think; "If her dishes are in the sink, I'm going to lose it." And guess what? They are. So you start yelling at her, and she's startled and freaked out, and starts yelling back.**

Or:

It's your birthday! You're a freshman in college and it's your first birthday away from home. Your friends keep asking you where everyone's going to go to celebrate that night. Birthdays were always a big deal in your family, with daylong celebrations starting with a special breakfast and ending with a soiree planned by your parents. You go from being a little annoyed to more and more angry as the day goes on, as people keep asking you where the party's at. You tell your friends you don't feel well and spend your birthday in bed, angrily surfing the Internet.

In all these examples, you had a set of expectations, or a "should" for behavior clearly laid out in your head—but without communicating those expectations to anyone else, you've essentially set yourself up for disappointment. Your coworker most likely has no idea how loud he is; gently letting him know that the cubicle walls are thin and that he might want to make his calls in a more private spot would likely solve the problem. It will also much more likely keep you from murdering him. Most of us assume that other people's expectations are similar to our own—but this is rarely the case, which is part of what makes interacting with other people so interesting. Our task as we move through life is to make sure that, rather than expecting other people to be psychic, we give them the memo of how we want to be treated. I don't mean you should assault others with your list of expectations in a princess-demanding-diva sort of way, but merely that you should keep in mind it's not others' job to do the detective work of finding out how we want to be treated. It is *our* job to communicate how we want to be treated. Does this mean we're always treated as we want to be? Of course not, because as we all know—say it with me—we can only control ourselves! But by communicating our expectations to others, we give ourselves the most sporting chance possible of being heard and understood. Now, by communicating clearly up top, are we robbing ourselves of an opportunity to be angry and disappointed with someone else? Absolutely we are. Are we also giving ourselves the opportunity to have our expectations met by the rest of the world? Absolutely we are. Which would you prefer?

Some of you are still squirming from the thought of confronting a coworker about moving his cell phone conversations elsewhere, and I get it. Never being confrontational in person is pretty much the norm these days, and don't even get me started on people who are fantastic at confronting others online but not in person. So, on to the next Badass Division tip.

Badass Division Tip: Confrontation

The word "confrontation" may make you picture a *Real Housewives* show with cameras ready to capture two women screaming into each other's faces in hopes of becoming big stars—but that's not what it has to be. A confrontation, to me at least, is merely how you request that someone behave differently in a specific situation. It can be done in a shouting match, it can be done passive-aggressively over Twitter, it can be done in writing, and it can be done calmly and rationally in person. But even when it's done calmly, that doesn't mean it won't be awkward. Confronting people is never easy or fun, but it is a muscle that gets stronger with exercise. The more you bite the bullet and talk to someone openly and honestly about how you'd like her to treat you differently, the more you'll find that confronting someone

usually won't kill you. Sometimes it's just a necessary awkwardness of life, and you only really learn that by trying it.

When I worked at a residential treatment program for angry/addicted/conduct-challenged/socially unskilled teenage boys, we worked a lot on confrontations and conflict resolution. Young men are often taught that it's okay, and even expected, for them to blow up at each other as a means of expression, but the staff wasn't having any of that mess. It was amazing to watch these boys go from incoherently raging if their shoes got scuffed to requesting a time-out to "ask that the nickname 'dumpbutt' no longer be used because it is hurtful and also I didn't even dump my pants; it was just mud." And while it was my job to teach them how to confront each other, I ended up learning a lot from how they handled being somewhat forced (as part of their treatment) to adopt these skills. From them I learned how complex intricacies of human interactions and anger and hurt feelings and respect and boundaries can be broken down into calm, simple, direct requests. From them I learned the difference between confronting someone in order to improve a relationship and confronting someone in order to inflict hurt. From them I learned that sometimes it's necessary to do something that's a little awkward in order to make things a lot better. From them I learned that practicing confrontation

QUICK SUPER YOU INTERNET/LIFE ADVICE

Don't say anything on the Internet that you wouldn't be willing to say to the person's face. That could include a polite but firm "Please leave."

skills truly is a muscle, one I watched them use on their thunder-struck parents. It was beautiful.

Now it's your turn. Here is how a Super You, intent on keeping herself important and safe and a strong member of the Badass Division, confronts another human being. Let's say you have a coworker, Bob, who constantly interrupts you and talks over you in meetings. This makes you annoyed and hurt, and you want him to stop. Okay: the first thing you need to do is figure out whether or not this confrontation is *necessary*. Sometimes, the squirmier, darker parts of us want to confront someone about something that's really more about ourselves than it is about them—but we either can't tell that it's actually our issue, or we want to spread our misery around a bit under the guise of standing up for ourselves. How do you figure this out? Well, imagine your office is in a reality show: if you were to confront Bob, would the viewers at home agree this is a problem to address, or would they be confused by your confrontation? When it comes to coworker conflicts, the issue actually could be more about whether Bob does better work than you, or the boss likes him more. If so, that's not really something to confront Bob about—that's something for you to accept. You have to pick your battles and realize when the shit belongs to you more than it belongs to Bob. But in the case of a coworker interrupting and talking over you, I agree that confronting him is a good idea.

The next step of confronting someone is *timing*. Good timing is essential for a healthy, calm confrontation. Are your feelings in check, or are you about to punch Bob and/or cry? Is Bob even avail-able? How calm is the environment in general? Overall, you want to aim for confronting Bob when you're both calm. Always, like a vampire, ask permission to speak with the other person before just storming into talk about feelings.

Now on to the next step: what do you want to *accomplish*? What's your ideal best outcome of this confrontation? This is another chance to check in on whether you actually want a behavior change or you just want to punish the other person. Punishment has no place in a proper confrontation. Thinking about what you want to accomplish will help you craft what to say, and you'll want to verbalize some concrete, observable behaviors that you'd like from the other person. Because if you ask Bob to "respect you more," you and Bob might have very different interpretations of what that means. Bob may not see interrupting you as disrespecting you. But, if you tell Bob that you'd like him to let you finish speaking in meetings, that is a specific behavior that can be measured.

Now we've reached the moment of truth. It's a calm Tuesday at work, and you go to Bob and ask him if you can speak to him for a moment. Your hands may be shaking—this stuff is awkward. What do you say?

> [Brief small talk about Tuesday.] Bob, I've noticed [insert concrete description of the behavior here, stated without assumptions about why it's happening]. I would like you to [a request for alternate behavior]. Does what I'm saying make sense to you?

That's it. Please note that it's incredibly important not to make assumptions about why the behavior is happening. Do not say to Bob, "I have noticed that you interrupt me during our weekly team meetings, probably because I'm a woman and you're sexist." Whether or not this is true, this is not going to do anything except insult Bob and put him on the defensive, even if your assumption is pretty low-caliber. Plus, you might be wrong.

If you're confronting someone you're closer to, you can add the optional step of telling the confrontee how the behavior makes you feel. Let's say you're confronting your friend Lucy about how she rolls her eyes and says "Champagne problems" when you complain about a fight with your husband. That could look like this:

> Lucy, I've noticed [insert concrete description of the behavior here, stated without assumptions about why it is happening]. When you [do the lame behavior, without saying "lame"], I feel [how you feel—keep this focused on your reaction to the behavior, and not why she does the behavior, and not "I feel that you're a jerk"]. I would like you to [a request for alternate behavior]. Does what I'm saying make sense to you?

This one's reserved for those we're close to because it may not always be necessary to let a stranger know how her cutting in front of you makes you feel. In fact, I'd advise against it.

So then what happens? Once you've done this tough stuff, it'll be up to the other person to decide how to respond. Bob, Lucy, or the stranger at the bank may apologize and correct his/her behavior

SUPERHERO GROUPS: A QUICK PRIMER

When it comes to random groupings of superheroes, there's more than just the Avengers.

➡ The Doom Patrol was a group of superheroes who felt angry and alienated by their superpowers.

➡ The League of Extraordinary Gentlemen, like the Avengers but set in Victorian England, features men from works of fiction like Captain Nemo, Professor Moriarty, and Dr. Jekyll.

➡ The Thunderbolts are a crew made up of reformed supervillains.

("Badass Division" doesn't sound so silly anymore, does it?)

immediately. You guys may end up hugging and understanding each other on a deeper level. Or he/she may balk and tell you to fuck off. When a person you've confronted rejects your request, that's a whole new tip.

Badass Division Tip: How to Deal with Terrible People

There are some people who just behave terribly. Maybe they're unhappy and want to make other people feel as bad as they do. Or maybe it's how they prove to themselves that they're important. I don't know, and I don't really care: they're just terrible. People who go out of their way to make things harder on other people come into and out of our lives all the time, so what can we do about it? How does a Super You deal with such assholes when she realizes that she can't really control anyone but herself?

Note: I'm speaking of low-level, garden-variety terribleness in friends, coworkers, acquaintances, and strangers. I'm not speaking of abuse at any level, physical or otherwise, in personal relationships. Threats of or actual abuse is an extremely important topic that falls outside the scope of this book. If you're struggling with an abusive relationship of any sort, please reach out to a professional, either via 911, the National Domestic Violence Hotline (1-800-799-7233), or a therapist.

There are two types of jerks: jerks you can avoid, and jerks you can't avoid.

Jerks You Can Avoid

If you've made a calm, concrete request for behavior change from a person and it has been denied, consider whether you have the option of removing yourself from the situation. If so, then you're dealing with a jerk you can avoid. So if someone tries to break in front of me in line, and she refuses to move when I ask her to go to the back of the line, I see two options: find another way to make myself heard—in this case, letting the cashier know that I'm actually next in line—or leave the line. Keep in mind that there's no fault or shame in leaving the line. Removing myself from a situation where I'm not being respected isn't giving up or letting the other win, it's me exercising the bit of freedom I do have: my presence and participation. I cannot and will not force another person into doing what I want, even if it's the right thing to do, so I'd rather remove myself from the situation than suggest I'm okay with what's happening by continuing to exist there.

Leaving the situation can play out in a few different ways. If you're in a social setting where an acquaintance is being a dick to you, and guffaws when you ask him to stop being a dick, leaving the situation means that you let the group know you're leaving and you leave. Or if this is a school project and someone is taking credit for your work, it could mean asking the teacher to let you move to a different group. In situations like these I try to visualize the amount of power—often in a little bar hovering above the jerk's head—each person has in a social situation. (If you've played the videogame *The Sims,* you know exactly what I'm talking about.) How much of my power do I want to hold on to, and how much am I willing to give to another person? For me, staying at a party where an acquaintance is being rude to me gives a jerk more of my power than I'm comfortable with. Requesting a different behavior, and then leaving if I don't get it, is how I take my power back. The power the other person has over me dissipates when I remove myself from the situation; this is essential, even if it means I'm inconvenienced. It's not that someone else had the power to make me leave a party or a checkout line—it's that I had the power not to let someone else's bad behavior ruin my day.

Jerks You Can't Avoid

If, out of some sort of obligation that matters to you, you're unable to leave a situation where you're being disrespected, you're in another territory entirely: in the land of jerks you can't avoid. This is where pulling out extra armor and adding it to your Super You uniform may not be such a bad thing. If you have a boss, coworker, or parent who's a bit of a jerk, and you feel you can't do anything about it, then it's your job to protect yourself. For this you can use jerk protection— which is similar to the cheap weapons and armor we talked about earlier, just more useful. Jerk protection has several pieces:

- ⚡ The Mask of Poker Face, your reminder to take deep breaths and not let a jerk's behavior cause you to overreact.

- ⚡ The Cape of No Responsibility, so you may cloak yourself in the knowledge that the jerk's behavior is about the jerk and has absolutely nothing to do with you. The Cape can also remind you that you do not deserve such treatment.

- ⚡ Armlets of Empathy, to remind you that this jerk is lashing out because he most likely feels sad/scared/frustrated with himself. Armlets of Empathy may produce feelings of pity toward your jerk, and this is okay. Feeling pity is better than feeling victimized.

- ⚡ Helm of Anger Management, to help you remember to employ whatever techniques calm you down the best, so that this jerk doesn't also get to take your good mood.

- ⚡ Boots of Escape, so you're always ready to seek your quickest way out.

There's one last jerk-armor item, which applies only to jerky behavior that, on closer inspection, turns out actually to have good intentions. Essentially, behavior is gift wrapped in some really shitty wrapping paper. This is the power of unwrapping.

Let's say a coach or teacher constantly barks at you to do better: basically, he sees potential in you, but doesn't know more elegant means of teasing out your talent. Or your mother makes snide comments about how terrible your pink hair looks—but that's actually a gift of "I love you and want things to be as easy as possible for you" wrapped in judgment and disdain. When I'm able to see that there's actually a good intention inside that shitty wrapping, it helps me to remember that, just as some people don't know how to wrap presents, jerks usually have really poor communication skills. On occasion I've thanked a jerky gift giver for caring about me so much, which usually throws them off a bit. This doesn't excuse his/her behavior in the slightest, as no one should act like a jerk. The point is merely figuring out how to accept a person whose behavior will not change—and getting the most out of it.

I had a boss who was incredibly critical of me for years, to the extent that he'd call me to yell at me about things that weren't even my job. I eventually realized there was a gift inside that yelling: he thought I was capable of perfection. I'm not, and no one is, but his wrapping paper screamed that I should be. So when he'd call to yell, I started lavishly thanking him for his confidence in my abilities. It didn't stop him from yelling, but it did weird him out a bit, and that was enough for me. Thanks to knowing how to unwrap his gifts, and to my extra armor, I survived that job; eventually, I also managed to leave it.

Badass Division Tip: Apologizing

Crafting a good, solid apology is both easy and incredibly difficult. It's difficult because it requires admitting that you're wrong, which even the absolute best version of yourself may not love doing. It's also difficult because it requires vulnerability. In terms of the transfer of power between people like those we were discussing earlier, to apologize is to voluntarily give away some of your power in order to make amends to another person. But in sharing our power with the person we've wronged—by owning up and taking responsibility— we ultimately create more lovely, grown-up emotional power for ourselves. And there's more good news: it's never too late to apologize. If you still have a squirmy sense that you should have apologized about something, even from long ago, then making that apology will have an added benefit: freeing you from that feeling.

Amy Poehler's wonderful book *Yes, Please!* discusses apologizing in a wonderful way, I highly recommend reading it. So sure, the impetus of apology is tough, but crafting the apology can also be easy, because it's most effective when it's simple and stark. Let me show you.

The first step in apologizing is saying the words "I am sorry." With the second step you must take responsibility for your part of whatever has occurred—and you must do so without blaming anyone else, giving excuses, or minimizing your behavior. This part is important. No one else's name should even come up when you are apologizing. A good way to demonstrate the importance of this is to imagine the following apology being made to you:

> **I am sorry I said something rude about your new boyfriend, but the girl I was talking to is such a gossip and kinda prodded it out of me and I didn't even know you were standing there and it's not a big deal really...**

If this were said to you, would you feel the person had taken responsibility for her actions? My guess is no. Now, imagine how you'd feel if she said this instead:

> **I am sorry I said something rude about your new boyfriend. It was unkind of me.**

Do you see (and feel) how different this one is? Simple. Stark. Nothing but ownership in as few words as possible. Regardless of why that woman said something rude, no one forced her to do it, and her whole story behind it isn't important to you—only her unkindness is. So if your behavior hurts others, be sure to say you're sorry and take responsibility for your actions. That's really all a bare-bones,

simple apology requires, which will be all that is called for in certain situations.

But we're not done yet. There are a couple of optional apology add-ons that can be very important if you've hurt someone you're close to—and the fact that these require you to show even more vulnerability makes them all the more important. Optional step three is explaining the feelings behind your behavior. But note that the intention of this explanation is neither to make excuses nor to engender pity; ideally the intention is more of an opportunity to increase understanding and empathy between you and the other person. So, again, imagine the following was said to you:

> I'm sorry I said something rude about your new boyfriend, but I've been PMSing real hard all day and you know how that is.

Would that make you feel better? Again, likely no. Knowing just what was going on with the speaker when she hurt you doesn't lessen the hurt. She'll have to dig a bit deeper, get vulnerable, in order to own her part. Now how about if she said this to you:

> I'm sorry I said something rude about your new boyfriend. It was unkind of me. It's not an excuse, but I think I've been feeling a little jealous that you've found someone you care about. But that's all on me; I still shouldn't have said it.

So, how would that land for you? Can you imagine then having a good discussion with your friend about feeling threatened, and about how friendships need to remain strong even when romance comes along? I'm hoping yes.

If you choose to explain in an apology the feelings behind your behavior, ask yourself if what you reveal will bring you closer to the other person, or if it would just serve to make that person feel sorry for you. It's important to repeat: knowing the feelings behind a person's shitty behavior does not excuse the behavior. It can merely serve as an empathetic bridge to foster discussion so as to move past the apology.

There's one last one. Optional step four of apologizing is offering to make amends. Obviously, this is not always appropriate, but if there's a mess to be cleaned up or a miscommunication to be cleared, you can't go wrong by offering to help make things right. Make your offer concrete and clear, then follow up on it.

A Scene from
My Blockbuster Superhero Movie

Interior: office—day

We see a laptop, printer, and some files sitting on a desk. A few posters are on the walls, of beautiful women, of bands, and of movies. The scene is calm. Suddenly, the door bursts open and two Jittery Gray Demons slink in. They are disgusting, all sharp teeth and sharper claws, and they look like they stink terribly. Think larger, nastier Gremlins. These are **Self-Doubt** and **Fraud**.

Fraud: I'm digging into this mainframe.

Self-Doubt: Awesome. I'm going for the looks.

Fraud sits at the laptop and is amazingly adept at typing, despite his claws.

Self-Doubt: [starts pulling down the posters of the beautiful women gleefully.] Ugly ugly ugly! Look how ugly you are compared to them! Everyone knows your thighs touch!

Jump cut to
Interior: a busy train—day

The train is packed but we are focused on one woman, late twenties, dressed professionally. This is **Emily**. She shifts from staring off into space, to frowning, to snapping to attention. She holds her wrist up to her mouth like a Secret Service agent, and speaks into her sleeve.

Emily: Oh shit, we have a terrorist attack under way.

Voice from Communicator: What? Now? How do you know?

Emily: I just know, damnit! Now find me a secure spot so I can get in there and fight.

Interior: office—day

Self-Doubt and **Fraud** have utterly destroyed the office. There are papers lying everywhere; everything is covered in goo. **Self-Doubt** has his feet up on the desk and is on the office phone.

Self-Doubt [in a falsetto]: I mean, that's exactly my point, pal. Have you really taken a look at her, I mean my track record?

Fraud: Tell him that you've coasted this far on luck and you don't know how you even got the job! [The demons high-five.]

Exterior: a busy street—day

Emily is running and out of breath. She lifts her wrist to talk into her communicator again.

Emily: There are no phone booths anymore, period. Find me a froyo shop!

Voice from Communicator: Next block up, on the left!

Emily dashes into a froyo shop, and dashes back out seconds later dressed as a superhero. She looks badass. She raises her wrist to her mouth again.

Super Emily: Put me in. This pitch meeting is in half an hour.

Emily disappears from the street.

Interior: office—day

Emily reappears in the wrecked office. She looks dejected for a moment and then straightens her shoulders. The Demons haven't noticed her.

Super Emily: Alright, boys, it's clobbering time. I've come too far for you assheads to bring me down now.

Self-Doubt: You sure you've come that far, really? I mean, at one point you were begging people to write for free. Why should anyone pay you to write now?

Fraud: And if you write anything about being a therapist, won't that violate your code of ethics?

Self-Doubt: And yikes, I thought when you stopped dyeing your hair it would stop looking so frayed and split endy.

Emily pulls her hair in front of her eyes for a second, then stops and shakes herself.

Super Emily: Nice try.

Emily pulls a backpack off her back and starts pulling out tools. She pulls out some positive mantras, some soothing music, a tiny pocket-sized friend who gives her a thumbs up, and finally, a sword. She holds it up above her head, and we see engraved on it the words NEGATIVE SELF TALK EXTINGUISHER.

Super Emily: The best version of me doesn't have to put up with this bullshit. [The sword comes down. Blood splatters.]

V.O.

Coming this fall to a theater near you. Be the person you always wanted to be. Be SuperYou.

Conclusion: Where Do We Go from Here?

hen I was younger, I desperately wanted to be small. Because I thought I was too big, I constructed myself as a walking apology, always trying to cram myself, physically and emotionally, into a smaller and smaller space. I begged the universe to make me small, to make me easy, to make me more understandable. I was begging in the wrong direction—I wasn't looking to understand myself, I was looking for others to understand me. That kind of thinking kept me feeling both small and enormous at the same time, kept me looking out into the universe and screaming, "Who am I?!"

If you've been seeking an answer to the same question, I hope this book has helped you determine the answer for yourself.

You are you. You are Super You.

You are valuable. You are complex. You are substantial—you take up space. And you don't need to be understandable to anyone but yourself. You're a damn superhero, for crying out loud. You have powers and you have weaknesses, but neither make up who you are. You are who you create yourself to be. And my lifelong mission is for all of us to start creating ourselves positively, honestly, and intentionally. To create ourselves in ways that demonstrate how we value ourselves, and how we're always changing and adapting. To live as little of our lives as possible on autopilot: always savoring, always taking in the world, and always adapting to it.

As I've written and read and reread this book, I've tried to read it as sixteen-year-old Emily would have read it, and then as twenty-five-year-old Emily would have read it. I hope I would have been convinced I was valuable by this book, even though the words "You are valuable" came from someone I've never met. I hope that I would have tried some of the techniques, even though I might have felt dumb for trying—or even more, might have felt dumb for needing to try. I hope I would have stopped my emotional noise long enough to peer into myself a little bit and realize some self-reflection wouldn't kill me. In this I'm trying to say—though I don't want to change the past, and I couldn't if I tried—I would love to think I could ease the journey for someone else.

For those of you (still) reading this, and those of you who've crafted superhero missions for yourselves, I hope that they're progressing—and if they aren't, I hope you feel you have the tools to tweak those missions to suit you better. I hope you remember that you're a work-in-progress, and treat yourself with the kindness and respect you deserve. I hope that you accept the person you are, with her strengths and weaknesses, and that you learn not to fret about the qualities you don't have. I hope that you learn to cross-stitch, if only to cross-stitch yourself (and maybe me?) a reminder that you can only control yourself. I hope you continue to stretch and grow and look toward your Bat Signal until the day you realize you've reached it—and then I hope you set yourself a new Bat Signal. I hope you stay occupied with yourself, in the loveliest of ways, until you are old and gray and still kicking ass.

There are infinite ways to spend a life. Though I choose to live my life by the ideas presented in this book, that doesn't mean it's the right path for you. All I am asking of you, Super You, is that you choose the best way to live your life—and then you pursue it. Regardless of what you do with today, it's going to be gone by tomorrow. You decide what to do with today.

These days, the only time I want to feel small is when I've had a long stressful day. Then I want the person I've grown to love and trust more than anyone to hug me, making me feel tiny and taken care of. But in order to get comfortable with being small, I had to get comfortable taking up space. Now, once I've felt comforted and small for a little while, I reemerge at my usual Super You size. Then I put on my cape and costume, and I fly. Come fly with me. There's room for all of us.

Acknowledgments

This book is filled with gratitude. Thank you to my agent, Wendy Sherman, for hooking me up with Laura Mazer at Seal Press, who has been a joy to work with. Thank you to my copyeditor, Kirsten Janene-Nelson, who traded nerdy anecdotes with me while helping make this book better. Thank you to Hannah Nance Partlow, who provided the illustrations and a ton of pep talks. Thank you to H Coffee in Los Feliz, where I wrote the majority of this book. Thanks to my Meltdown family for being my Meltdown family. Thanks to Pete Holmes for creating a very early book cover that I sadly couldn't use. Thanks to my parents and my sister, who are simply the best family anyone could ask for and the reason I am the person I am today. And last, thank you to my husband, Kumail, who is my everything.

About the Author

Emily V. Gordon is a former therapist and current writer, producer, and podcaster. She co-hosts a podcast about video games and more called The Indoor Kids, and writes advice columns and essays for websites like Huffington Post, Rookie, Refinery 29, Hello Giggles, and TV.com. For the past three years, she has been the producer of The Meltdown with Jonah and Kumail, a live stand-up show in L.A., and is the executive producer of the TV version of The Meltdown, which has run for two seasons on Comedy Central.

Selected Titles from Seal Press

What You Can When You Can: Healthy Living on Your Terms, by Roni Noone and Carla Birnberg. $14.00, 978-1-58005-573-4. This companion book to the #wycwyc movement teaches you how to harness the power of small steps to achieve your goals for healthier living.

Beautiful You: A Daily Guide to Radical Self-Acceptance, by Rosie Molinary. $16.95, 978-1-58005-331-0. A practical, accessible, day-by-day guide to redefining beauty and building lasting self-esteem from body expert Rosie Molinary.

Snap Strategies for Couples: 40 Fast Fixes for Everyday Relationship Pitfalls, by Dr. Lana Staheli and Dr. Pepper Schwartz. $16.00, 978-1-58005-562-8. *Snap Strategies for Couples* offers 40 practical, immediate fixes (or "snaps") for common problems that partners can use to end the fighting, leave the baggage behind, and move their relationships forward.

Stop Signs: Recognizing, Avoiding, and Escaping Abusive Relationships, by Lynn Fairweather. $18.00, 978-1-58005-387-7. A go-to manual for women containing the life-saving information needed by anyone who is living with abuse, knows someone who is, or wishes to avoid becoming involved in a potentially life-threatening relationship.

The 3-Day Reset: Restore Your Cravings For Healthy Foods in Three Easy, Empowering Days, by Pooja Mottl. $22.00, 978-1-58005-527-7. These 10 simple resets target and revamp your eating habits in practical, three-day increments.

Reality Bites Back: The Troubling Truth About Guilty Pleasure TV, by Jennifer L. Pozner. $18.00, 978-1-58005-265-8. Deconstructs reality TV's twisted fairytales to demonstrate that they are far from being simple "guilty pleasures," and arms readers with the tools they need to understand and challenge the stereotypes reality TV reinforces.

Find Seal Press Online
www.sealpress.com
www.facebook.com/sealpress
Twitter: @SealPress